# The
# Fugu Plan

# The
# Fugu Plan

The Untold Story of the Japanese and the Jews
During World War II

## Marvin Tokayer and Mary Swartz

gefen
publishing house בית הוצאה לאור
JERUSALEM ◆ NEW YORK

First published by Paddington Press, Ltd., 1979
First Weatherhill edition, 1996
First Gefen Publishing House Ltd. edition, 2004

Cover Design: S. Kim Glassman, Jerusalem

5  7  9  8  6

Gefen Publishing House
6 Hatzvi Street, Jerusalem 94386, Israel
972-2-538-0247
orders@gefenpublishing.com

Gefen Books
600 Broadway, Lynbrook, NY 11563, USA
1-516-593-1234
orders@gefenpublishing.com

**www.israelbooks.com**

Printed in Israel                    *Send for our free catalogue*

ISBN 965-229-329-6

**Library of Congress Cataloging-in-Publication Data**

Tokayer, Marvin, 1936-
The fugu plan. Includes Index

1. Jews in Shanghai-Politics and government. 2. World War, 1939-1945-Jews-Rescue-Japan.
3. Japan-Politics and government-1912-1945. I. Swartz, Mary, 1942- joint author. II. Title

DS135.C5T64 • 940·53'1503'9240951132 • 78-21125

# CONTENTS

Acknowledgments                                    VII
Introduction                                        IX
Introduction to the Current Edition               XIV
Introduction by David Rubinson                    XVII
Chronology                                          14

PART ONE    From Europe to the Orient 1939-41:
            The Birth of the *fugu* Plan            19

PART TWO    Japan 1941:
            Security in an Alien Land              121

PART THREE  Shanghai 1941-1945:
            The Challenge to Survival              190

            Epilogue                               271
            Glossary                               277
            Index                                  279

*To Mazal who made the possible a reality*

# ACKNOWLEDGMENTS

IT WOULD BE almost impossible to acknowledge all who deserve it, but we offer our thanks also to the many unmentioned people who have been of help.

If the reader gains any perspective of the years and events of 1939–45, it is a reflection of the vivid glimpses afforded me by Ezekiel Abraham, Zelig Belokamen, Millie Campanella, Dr. Abraham J. Cohn, Rabbi Joseph D. Epstein, Benjamin Fishoff, Joseph Genger, Jan Goldsztejn, Nathan Gutwirth, Leo Hanin, Michael Ionis, Horace Kadoorie, Sir Lawrence Kadoorie, Irving Rosen, Alex Triguboff and Dina Waht. They shared memories, feelings and experiences, perhaps at great personal cost.

A number of scholars, including the late Professor Setsuzo Kotsuji, motivated and encouraged me with useful facts and insights. I am also grateful for information obtained from Senpo Sugihava, Mitsugi Shibata, Mitsuzo Tamura, Mrs. Koreshige Inuzuka and Hiroo Yasue.

Mr. Michael Kogan deserves a special expression of gratitude for the many hours spent discussing with me the history of those years, and for the use of his collection of top secret and highly confidential Japanese Foreign Ministry documents.

For their love, devotion and friendship, my personal thanks go to Walter J. Citrin, President of the Jewish Community of Japan and all the congregants and members. Their valuable recollections and constant impetus were refreshing moments during arduous years of research.

No amount of appreciation can repay my debt to the World Jewish Congress, Joint Distribution Committee, YIVO Library,

National Archives and Records Service and the Library of Congress for research help and use of their papers. When the cost of translating Japanese documents became prohibitive, the Memorial Foundation for Jewish Culture lent financial support.

I have learned much from three giants of Far Eastern Jewish history. Dr. Herman Dicker who was the pioneer writer in this field and whose contributions formed the basis of present and future works, is the beacon in the dark for those who wish to know the subject. A special debt of gratitude is due Dr. David Kranzler who has devoted many precious years in the pursuit of learning and disseminating the history of the Jewish refugee community in Shanghai, and the Japanese policy toward Jews. I leaned heavily on his *Japanese, Nazis and Jews* – a fully documented and comprehensive description and analysis of this period – and he graciously gave of his experience, data and advice. Professor Rudolf Loewenthal provided encouragement in my research, and allowed me to consult his valuable thesis, *Japanese and Chinese Materials Pertaining to the Jewish Catastrophe*.

Writers will occasionally overlook the fact that the foresight and perception of the publisher is perhaps equal to the work itself. Paddington Press was enthusiastic about the idea of this book when not even an outline was available and before one word was typed onto a page, and my special thanks go to Richard Ehrlich of Paddington Press and Alan Joseph who first introduced us.

Last, but not least, I humbly accept the blessing of my marriage because it was my wife who typed the first manuscript and whose inspiration and tranquility have contributed to every present achievement and will see me through whatever the future brings.

# INTRODUCTION

BETWEEN 1934 and 1940 a secret policy was devised in the highest councils of the Japanese government. It could have saved a million Jews from Hitler's Holocaust and even halted the war between Japan and the United States before it began. This was the *fugu* plan – Tokyo's means of enrolling the talents and skills of European Jewry, plus the capital, influence and sympathy of American Jewry, in the building of Japan's twentieth-century empire, the Greater East Asia Co-Prosperity Sphere.

In the 1930s the Jewish people seemed – to the devisers of the *fugu* plan – to have exactly what Japan lacked. Her empire – growing rapidly by conquest – needed the capital and financial skills exhibited, for example, by the Rothschilds, Bernard Baruch and Jacob Schiff, and there was a particular shortage of experienced industrialists and technicians who would be willing to settle in the wilderness of Manchukuo (Manchuria) – Japan's newly acquired north China "colony" – to develop the area into a secure buffer zone against the menace of the Soviet Union. Finally, Japan sought to improve her image in the world and reverse the drift of Western, especially American, foreign policy which had begun to go against her. That task, she believed, was one for which the Jews were best suited, since, it was said, they controlled so much of the United States press, broadcast media and film industry.

In return for Jewish assistance with her problems, Japan was prepared to offer exactly what the Jews needed most: a safe haven from the increasingly brutal anti-Semitism welling up against them in Europe. Japan had neither a tradition of anti-Semitism, nor any interest in it, and in *Shinto* Japan, Christian antipathy toward Jews had no meaning whatsoever. To the devisers of the *fugu* plan,

IX

a Japanese–Jewish involvement seemed an arrangement made in heaven.

On earth, it was another matter. From the outset the creators of the *fugu* plan had undermined their own scheme with two very mistaken beliefs. The first was a gross misunderstanding of the nature of the Jewish people as a whole. (It could scarcely have been otherwise. For years, the primary source of Japanese "knowledge" about world Jewry was that notoriously anti-Semitic piece of fiction masquerading as fact, *The Protocols of the Elders of Zion*.) Their second misconception concerned the importance of Jews, as economic factors and policy shapers in the Western world. With these two basic mistakes built into the foundation of their plan, the Japanese could not help but build askew. In spite of vast amounts of research, Japanese officials were never able to comprehend certain crucial features of the Jewish situation. The most important of these was that the American Jewish community considered its ties to its political family, America, at least as strong as its ties to its religious family in Europe. Not understanding this, the executors of the *fugu* plan did not understand, for example, that when they made their proposal to Rabbi Stephen Wise in the winter of 1939, they were confronting not only the principal leader of American Jewry but a Jew whose loyalty to and love for the United States was almost Biblical in its intensity. Had they recognized this and approached him accordingly, the outcome of the Wise meeting, and of the *fugu* plan itself, might have been very different.

My own involvement with the *fugu* plan, though I was unaware of it at the time, began in 1968 when I moved with my family to Tokyo. No sooner had I taken up the position of Rabbi of the Jewish Community of Japan than I realized I had a congregation of "talking books." With the end of World War II and especially with the Communist takeover of mainland China in 1949, virtually all the Jews who had been part of the large foreign community in Shanghai fled. Many of them, particularly those who had lived in Asia all their lives, moved to Tokyo. At first, I would simply chat with these people, of my days at Hebrew High School in New York when many of my teachers had made references to their own experiences as refugees in Shanghai and Japan. As my congregants in Tokyo spun out their anecdotes, I was fascinated by their tales and in awe of their powers of survival. When I realized that no one had yet put together a collection of these remarkable experiences, I began interviewing my congregants in a more organized fashion. For three years, I took notes, taped interviews and gained familiarity with the sometimes scarcely believable story of the flight of thousands of Polish Jews away from the threatening hand of one Axis nation right into the apparently welcoming arms of another. Then, in the early 1970s, I was shown the Kogan Papers.

The Kogan Papers are a bound set of prewar Foreign-Ministry documents which had been found in the back of a second-hand bookstore in Tokyo and subsequently turned over to a Jewish resident named Michael Kogan. Each of the ten volumes was stamped *maru hi* (secret). The originals of the reports, studies and orders that made up the Kogan Papers had, like all the Japanese government's documents, been confiscated by the Allied Occupation Forces shortly after Japan's surrender, and moved to the Library of Congress in Washington. However, because for the most part all such documents were made in duplicate, it was not uncommon for these extra copies to turn up for sale, as the Kogan Papers did, during the early postwar period. Kogan, fluent in Japanese, had scanned some of the onion-skin pages absolutely bewildered. What was this nonsense about a "Jewish settlement in Manchuria"? He himself had lived in Harbin, the capital of Manchuria, while the Japanese were in control of the region; certainly he had heard of no such thing. Michael Kogan came to discuss the documents with me at a time when a Japanese colleague, Hideaki Kase, happened to be in my office in connection with an article he was translating for me. It is, indeed, a very small world: Kase was the son of the secretary of the prewar Japanese foreign minister Yosuke Matsuoka. Intrigued, he studied the whole set of volumes at length and found that Matsuoka had played a considerable role in the subject matter of those Papers – an involved scheme for manipulating world Jewry that was informally referred to as "the *fugu* plan."

Up to the time that Kase reported the contents of the Kogan Papers, I had merely been amassing a collection of reminiscences of a group of Jewish refugees about their lives in Japan and Shanghai during the thirties and World War II. Now I realized that these people, along with many others, had been unwittingly involved in a much more complex series of events. Using the Kogan Papers as a starting point, and with the help of the archives in the

Diet Library as well as various clerks in the Japanese Army and Navy and in the Foreign Ministry, I set out to track down as many people as I could find who had actually been involved with the *fugu* plan. Though Koreshige Inuzuka, a Navy captain who was one of its original creators, had died his wife was not only alive but was very responsive to my request for information. So was the son of Colonel Norihiro Yasue, another officer involved with the plan from the start, and so was the former Shanghai vice-consul, Mitsugi Shibata, and the *fugu* plan's New York liaison, Mitsuzo Tamura, and every one of the Jews mentioned in the documents whether they lived now in Israel or Hong Kong or even practically next door to me in Tokyo.

It was a fascinating investigation. I sat for hours with, for example, Shibata, asking questions, changing the tapes on the recorder and learning the human background to the officialese of the Kogan Papers.

"What was your reaction," I asked him, "to the plans put forth by the Nazi, Colonel Meisinger, at that meeting in Shanghai where .the 'final solution' was first discussed?"

Shibata rubbed his rounded chin briefly. After thirty-odd years, he remembered it clearly. "I was simply horrified. The atrocities I had heard rumors of were being outlined right in front of my eyes. But I felt so helpless. I am a loyal Japanese! These were our allies. I had to go along with what my superiors were planning, no matter how horrible it was. It was not until later, when I was sitting in the garden of the Japanese Consulate near the Garden Bridge, that I realized what I had to do."

Shibata and the others consulted their personal journals for half-remembered names and incidents. Without exception, in spite of an initial awkwardness in discussing what they had planned and done, everyone was totally candid and forthcoming.

In 1976, I left my position in Tokyo to return to the United States. But because I believed that the story of the refugees and of the *fugu* plan with which they were so intricately involved, deserved better than to be heard only by my friends and future congregations, I asked the help of Mary Swartz, a member of the Tokyo Jewish community and a professional writer. Coincidentally, she was also returning to America about the same time, and the stage was set for the collaboration that has produced this book.

The question of historical fact versus historical fiction arose early in our manuscript preparations. We both felt strongly that since the entire series of events is *factual*, we would not change anything for the sake of drama or character development. However, in order to convey the flavor of the refugee experience, we did decide to coalesce some of those hundreds of anecdotes that had been told to me by the Jews from Shanghai, around nine composite characters. As a result there are nine fictional characters: Avram Chesno, Gershon Cohen, Yankel Gilbewitz, Moishe and Sophie Katznelson, Cheya and Getzel Syrkin and their son Dovid, and Ephraim Orliansky. Through them we have described the actual experiences of some of the thousands of Jewish refugees who survived the Holocaust in Japan and Shanghai.

Other than these nine, all characters in the book are real and, within the reasonable bounds of recounting history, they spoke and acted as presented here.

MARVIN TOKAYER
1979

# INTRODUCTION TO THE
# CURRENT EDITION

Twenty-five years have passed since *The Fugu Plan* first appeared. In 1979, so little was known of Japan's plan to resettle up to a million European Jewish refugees in its puppet state of Manchukuo that the *New York Times* published a news story about the book. Now, the *fugu* plan is widely recognized as one of the few positive, if strange, twists in the tortured fate of European Jewry.

Over these years, one person has come to be the human face of the *fugu* plan: Chiune Sugihara. From November 1939 to September 1940, Sugihara was officially the Japanese consul in Kovno (or "Kaunas"), Lithuania. In reality, Sugihara had been sent to Kovno to gather intelligence about Soviet and German troop movements in the area. Because he was there, however, and because of who he was, Sugihara became one of the crucial players in the *fugu* plan – a scheme that, by the war's end, would save the lives of thousands of Jews, as well as the entire Mir Yeshiva, whose scholars would survive to inspire a new era of Jewish learning in the U.S. and Israel.

Books and articles in English, Japanese, Hebrew and Chinese, running the gamut from scholarly to mass-appeal, are now being written about Sugihara - "the Japanese angel". In Japan, the name 'Sugihara' has become a symbol of one who takes care of others. His life is the subject of a secondary school English language text. A plaque at the *gaimusho*, the Japanese Foreign Ministry, commemorates his humanitarianism, in spite of the fact that he had disregarded orders from his superiors. In Israel, Sugihara is honored by Yad Vashem among the "Righteous of the Nations". And in the spring of this year, PBS will air, nationwide, an award-winning documentary, "Conspiracy of Kindness" about Sugihara's life and the lives of a few of the many people he saved.

Over the past 25 years, we have learned a great deal about this man. Chiune (or Senpo, he used either of two first names) Sugihara was born with the century, on January 1, 1900, and was raised in the *bushido/samurai* philosophy of his mother's family. Though his father – in pre-war Japan, the unquestioned authority in such matters – directed him to study law, Sugihara's own interests were in foreign languages and cultures. Circumventing his father, he applied to the *gaimusho* and was sent to Harbin, Manchuria, to study Russian. For the next ten years, Sugihara remained in Manchuria, marrying and later divorcing a Russian woman, and only rarely returning to Japan for brief visits. Starting with his posting to Lithuania in 1939, he spent eight years in Europe, going wherever the *gaimusho* saw fit to move him: Berlin, Prague, Konigsberg, and finally, at the war's end, Bucharest, Romania. There, he was arrested by the incoming Soviet forces and, with his wife and three children, interned for two years before being allowed to return to Japan.

In post-war Tokyo, there was little work available for a former, low-level diplomat. Sugihara managed to keep his family together only with small jobs that made use of his language skills. He worked intermittently at the American PX; he served as an announcer for the foreign language bureau of NHK, Japan's national radio; he free-lanced translation and interpreting services; and finally, in an almost unbelievable quirk of fate, he was hired by a Ginza clothing store whose owner, Anatole Ponve, had been one of the leaders of the Kobe Jewish community, which had cared for the 'Sugihara refugees' when they first arrived in Japan in 1940. But in spite of seeing Ponve virtually every day, Sugihara never mentioned his own role in the rescue of the Jewish refugees.

I asked him about that a few years before he died.

"I never knew what happened to the refugees," he said. "I never knew if they got past the Soviet Union, if they actually came to Japan, if they ever found safety. I didn't want to discuss it because perhaps I had only led them to their death. I was afraid to bring it up."

Did he know, I wondered, about the *fugu* plan?

"I only knew about that when you told me. If I had known, it would have been much easier for me. I wouldn't have felt the sole burden of responsibility for issuing the visas."

Finally, I asked him the one crucial question: Why did he do it? To the best of anyone's knowledge, before July 1940, Sugihara had never had any personal contact with Jews. Why, then, did he risk his career and possibly his life to save the lives of these refugees?

He looked at me as if he didn't really understand the question. "I just did what we as human beings should do. One of my best teachers, in Harbin, once told me: You do the right thing because it is the right thing. Not for gain. Not for recognition. Just because it is the right thing. The refugees were people who needed my help. I could give help to them. It was the right thing to do. That's all."

In the midst of the horror of 1940, it was the extreme good fortune of thousands of Jewish refugees, and tens of thousands of their descendants, that a rare man such as Sugihara was there when their lives depended on it.

Marvin Tokayer
2004

# INTRODUCTION BY DAVID RUBINSON*

In the late sixties, after his duty in Korea and Japan as one of the few Jewish air force chaplains, a young rabbi far from his native Brooklyn began serving his new congregation at the Jewish Center of Tokyo, Japan. Being an inquisitive and curious young fellow, in the Talmudic tradition, he asked questions. Who were his congregants? How had they ended up in Japan? Even in the context of the Diaspora, and the extremes of Holocaust survival, this group of Jews in Tokyo, twenty five years after Pearl Harbor, proved to be a fascinating repository of stories and history; what the rabbi later called "a congregation of talking books." The rabbi loved stories. He loved telling them and he loved hearing them.

One story was about thousands of mostly Polish Jewish refugees who had been saved from sure death by a Japanese man, in Lithuania in 1939/40. Even more amazing, the Jews had escaped to Japan, from there to Shanghai, and ultimately to hundreds of other points on the globe. Another story was about a secret Japanese government plan to save the Jews of Hitler's Europe.

Totally enthralled, Rabbi Marvin Tokayer began a quest that has endured these many years. He studied Japanese, Japanese history and religion, and discovered the amazing, extensive, and largely untold history of the relationship between The Jews and The Japanese. He learned all about Jacob Schiff, a Jewish banker, who became an icon in Japan in the early 20th century, by lending Japan the incomprehensibly vast sum of 196 million dollars to defeat

---

* David Rubinson is Executive Producer of the film *SUGIHARA Conspiracy of Kindness*.

Russia in the Russian-Japanese War of 1903. He learned about the Jews of Harbin and Manchuria, and the intricacies of the Japanese plans for world expansion and empire. He discovered what was called the Fugu Plan, and how it could have changed the course of history. He went out and personally interviewed everyone he could find who was connected with these amazing stories, and at long last, he found himself face to face with Chiune Sugihara, the man who had saved the Jews in Eastern Europe some thirty years before.

In human history, greed and the lust for power are as old as our first footprints in the sand. Why do the stories in *The Fugu Plan* continue to fascinate us so much now, some sixty years after the Blitzkrieg, much as they fascinated the young rabbi?

We Humans have decided that this Earth is ours, given to us to do with as we please. We act as if Human Beings are The Chosen, and the Earth is our dominion. We see ourselves, not as fellow beings sharing the Planet Earth with other equal beings, but define ourselves instead by our differences– our physical appearance, our religion, our politics or our material possessions.

We define ourselves by what we have, what we do. We act, not from the essential human traits of compassion and caring for others, but from expediency, entitlement, utilitarianism and pragmatism, and we Humans, individually and collectively as nations, make daily choices based solely on — what is good for ME? What do I GET from this?

Not- how do I feel, deep inside – what is my gut feeling?

Not from a deep sense of empathy and shared humanity.

You can make money if you *do* this. You can be famous if you *do* that. You can prove to everyone and to yourself how important or powerful you are. You can WIN or you can HAVE or you can TAKE. And since winning and having and taking make up so much of our lives, we do those things, and we make those choices. And we never stop and wait and feel. We have lost touch with our capacity for compassion that defines us as human beings, for ourselves and thus for anyone else.

*The Fugu Plan* is, among many things, about people who make choices. Some of the people act from self-interest or hope of gain or fame or power or salvation. Some others from a deep, inner and basic conviction, compelled by their innate humanity. *The Fugu Plan* is about how these various choices had profound repercussions on the lives of many thousands of fellow Humans, and upon the world itself.

In a time when war and massacre, starvation and disease, greed and domination threaten to rule the planet, the stories of *The Fugu Plan* show us how Humans can act differently, and by so doing, can change the course of History. One of these stories, largely untold even today, is about the actual "Fugu Plan" itself.

In the 1930s, the most influential Japanese military officers, as well as bankers, industrialists, politicians and aristocrats, debated the most effective methods to fulfill their desired destiny of a world empire. Certainly, they had achieved enormous success, including the invasion and capture of Manchuria, by military means. But some members of the group had another idea. There was a choice, they said.

Why not spend the money, resources, and time in a better way? A way that would be more constructive, not so wasteful of human life, perhaps longer lasting, and definitely cheaper? Why not dominate the world by trade instead of military expansion or war? But to do this, the Japanese decided that they needed to conscript who they strongly believed to be the best of the world's tradesmen and manufacturers, people who in the view of the Japanese, knew how to make quality goods, raise financing, develop markets, and who had powerful friends in America. They decided that they needed The Jews.

Thus was born the "Fugu Plan"– designed to take in Europe's Jews, deliver them from the Nazis and those seeking to exterminate them, and bring them by the tens of thousands to Manchuria and Japanese territory. The Japanese could populate the sparse land they had conquered but could not occupy, and, at the same time, staff themselves with talented people who could build their businesses, provide expertise in manufacturing, run their factories, and carry on international trade, especially in the USA.

The Japanese made their offer to the World Jewish Congress in New York. To their amazement, and disappointment, they were unceremoniously turned down. The militarists won the debate, the "Fugu Plan" failed and died.

Another story that Rabbi Tokayer heard regularly was about the Japanese consul in Lithuania. Few could even remember his name, and many had just scraps of paper or fleeting memories. One thing they all agreed was that a Japanese man had given them what no other representative from any other nation on earth was willing to give, in that horrifying and deadly time after the Nazi invasion of

Poland. He opened a door when all were closed. He gave them visas. A way out. He gave them their lives.

Rabbi Tokayer had never heard this story before. A Japanese savior of Jews? Jews escaping to Japan. He began to dig for any scrap of information. And what he found changed his life, as it changed mine, and those of so many of us who have read this book.

He discovered that the Japanese foreign ministry had sent its best German and Russian speaking career diplomat to Kaunas (Kovno), Lithuania in 1939, to "gather intelligence" on Nazi and Soviet troop movements. Lithuania in 1939 was, for a very brief period, a free nation, a safe haven buffering Nazi occupied Poland to the West, and the USSR to the East. Jewish refugees from Poland were streaming into this last remaining safe haven in Eastern Europe.

By a strange twist of luck, and some daring rule bending, some Jews of Dutch nationality discovered that they did not require visas to enter the distant Dutch protectorate of Curacao, invitingly close to the United States. They could not travel to Curacao by going west or north, all Nazi-conquered land. They would have to travel east, many weeks' journey on the Trans Siberian Railroad, past the Gulags, the slave labor camps, to the Russian port of Vladivostok, and then via Japan.

The destination was far less important than just getting OUT of Nazi dominated Europe. Get out and then worry about where to go from there.

But the world was populated much as it is today, by people lacking compassion, who acted in pure self-interest, expediency, and greed. There wasn't a nation on earth that would help them, not one of the thirty foreign embassies and consulates in Lithuania, not the American Embassy, not the British nor the French. There were excruciatingly few human beings anywhere who would even risk being perceived as helpful.

What was in it for them? What would they GET? There were orders to follow, and careers to protect, and there was money to be made. And the chances of a Jew finding a Japanese savior in Lithuania– what were the odds of that?

And so, while the world turned its back, and his government forbade him to help, with the Red Army now occupying Lithuania, and the Nazi Army gathered on the Lithuanian border – Chiune Sugihara looked out the window of his small house in Kaunas, at a motley crowd of panicked Jewish refugees desperate for the visas that would give them their lives, and he looked into his heart.

At last Rabbi Tokayer, after years of searching, letter writing and pleading, got to meet and interview Chiune Sugihara, living in poor obscurity. The rabbi finally asked Sugihara: Why did he do it? Why did he decide to save those people?

Chiune could not comprehend the question. What did he mean? Why did he do it? The question made no sense.

He did it because it was the only thing to do of course. These people were to die if he did nothing. There WAS no question. He did what any other man would have done, said Chiune Sugihara.

And that is why this book is so terribly relevant, significant, and important right now.

If one person who reads this book, stops and says: "I can do that."

"I can act from my deep humanity and sense of compassion and love."

"I can forget the expediencies of the world, the pragmatic and the profit making, what I am told to do, and even what is best for me, and just do what I know inside is the right thing to do."

Then the world will immediately, even if infinitesimally, change course.

Sugihara's visas saved thousands. The living descendants of those he saved now number over fifty thousand human beings.

One book read, one deed done, one mind changed, one small shift in the course of events, and who knows what vast repercussions can result?

After all, this book started with a young rabbi from Brooklyn at a synagogue in Tokyo.

David Rubinson
2004

With deepest gratitude and profound
respect for my good friend Moishe

# CHRONOLOGY

**1932**  **The Year of the Monkey**

MARCH   Founding of the "Independent State of Manchukuo."

**1933**  **The Year of the Cock**

JANUARY   Hitler comes to power in Germany.

FEBRUARY   Matsuoka leads Japanese delegation out of League of Nations.

MARCH   Establishment of Dachau concentration camp.

APRIL   German government dismisses Jewish civil servants; beginning of boycott of all Jewish-owned businesses in Germany.

AUGUST   Simon Kaspé kidnapped in Harbin.

DECEMBER   Simon Kaspé found dead.

**1934**  **The Year of the Pig**

JULY   Japanese Foreign Ministry announces plan to invite 50,000 German Jews to Manchukuo.

**1935**  **The Year of the Boar**

SEPTEMBER   Nuremberg racial-purity laws passed by German Reichstag.

**1936**  **The Year of the Rat**

OCTOBER   Mussolini and Hitler form Rome–Berlin Axis alliance.

NOVEMBER   Publication of first volume of *Kokusai Hinmitsu Ryoku Kenkyu* (Studies in the International

Conspiracy). Anti-Comintern (Communist-International) Pact signed between Japan and Germany.

**1937**  **The Year of the Bull**

JULY  "Marco Polo Bridge incident" provokes war between China and Japan. Japanese bombing of Shanghai and "Rape of Nanking."

DECEMBER  First Conference of Far Eastern Jewish Communities, Harbin. Kotsuji publishes Hebrew grammar in Japanese.

**1938**  **The Year of the Tiger**

MARCH  Germany invades Austria. Yasue assigned to Dairen as chief of military mission.

JULY  Evian Refugee Conference – attending nations refuse to offer refuge to German Jews.

AUGUST  International Committee formed in Shanghai to help refugees.

NOVEMBER  Cultural Agreement signed between Japan and Germany. Wise anti-Japanese letter to Zikman. First record of term *fugu* used at official meeting. *Kristallnacht* in Germany. Japanese government formally establishes Greater East Asia Co-Prosperity Sphere.

DECEMBER  Second Conference of Far Eastern Jewish Communities, Harbin. Five Ministers' Conference in Tokyo establishes Japan's policy toward Jews.

**1939**  **The Year of the Hare**

FEBRUARY  Foreign Minister Arita's public statement that Japan will not discriminate against Jews.

MARCH  Germany occupies Czechoslovakia.

APRIL  Inuzuka posted to Shanghai. Tamura first meets with American Jewish leaders.

MAY  Kaufman's "state visit" to Tokyo. Jews in Shanghai ask Japanese to prevent further immigration of refugees from Europe.

JULY  *Study and Analysis of Introducing Jewish Capital* approved by Japanese government.

| | |
|---|---|
| AUGUST | Japan puts severe restrictions on refugees wanting to enter Shanghai. Stalin and Hitler sign Non-Aggression Pact. |
| SEPTEMBER | Germany invades Poland. Britain and France declare war on Germany. Sugihara assigned as consul in Kovno, Lithuania. |
| OCTOBER | Kotsuji begins working for South Manchuria Railway. |
| NOVEMBER | Tamura meets with Inuzuka in Shanghai. |
| DECEMBER | Tamura–Wise meeting, New York. Third Conference of Far Eastern Jewish Communities, Harbin; Kotsuji delivers speech in Hebrew. |

## 1940 The Year of the Dragon

| | |
|---|---|
| APRIL | Germany occupies Denmark and Norway. |
| MAY | Germany occupies Holland and Belgium; Dunkirk evacuation. Churchill becomes prime minister. |
| JUNE | Wise writes Kindermann to say he might consider Japanese settlement plan with State Department consent. Italy enters war. Germans enter Paris. U.S.S.R. annexes Lithuania. |
| JULY | Matsuoka becomes foreign minister. Tojo becomes war minister. Japanese government secretly agrees to form Tripartite Pact with Germany and Italy. Kobe Jewcom formed. |
| AUGUST | Sugihara issues transit visas in Kovno. |
| SEPTEMBER | Sugihara forced to leave Lithuania. Tripartite Pact signed. |
| OCTOBER | Yasue dismissed by Tojo. |
| NOVEMBER | Jews in Shanghai and Harbin cable US organizations on behalf of Japan. Warsaw Ghetto sealed off. |
| DECEMBER | Mir Yeshiva and many refugees in Lithuania request exit permits from U.S.S.R. Dairen Jewish Community honors Yasue at banquet. Matsuoka meets Zikman on New Year's Eve. |

**1941**  **The Year of the Snake**

JANUARY  Exit permit lists posted, Vilna.

FEBRUARY  Mir Yeshiva, Amshenover rebbe and other refugees arrive Kobe. Newman, in Shanghai, gives silver cigarette case to Inuzuka.

MARCH  Matsuoka leaves on trip to Berlin and Moscow. Japanese Embassy in Moscow stops issuing transit visas. Warhaftig's "visas-for-tickets" plan fails. Eastjewcom founded in Shanghai.

APRIL  Matsuoka signs Non-Aggression Pact with Stalin. Germany occupies Yugoslavia.

MAY  Warhaftig arranges for refugees to be allowed into Shanghai if necessary. Interrogation of rabbis in Tokyo. Meisinger arrives in Tokyo to head Gestapo in Japan and China.

JUNE  Germany invades U.S.S.R., occupies Lithuania.

JULY  Stricter U.S. immigration regulations go into effect. Matsuoka replaced as foreign minister.

AUGUST  Refugees in Kobe relocated to Shanghai.

SEPTEMBER  45,000 Jews in Vilna confined to two ghettos.

OCTOBER  25,000 Jews in Kovno killed by Nazis. Tojo becomes prime minister.

NOVEMBER  Naval/air fleet leaves Japan for Pearl Harbor.

DECEMBER  Japan attacks Pearl Harbor. Japan occupies all of Shanghai. Hitler declares war on U.S. Japan captures Hong Kong.

**1942**  **The Year of the Horse**

JANUARY  Japanese government rescinds policy of Five Ministers' Conference.

FEBRUARY  Inuzuka assigned to sea duty. Japan captures Singapore.

MARCH  Japan overruns Dutch East Indies.

APRIL  Bataan Death March.

MAY  Joint Distribution Committee sends last cable from U.S. to Shanghai.

JUNE  Meisinger arrives in Shanghai.

JULY  Nazis and Japanese in Shanghai plan extermination of Jews.

SEPTEMBER  *Pao Chia* police formed, Shanghai.

| | |
|---|---|
| **1943** | **The Year of the Sheep** |
| JANUARY | Anti-Semitic exhibits in major Tokyo department stores. |
| FEBRUARY | Proclamation of "designated area for stateless refugees" in Shanghai. SACRA formed. Margolies interned in Pootung camp for enemy nationals. German Sixth Army surrenders at Stalingrad (considered turning point of war). |
| MARCH | Anti-Semitic exhibits in major Osaka department stores. |
| APRIL | Warsaw ghetto uprising begins. |
| MAY | Warsaw ghetto liquidated. |
| DECEMBER | Margolies repatriated to U.S.; sends "Happy Birthday" telegram to Shanghai. |
| | |
| **1944** | **The Year of the Monkey** |
| MARCH | Joint Distribution Committee funds begin arriving in Shanghai. |
| APRIL | Tientsin Jewish Club peace-feeler. |
| JUNE | Allied landing in Normandy. |
| JULY | Tojo resigns. |
| OCTOBER | Battle of Leyte Gulf virtually destroys Japanese Navy. |
| | |
| **1945** | **The Year of the Cock** |
| MARCH | First fire-bombing of major Japanese cities. |
| APRIL | Roosevelt dies. Hitler commits suicide. |
| MAY | Germany surrenders. |
| JULY | Shanghai ghetto bombed. |
| AUGUST | U.S.S.R declares war on Japan. U.S. drops atomic bombs on Hiroshima, Nagasaki. Japan surrenders. |
| SEPTEMBER | Formal surrender of Japanese troops in China at Nanking. |

# Part One

# FROM EUROPE TO THE ORIENT 1939–41

## The Birth of the Fugu Plan

**1** SENPO SUGIHARA, Japanese consul in Kovno, Lithuania, sat half-awake on the edge of his bed. He shivered in the chill of early morning. It was 5:15 – no hour for any civilized person to be stirring. What woke him? Usually it was his wife who responded to noises from the children. But she, and the children, were still sleeping soundly. Yet there had definitely been a sound . . . and there it was again: a shushing, rustling, almost whispering stir from just outside the house.

Sugihara wrapped his *yukata* more closely around him, padded across the floor and peered out of a window.

"*Chik-sho!*" He immediately jumped back. The army was out there! The invasion had come overnight! They were forming ranks, under his window! Sliding across the bare floor, he quickly woke his wife. Within seconds he had shuttled her and the children into the security of the closet. Then he alone returned to peek out of the window.

At second glance, it was not such a military scene. True, there were a great many people, and most of them men, but they were not preparing for battle. They were simply staring – staring up at his bedroom window.

"*Nan-de o? Do desho-ka?* What are they doing here? What do they want with me?"

But even as he whispered the questions to himself, he knew the answers. Far from being soldiers, those gaunt, poorly dressed men were civilian refugees, Jews. Originally from Poland, driven out of their homes by the Nazis, they had been living for the past several months on air and charity in the larger towns of Lithuania.

Sugihara released his family from the closet, though warning everybody to stay out of sight of the windows, and sat down on his bed to think. Once over the shock of suddenly finding so many of the refugees virtually under his nose, he could easily comprehend why they had come. For a moment, he even wondered how he could ever have imagined that they would do otherwise. Now he had to decide what his answer was going to be to their inevitable request.

Despite his heavy shoes, Getzel Syrkin's feet were unpleasantly damp from standing in the wet grass half the night. He felt his wife's weight against his shoulder as she dozed on her feet. Last night, traveling on the jerky train from Vilna to Kovno, they had had no sleep. Their arrival had only led to this – standing around waiting for some unknown figure to wake up. Getzel shivered. It was surprisingly chilly for August.

How strange that it should be August again, he thought, overwhelmed, as he had been for nearly a year, by the rapid pace of events swirling around him. Last August at this time, 1939 it was, he would have been asleep in his own house, in the small town where his father, and grandfather, and who could count how many fathers back from there, had all lived and died. Last August he had thought he too would live in Alexandrov. Then, in September, they had come – the machine men with their machine guns – and he had thought he would at least die in Alexandrov. Well fed, blond, energetic, they seemed so sure that they alone had the right to say who was to live and who was to die. It was unbelievable how often they decided the latter. They would shoot a person, just where that person happened to be standing for no reason anyone could see. And then they just left the body where it fell. So a person who had been a relative or a friend or even an enemy, but anyway a known human being, suddenly became just an impediment, an object that one stumbled over in one's haste to obey the Germans' commands.

"Is anyone cold?" the leader of the Nazi platoon asked when all the Jews they could find had been herded into the market square. Such a simple question. But when you had been goaded out of bed in the middle of the night by a bayonet-wielding teenager and rushed, in just pants and shirt, out into the streets, with people screaming and guns going off all around you, and your children crying, and even your wife unable to do anything about what was happening . . . who knew the answer to even such a simple question at such a time?

"You must be too cold to speak," the commandant had said. "Let us make a few fires to warm you."

So they made a few fires. They burned the synagogue and the school. They burned most of the shops, including Getzel's tiny tailoring shop, and some of the houses. Then the commandant made a brief speech, ending with the order that all Jews were to be out of town by 7:00 that morning and any who weren't would be shot.

Getzel had never been an "outdoors man". His favorite pastime had been to go to the *shul*, the small synagogue only a few buildings down the street from his tailoring shop. Seated there, across from the man who had been his study partner since childhood, surrounded by other men similarly engaged, he would delve into the precise interpretations of one of the 613 commandments by which observant Jews had organized their lives since the time of Moses. Reasoning, examining, trying to comprehend arguments propounded long ago by rabbis from Mainz to Troyes, Getzel felt fully at home, firmly rooted in the proper time and place, his spirit nourished as much by the familiar routine as by the meaning he found in the Law.

Suddenly, literally overnight, all that had disappeared: the *shul*, the old, hand-worn texts, even, he realized as the sun, incomprehensibly, rose, even his life-long study partner, the victim of one of the fires in that terrible night. All the domestic and religious supports that had given Getzel his own particular niche in the world were being destroyed. Nothing remained except his son, thank God, and his wife Cheya who was now quietly snoring against his left shoulder.

He glanced down at her, thin hair and skin like a half-cooked bagel. He had lived with Cheya for so long he sometimes thought that he no longer really saw her when he looked at her. He had been amazingly fortunate to have her for a wife – a circumstance due, he knew, more to her poor father's inability to make a dowry for the fourth of his daughters than to Getzel's own personal appeal or stature in Alexandrov. A beauty she was not: even when she'd been pregnant with the children they'd lost and the one son that had lived, she had been too thin. But she had a good head for business, and she had sense. It was Cheya who managed the accounts of the poor tailoring business by which Getzel struggled to support his family – and Cheya who coped with the day-to-day problems of their meager existence. Yet she never scorned him for his lack of commercial ability or for the resultant lack of material comfort in their lives. And she always gave him the respect a husband was due.

But the horror that their life, like the lives of their neighbors, became after September 13, 1939, was incomprehensible even to Cheya. No one knew where to go. Thrown bodily out of the only homes they had ever known, the Jews of Alexandrov joined the Jews of dozens of other little towns, trudging the dirt roads of Poland. Many, fearing the Russians (who were already in control of eastern Poland), more than the Germans, headed for Warsaw. Others, like Getzel and Cheya, with their six-year-old son Dovid, thought only of escaping the unreasoning brutality of the Nazis. Refuge was so far away. For Getzel, the trek through the mud and rain, and increasing cold as September sank into October, was an unending nightmare, one made worse by having to wake up every morning to another day of it. Terrified of every strange place – and every place was strange – Getzel could only numbly keep putting one foot in front of the other. Totally unprepared by his thirty-eight years to cope with the unfamiliar, Getzel was unable to get his bearings in this overwhelmingly unfamiliar world that stretched out endlessly beyond the borders of his native village. All his attention was concentrated merely on keeping up with the rest of the straggling mass of refugees informally united only by pace and direction. The subconscious realization that half these people also had been shocked into the same state of virtual incapacity made no difference. Getzel Syrkin sank into himself, leaving Cheya almost completely responsible for the needs of the family. Aware and bitterly ashamed of the state he was in, he could nevertheless do nothing about it.

Fearful or not, they could only keep going. First they crossed German-held Poland, now completely overrun with Nazi soldiers; then through the sector controlled by Russia, where at least they didn't shoot a person just for having been born a Jew; and finally after weeks and weeks, they reached still free Lithuania. Here, at last, a Jew could get help from the Jewish relief societies, just because he had been born a Jew.

Getzel moved slightly, waking Cheya.

"Nothing?" she said.

"Nothing. He's not awake yet."

"Let him sleep till noon," she said, "if only when he wakes up he will give us the permits."

"*Im yirzeh ha-Shem* . . . God willing . . ."

Getzel's voice was a whisper, scarcely louder than a fervent thought, but a few feet away, Moishe Katznelson heard the words. Scarcely fourteen years old and raised, until not quite a year ago, in a happy, religious family, Moishe had not yet lost his feeling for the power of God. Everything else, but his sister, Sophie, he had lost. The September before, his home in Kucholze had been left behind in the Polish night as he and his three sisters had fled, hidden in the hay of a borrowed milk cart. His mother pretended to be the milkman. His father, on foot, had caught up with them a few miles outside just as the sun was coming up. It had been an adventure, then. They were all together. And his father, as always, seemed in command of the situation. They had walked or ridden, bartering a few possessions brought along for the purpose, for food, but saving their money just in case, as his father had said, "we need help in finding our way over the border."

They had reached the frontier late in the afternoon, joining several other refugees waiting in a wooded area near the open swath that formed the border. Moishe's father left the five of them and went ahead "to arrange things." It was dark and a chill rain had begun before the money changed hands and the crossing was arranged. Following the hooded light of a guard, the Katznelsons stumbled over one another, heeding the guard's warnings to stay close together. Suddenly there was a blinding burst of light and soldiers were all around, yelling, and dogs, too, barking and biting.

His mother's voice, his father's voice screamed out of a tangle of bodies, shouts, shots and beams of light cutting wildly across the field.

"Run, Moishe! Over the border! Fast! Run, Moishe, Sophie, Malke, Sara. Keep going! Don't stop! Cross the border! Cross the border! We'll follow."

Moishe grabbed the hand of his nearest sister and ran across the stubble of the field. Tripping over clumps of earth, they ran and ran to the safety of the trees beyond the field. And there they waited for Father and Mother and Malke and Sara. But no one came. None of Moishe's family and none of the others that had been led into the trap. The darting lights moved away from the open field, swinging back in the direction the Katznelson family had come from. The screams and cries became fainter. Then, for a moment, the sound of the car engines. Then silence . . . and the rain.

"Moishe?" Sophie was ten, the baby of the family. "Moishe,

where are we? What happened to Mama? Where are Malke and Sara?"

"We are across the border," Moishe heard himself saying. "The others will come later. They will meet us later."

He almost reassured himself. The part of him that was still a boy had faith that when his father said something would be, it would be. And since he had clearly heard his father shout "We will follow," it was absolutely certain that the rest of the family would be coming. But the part of Moishe which had accepted the responsibilities of manhood at his *bar mitzvah* only a few months before, refused to suppress the sounds of the shots which had been followed so incontrovertibly by silence. Perhaps what his father had meant was that they should keep going all the way to their original destination, to Vilna. Perhaps he had meant that they would all meet in Vilna. But where was Vilna?

"I'm cold, Moishe," said Sophie, and then beginning to cry, "I want to go inside someplace and get warm."

Moishe looked at her, shivering in the rainy night. Suppose they didn't go on but crept back instead – back across the open field, back to find the others. Then they could all be together again.

But suppose the family wasn't there, he thought. Suppose they had escaped somehow? Then he and Sophie would be on the wrong side of the border, holding everybody up. His father had said: go over the border, keep going, don't stop. All right then – they had crossed the border. Now they would keep going until they reached Vilna.

Moishe took Sophie's hand. "We'll warm up if we walk," he said.

"Where are we going, Moishe?" she asked again.

"Vilna," he said firmly. And in too soft a voice for her to hear, "To Vilna and to Father, *im yirzeh ha-Shem*."

With the will of God – and, more tangibly, with the help of other refugees who were never so tired or destitute that they couldn't share something with the two children – Moishe and Sophie Katznelson finally reached Vilna. There, the well of support that was fed by streams of money from Jews all over the world relieved them from the daily pressures of finding food, and shelter from the increasing cold. But as a result, there was absolutely nothing for Moishe to do . . . but wait. A steady, sad line of refugees continued to enter Vilna, so no doubt his father would come soon. But suppose his father and the rest came, even tomorrow? Where would they go from Vilna? Moishe sat around the International Joint Distribution Committee's relief kitchen with men older than he, but he soon realized that they had no better idea than he where to go from here.

Moishe wracked his brain, mentally exploring all the countries in the world he had ever heard about, then, finding a world map in the library attached to the Great Synagogue of Vilna, discovered a great many more. He had never imagined there were so many countries! Pink, yellow, blue, green – it was such a beautiful world. After studying the map carefully, Moishe suggested half a dozen possible destinations for the Katznelson family to the secretary of the Hebrew Immigrant Aid Society, the main organization in charge of relocating Jewish refugees. At first, the overworked woman, exhausted from the frustrations of trying to find places for Jews in a world that simply did not want them, explained to him why each of his proffered destinations was impossible. But when Moishe returned with another list of countries, she angrily told him to leave her alone – then put her head down on the stacks of paper on her desk and burst into tears for no reason he could see. After that, all Moishe could do was keep his ears open for any possibility while his eyes were watching out for his family.

Yesterday he had been rewarded. Killing time, sitting on a bench in the courtyard of the Great Synagogue, he had overheard one yeshiva student telling another about getting a permit to go to a place called "Kurasow." The funny thing, the student said, was the permit – a "visa" they called it – wasn't any good. They wouldn't really let you into "Kurasow." But, if you had one of those "visas" – or even if you said you were going to get one – you could get a *real* "visa" to Japan. You couldn't stay for long in Japan – Moishe tried unsuccessfully to remember just where Japan was on the map – but from Japan, some people were going to . . . America!

America: the rich, the free, the place where nobody starved and no one was ever rejected. America: the good life for everybody – students, laborers, shop keepers, geniuses, cripples and fools alike. Like the end of the rainbow, America was almost impossible to reach. But once you were there, once you were in. . . . The irreligious believed in America more than in God. Even the yeshiva students couldn't say the name without pausing an instant.

Moishe had listened, had heard where the Japanese Consulate was and how to get there. That night, leaving Sophie in the free boardinghouse run by one of the Jewish relief agencies, he had crept onto a train for Kovno.

Now he watched the huge crowd expand visibly as the warm light of the sun spread out from the horizon. Maybe Japan was a big country. Maybe the man inside that white cement house could give everybody "visas." He alone needed six. Where was Japan, anyway? But it didn't matter. If you could get from Japan to America, it didn't matter where Japan was. "America. If we could really get to America. *Im yirzeh ha-Shem.* . . ."

A rustle of whispers ran through the crowd when a figure appeared briefly at the second-story window of the house. Then everyone became instantly and completely still. This was a way out. If only, if only. . . . There was no sound but the shallow breathing of four hundred people and the early morning chirruping of birds in the eaves of the Japanese Consulate.

Away from the sight of the motionless crowd, Consul Sugihara sat on his bed and reflected on what had led up to this. Three days ago, there had been one person, and he not literally a refugee. A young Dutch student in one of the Jewish yeshiva schools – one shy, respectful young man – had come to ask for a transit visa for Japan so that he might stop off en route to the Dutch colonial island of Curaçao in the Caribbean Sea. It had all been very proper: the student, Nathan Gutwirth, had a Dutch passport and in it the honorary Dutch consul in Kovno had stamped and signed an affirmation of the fact that Curaçao did not require an entry visa. That was strange, Sugihara had thought at the time, because, to the best of his knowledge, all the countries of the world now required entrance visas. Even Shanghai, the one place traditionally open to everyone under any circumstance, no questions asked, had, under Japanese occupation, instituted visa requirements the year before. However, what Curaçao required was the business of the Dutch, not the Japanese. So Sugihara stamped the multi-lingual transit visa into Gutwirth's passport, filling in the date of issue and duration of validity. Then he signed his name and legalized the whole thing with the bright orange–red official stamp of the Imperial Japanese Consulate.

Actually it had been a pleasant change of pace. In the eleven months he had been in Kovno, Sugihara had not been asked to do a single thing concerning trade or diplomacy. Of course, he hadn't really been sent to do the work of a consul. He'd been sent out to spy. Tokyo did not trust its German allies. Sugihara's mission was to keep track of German troop movements, to be the extended ears and eyes of the Japanese military attaché in Berlin who was, Tokyo believed, purposely kept in the dark as to Germany's military plans. However, Sugihara, in his early thirties and too young to have risen high in the ranks of the Foreign Ministry, still considered himself to be a diplomat, not a spy; so for once he was pleased to be doing something in his normal line of business.

Within twelve hours of Gutwirth's polite departure from the house three more young men had appeared. Two had passports containing the phrase, "No visa to Curaçao is required." One of them did not have even that – though with heartfelt conviction, he assured the consul that he would soon get it. Beginning to see a trend, though one he did not understand, Sugihara pleaded that he needed time to do the paperwork: the three young men should return the following day.

Sugihara had never been involved with the apparently universal problems of those people called "Jews." He had read about them once, in high school, in a Shakespearean play. During the several months he'd lived in Manchuria, he had met some people who, he'd been told, were Jews. And of course he was well aware that Hitler blamed Jews for all of Germany's problems and that Russia also found them useful as political scapegoats. But until this moment, the "Jewish problem" had never been in any way *his* problem.

Until this point it had seemed to Sugihara that "the Jewish problem" had always been simply a question of politics. In political matters, he was quite content to follow the directions of his superiors in the Foreign Ministry. But seeing actual people rather than words, and finding these people standing not in some far-off place but right under his nose, put the "Jewish problem" into a moral and human perspective. While he thought about it, Sugihara began drafting a cable to the Foreign Ministry in Tokyo: did he have permission to issue a number of transit visas for people reportedly bound for Curaçao?

Until Tokyo replied to his cable, there was nothing Sugihara could do. Outwardly unperturbed, he politely fended off the refugees who appeared in his office with that strange notation, "No visa to Curaçao is required," stamped on their papers. But as their numbers increased, so did his inner bewilderment: what had the student Gutwirth done, or what had the honorary Dutch consul done, to start this train of events?

It had been early July 1940 when Nathan Gutwirth had at last faced up to the fact that he had to do *something*. Born in Belgium twenty-four years before and raised in Holland, Gutwirth had been studying for nearly four years at the renowned Tels Yeshiva in central Lithuania. But clearly, that intellectually exciting and extremely satisfying part of his life was rapidly coming to a close. The previous May, Hitler's soldiers had marched through Holland with the speed, and resulting devastation, of lightning. The last letter from his mother had a terrified, almost indecipherable plea for him to save himself from the brutality of the German war machine. Nathan Gutwirth had spoken to his teachers and to the principal of the school. His problem was not, after all, unique: the Tels Yeshiva drew its students from all over Europe and now all of them equally were caught in the noose that was slowly tightening around Lithuania. Sympathetic as the rabbis were, and fearful of the worsening situation, they counseled against even attempting to do anything. "We can only hope and pray that we live through these times," they advised. "In the meantime, we should make no trouble, ask no questions, and by all means not call attention to ourselves. To go unnoticed is the best way of surviving."

So while Germany tightened its hold on Holland and Belgium, while Britain was driven back to the Channel and Dunkirk, Nathan Gutwirth did nothing. By the end of June, the Germans were in Paris, but, more important to the Tels Yeshiva, the U.S.S.R. had formally annexed Lithuania. It had all been arranged on paper – no invasion, no bloodshed. But the Jews were, once and for all, trapped.

In early July, Gutwirth began a correspondence with the nearest Dutch ambassador, L. P. J. de Dekker, in Riga, Latvia. As a Dutch citizen, he asked, would it be possible for him to get a visa to the Dutch colony of Curaçao? (Since that island was only some nine hundred miles from America, Gutwirth hoped that once he got there it would not be too difficult to get a visa to the United States.) De Dekker's response came promptly. Gutwirth would need no visa to go to Curaçao. But Holland had no diplomatic relations with the Soviet Union. It was theoretically impossible for him to try to pass through that country, and extremely dangerous for him to try.

But Nathan Gutwirth had another problem to confront before dealing with Russia. "I am not in this predicament alone," he wrote back. "Is there some way my fellow students and teachers – who are not Dutch citizens – could also get visas to Curaçao?"

"Visas to Curaçao are not based on Dutch citizenship," de Dekker replied. "The official regulation concerning entry into Curaçao is that no visa is required for anyone. What is required is a landing permit issued by the governor of the island. Definitely, the governor will *not* issue your friends any such permit. However, according to the letter of the law, Curaçao does not require a visa. And there is no reason why this fact should not be stamped into the passport of any traveler who should desire it."

Nathan Gutwirth caught the ambassador's drift, and he responded to the letter the same day he received it: "Would it be possible for you to inform your consuls here in Lithuania that they are permitted to do this?"

De Dekker's reply came equally fast. "Not only is it possible," he said, "but I have already instructed every Dutch consul in the area to do exactly that – in passports, on identity papers, in fact, on any clean sheet of paper bearing the refugee's name. I fear the Russian problem is insurmountable. And I have no idea how you will get anywhere else even if you do manage to cross Russia. But I wish you – all of you – the best of luck."

De Dekker had been as good as his word. When Nathan Gutwirth went to see the honorary Dutch consul, Mr. Zwartendyk, who was actually the manager of the Philips Company's office in Kovno, Zwartendyk was waiting for him with a rubber stamp already made up: "No visa to Curaçao is required." As he stamped Gutwirth's passport he assured the young man he would do the same for any Jew trying to escape from Europe.

The background to that diplomatic stamp had never been explained to Consul Sugihara, but it wouldn't have mattered. Now, as he sat on the edge of his bed listening to the muffled sounds of four hundred anxious people just below his window, Sugihara realized that the time for contemplating the past, no matter how it had happened, was over. The Foreign Ministry's reply to his request to issue transit visas had come last night – an unequivocal "no." Transit visas could be issued only to people holding firm declared destination visas. There was no change in this policy of several months standing and there were to be no exceptions.

From the kitchen, Sugihara heard his youngest child, still upset by his frightening awakening, begin to whimper, only to be hushed by his mother. If the Jews couldn't guarantee that they could leave Russia for Japan, Sugihara knew, they would never be allowed into Russia in the first place. Other than Russia, there was no way for them to leave Lithuania. And there was not the slightest doubt in his mind that if they stayed in Lithuania, many, if not all, would be killed in the war that was bound to come. Politically, the Jews were not his problem. Still, when he had considered the political implications of Japan assisting the Jews, he wondered if Germany might not actually be pleased to see the back of some of this "problem."

Morally, ethically, from the standpoint of basic humanity, Sugihara had no doubts. These people were not enemies. They weren't soldiers. They weren't revolutionaries. They weren't even common criminals. They were innocent, desperate refugees. In their helplessness, they were asking merely the simplest form of aid from Japan. How could Japan – imperial Japan which even now was championing the right of all wrongly oppressed peoples in Asia – deny her help to these people?

Consul Sugihara was an officer in the Foreign Ministry. But beyond his allegiance to his bureaucratic superiors, even beyond his allegiance to Foreign Minister Matsuoka, Sugihara, like all Japanese, believed his primary allegiance was to the one man who embodied all that was noble, strong and pure in Japan: the emperor. Certainly the emperor, Sugihara thought, would not hesitate to deal sympathetically and benevolently with these poor unfortunates. And just as surely, the emperor would expect his subordinates to do as he himself would do.

Sugihara reworded his cable, this time to be sent to Foreign Minister Matsuoka himself. Then he confronted the even harder task of trying to determine what he could say to all those people standing just outside his window.

**2** IN THE EARLY AUTUMN of 1939, shortly after the start of World War II, Jewish refugees from Poland began streaming into the Baltic state of Lithuania – a state still free of German occupation. Within days, the international Jewish self-help organization known as the Joint Distribution Committee, or JDC, established relief kitchens in all the major towns of the country to serve the refugees who within six months numbered close to ten thousand. One of the kitchens in Vilna, the capital, was known by its refugee patrons as the Club. It was to the Club that Avram Chesno had to turn his steps every morning. Avram Chesno hated the Club. For the four months he had been in Vilna he had hated the very existence of it, the reasons for its being there. He hated the stale smell of tobacco smoke that never left because the stale, smelly smokers never left. The Club, originally nothing more than a section of the ground floor in a small office building, was more than a relief kitchen: it was the coffee house, discussion room, meeting hall and social center for the entire lower economic echelon of Vilna's refugee community. Here was where you came when you had nowhere else to turn and nothing else to do. That was precisely what Avram Chesno hated most of all about the Club – it was evidence that he had no other place to go, that circumstances had locked *him* into such a helpless situation.

Avram poured himself a breakfast of weak coffee and moved toward one of the long, stained and sticky tables. Around the room were clumps of gaunt men dressed in clothes that had been chosen by necessity rather than fashion or preference; men whose lined faces and overgrowth of hair and beard made them look older than their years. There were few who were outside the age limits for military service, younger than eighteen or older than fifty. Avram mentally compared their faces with the reflection he had seen as he glanced into a shop window the day before. He had always maintained a private conviction that he was a good-looking man. Tall, well proportioned and solidly built, he had enjoyed an active life of hiking and swimming – even soccer until a badly broken shoulder took him permanently out of the game. His wavy red-brown hair – still plentiful at forty-one, though he supposed that wouldn't last much longer – had set off the ruddy skin of his clean-shaven face. Not like your typical Polish Jew at all, he had thought in honest moments of vanity. Not that Avram would have allowed anyone to call him an anti-Semite. It was only that he was extremely glad not to have the grossly hooked nose that so many Polish Jews seemed cursed with.

Luckily, he had never had such a thing attached to *his* face, and it had not spontaneously generated as a result of the past nine months' experience. But, catching sight of his reflection in that shop window, he realized that his anxious eyes, his sunken cheeks and a full growth of grey beard gave him more in common than he liked with the other refugees at the Club.

Relegating his physical appearance to the back of his mind, Avram slumped into his chair, tired already, though it was not yet 9:00 A.M., and asked himself the same question he had asked himself every morning for the past four months, one week and two days: "What am I *doing* here? Alone, uncomfortable, inexpressibly bored and *here*, in such a place. What, in the name of God, am I doing here?"

It had begun on September 7, a Thursday. An order was broadcast by the Warsaw Military Command that all males of military age must leave the city immediately, before the German seige, already seven days old, had fulfilled its purpose. Avram was forty-one; he had no choice. What he remembered most strongly of that tumultuous day was kissing his wife Ruth goodbye – standing in the dark-paneled entrance hall of his house, brushing her light brown hair away from her face, taking in her beauty and the love in her eyes. He remembered reassuring her for the fiftieth time that he would be away for only a couple of weeks, thirty days at the most, because everyone knew that the British even then were preparing to come to rescue Poland. He would be back soon, to her and to her parents. Back to the comfortable middle-class professional routine of a high-school science teacher in the suburbs of Warsaw.

In spite of the reassurance he had hoped he was conveying to her, he was worried. There was no denying the violence of the German attack or the incredible speed of it. Hitler's madness had not sprung up overnight so that it could be expected to wither in the light of day. In Warsaw, Avram had been aware of the growing nationalism of the country next door and Hitler had had his effect on Poland. Even Avram's Christian colleagues at the school – intelligent, well-educated men with a solid grasp of history – had been swayed. Nothing obvious, of course. As the Warsaw government, during the thirties, increased its own harangues against the Jews and began imposing petty, and not-so-petty, restrictions on them, Avram's Polish Christian friends expressed their regret to him for all this. They were embarrassed by their own government, they said. It was regrettable that the Polish peasant mentality was still so strong, they said. We do not share this nonsense, they said. But as time passed, Avram was gradually isolated. His class schedule was changed without his being consulted. Meetings were held without his being notified. More and more the other teachers seemed to be avoiding him; less and less did either his opinion or his feelings seem to matter.

On particularly humiliating days, especially when the autumn rain or winter sleet made life even more depressing, Avram Chesno found himself dreaming almost uncontrollably of the land across the Atlantic. Not New York – which so many European Jews were struggling night and day to reach – but California. California, where cities had room to spread out in an exhilaration of space. California, where the air was clean and dry and the scenery unbelievable. When Warsaw was drowned in rain, California would be bathed in sunlight. When Warsaw was frozen, California would radiate warmth. America as a whole offered a freedom, an openness, a whole range of material and professional possibilities that Avram knew he could never find in Europe. But to Avram of all America only California – and particularly Southern California – offered enough to induce him to break his ties to his homeland in order to seize it.

But he hadn't. The California dream had been interrupted, in 1932, by the reality of a girl whose beauty, warmth and wit he had found irresistible. He had married "his Ruthie" in a synagogue – the first time he had been in a synagogue since he had left his parents' home at the age of twenty and the last time, excepting a brief visit each year on the High Holy Days. Ruth would cheerfully have gone with him to California then, in 1932, when a well-educated teacher from Poland could have aquired an American visa even if he was a Jew. But Ruth felt responsible for her parents and they, with all the stubbornness of old age, flatly refused to leave Warsaw. They had been born in Europe; everything and everyone they knew was in Europe; they would die in Europe.

In moments of honesty with himself, Avram Chesno realized that much as he loved his in-laws, he was waiting for them to die. This was not an aspect of his self awareness that he was proud of, nor one which he wished to share with his wife. So emigrating to California simply ceased to be a topic of household discussion and remained only a dream.

Then on September 1 the German invasion put an end even to the dream. The Nazis were showering up to thirty thousand shells a day on Warsaw and that the capital could hold out against them even till the seventh was incredible. The order for men to evacuate, though terrifying in its implications for those remaining behind, was not completely unexpected.

"I didn't tell you before," Avram had said over breakfast the morning following the order, the last meal they had together, "but I have withdrawn almost all our money from the bank."

To his surprise, Ruth merely nodded.

"I know. I went to the bank a week ago, thinking to do the same. They told me you had beaten me to it."

Avram looked at her across the breakfast china. After seven years of marriage, her calm common sense and competence still amazed him.

"I don't know where you put it," she confessed, trying to smile.

"In the small wooden trunk on the top left shelf of the bedroom closet," he said. "Ruth, there is something else in the trunk. I bought a gun, a small revolver, and a box of bullets. I really don't think you will ever have to use it. The Nazis want the land and they want political control, but they have no reason to make war on women and their elderly parents."

In spite of his anxiety, Avram tried to lighten what he was saying. Ruth turned her face aside and closed her eyes.

"Just come back, Avram. Just let it all be over soon and you come back to me, to us. How long will you have to be away? How will I know where you are? How can I get in touch with you? And suppose something happens to us here – how will you know where to find us?"

He didn't have the answers. All he could do was repeat what he had said the night before. "I will try to get to Bialystok. One of my former classmates from university is there and I am sure I can stay with him. You have his address? I gave it to you last night."

She nodded. She had the address, but what she wanted was reassurance. All he was giving was reality.

"Ruthie, I don't know what conditions will be like. Try to keep in touch with the school. If I can't reach you directly, I'll try to reach you that way. Ruth, it's only a question of *weeks*," he said, as she began to cry. "I'll be back with you, you *know* I'll be back. . . ."

In the two days following the order to evacuate Warsaw, over a hundred thousand men between the ages of eighteen and fifty went out from the city. Almost all of them – Jews and non-Jews alike– headed east to the relatively safe sector of Poland which Hitler had awarded to Russia in return for her compliance in Germany's take-over of the rest.

Avram at first tried to take the train heading toward the border. But the train was stopped and all passengers off-loaded at Lochow. It was there, in Lochow, that he began to realize that, superficial as it might have been, the façade of acceptance he had been living with in Warsaw was not a part of the provincial scene. He was well dressed and had a pocketful of money, but he was spat upon, shoved, denied service in restaurants, even forced out of the line waiting for the country bus – all in the moment of realization or suspicion that he was a Jew. Avram was incensed! As a child he had some-times encountered things like this. But as an adult, as an educated comfortably well-off professional, he had escaped these indignities.

The closer he came to the border, the happier he was to be going to Bialystok – not that he had any love for the Russians. But at least Bialystok was a city – not like the one-horse peasant towns he'd been passing through for over a week. His classmate was a part of the sizable Jewish community there. Bialystok, he thought, ought to be a good place to stay for a while.

It hadn't turned out quite that way. Bialystok was only another stage in the thickening nightmare of disruption, separation and fear. A steady torrent of refugees poured in from the Nazi-held west, crowding the Jewish quarters beyond capacity and driving already inflated food and housing prices almost beyond reach. Avram was greeted and accepted into the family of his former classmate; but he quickly understood that his contributions to the household budget were considerably more important than his sparkling wit or recall of the good old days.

With their seizure of Bialystok Province the Russians had begun rebuilding the society according to Stalin's blueprints. Judaism, while officially protected as a culture, was suspected as an "exclusivist" and counter-revolutionary religion. A successful Jew, like Avram's classmate, was doubly damned for being a "bloodsucker on the body of the working class."

At first Avram went almost daily to the telegraph office, sending off cable after cable telling Ruth how he was doing and asking after her. For weeks, there was no response. Avram was beside himself with anxiety. Finally, an answer came – but so brief, almost inconsequential, as if she had been afraid that anything more would be blocked by the censors. She missed him. She was well, and her parents were well. Life was more difficult than before, but not impossible. That was all! Heedless of the censor, Avram wrote back voluminously. From her meager replies, he realized very little of it got through.

With the approach of the year's end, Avram could no longer pretend to himself that the British could or would rescue Poland from the Nazis. What was now would be in the future: Germany held Warsaw like a piece of sponge in an iron vise. Ruth was there; he was here. There was a distinct possibility they would not see each other again for a long, long time. Avram spent the bitter cold December days trudging the streets of Bialystok, seeing nothing of the city, the people, the shops and markets, only seeing in his mind Ruth's fair skin, laughing eyes and lithe body. He would spend half a morning thinking just of her hands – their smoothness, their warmth, how they looked nestled in her lap while she was listening to one of his stories, how they felt when she first came into the house on a cold winter day and put them against his cheeks. It was inconceivable that he would never see her again, never hold her again. Avram went home late and left early. He never laughed.

In early March, he hit bottom. Standing near the eighteenth-century Podlasie Versailles Palace, permitting the weak winter sun to burn off at least a little of his depression, he recognized a face from his own block in Warsaw. Avram started walking quickly toward his neighbor, asking questions before he reached him.

"Hello! Have you any news? I haven't heard from my wife in a long time . . ."

Recognizing Avram, the man began to respond with pleasure at finding a familiar face so far from home. But as Avram's questions continued, the neighbor's smile faded. "Do you know how our wives are doing?" Avram kept on asking questions. "Our families? I have been trying . . ."

He stopped and began again more quietly. "What's happened? To my wife, to my home? Tell me. Please."

Slowly, miserable to be the bearer of such news, the neighbor told him. "About three weeks ago, Mr. Chesno, there was a fire on our street at your end. My nephew, who only recently escaped here from Warsaw, told me.

"He said the police insist it was accidental. He himself believes it was done on purpose, by some young hooligans wanting, as they put it, to 'settle the score with the Jews.' Your house and – I am so sorry – your wife did not survive the fire. Also, the two other, elderly people there were killed."

Avram lowered his eyes, releasing the man.

"I am sorry, Mr. Chesno. If there is anything . . ."

Avram did not hear the words or see the sympathy on his former neighbor's face. Grief clouded his vision so that he stumbled away from the sidewalk. He found privacy behind a large evergreen tree before he broke down.

For seven days, Avram did nothing but remember Ruth. He cared nothing for himself, ate scarcely at all, neither bathed, nor shaved, nor changed his clothes. By the eighth day, the poignancy of her death had been dimmed, the sense of loss not diminished but at least familiarized. Avram awoke feeling for the first time his own physical griminess. He bathed, shaved, dressed in clean clothes and joined his host for morning coffee. Then he returned to his bedroom to think.

He had no desire to go back. Without Ruth, Warsaw was nothing more than a city he didn't care for under a regime he despised. Living here in Bialystok with his friend was becoming more difficult. It would become completely impossible once his money ran out. Realistically, he had only one alternative. With the first break in the cold, Avram Chesno set out on the path followed by thousands of his fellow refugees, a path that led to Vilna. His former classmate envied Avram the refugee status that permitted him to leave the Soviet Union, but he was not sorry to see him leave.

"Hello, again. May I join you?"

Avram looked up from the sticky table to see a tall, heavy-set man

38

hovering over him, trying forlornly to smile.

"Yes, of course. Orliansky, isn't it?" The two had met three days ago at the post office – the day an excited Ephraim Orliansky had received a thick envelope from America.

"You looked happier the last time I saw you," Avram added as the man sat down.

"I have been to the American Embassy. In fact, since I saw you, I have been to the Japanese Consulate in Kovno as well. But I had higher hopes from the Americans."

Orliansky sighed and lost himself in the depths of his tea glass, seeming to forget Avram entirely. But preoccupation with distant thoughts was one of the commonest symptoms of the diseased state of being a refugee. Avram said nothing and waited.

"Do you know," Orliansky resumed the conversation, "what you need to have, just to *apply* for a visa to America? A certificate of good conduct from your local police covering the past five years. Can you imagine that? I am running for my life, carrying two babies, shepherding another and my wife through the woods, and on the way I am supposed to drop by the police station and ask the fellow who is driving me out if he would be so kind as to attest to my noncriminal status for the past five years. 'Oh, and by the way, Mr. Police Captain, I also need copies in duplicate of all public records concerning myself, my wife and our three children; birth certificates, school certificates, marriage registration. Be a nice fellow and put all that together for me, won't you?' Either they are living in a dream world or we are. And if it's us, I'd like *very* much to wake up!"

Orliansky's story was nothing new to Avram. Months before, he had presented himself at the American Embassy thinking that, in spite of all he had heard, the United States might be interested in making a new citizen out of a Warsaw science teacher. She wasn't. No reason, no explanation; just "application rejected."

"Apply again in a few months," the visa officer had said; but that was the only consolation he had had to offer.

Avram's disappointment would have been greater if his hopes had been higher in the first place. He should have gone to California years before, dragging Ruth's parents by the neck if necessary, or simply presenting them the alternative of coming along or staying behind alone. If he had done that, he'd now be on a beautiful beach or teaching in one of the clean, flat-roofed schools that seemed to be the norm all over the state. But he hadn't. So ever since he had fled Warsaw, long before he had even reached the American Embassy in Vilna, the dream of California seemed to have less and less substance, less and less possibility of being realized.

Orliansky had his own problems, though, and Avram knew the man hadn't sought him out to listen to *his*.

"So you can't even apply?" he asked.

"Oh yes! Can and did! Fortunately, we could safely assume that Mr. Bailey, the visa officer at the Embassy was not familiar with the personal signature of a police captain in such a tiny town as Kuczbork. The Hebrew Immigrant Aid Society managed to get copies of all our birth certificates from Warsaw just before their office there was shut down. And I have an uncle and a cousin in America who guaranteed our support so we would not become what they call 'a public charge.' So, Mr. Chesno, you are looking at the proud holder of a bonafide place on the waiting list for an immigration visa to the United States of America!"

Orliansky raised his tea glass in a toast to his own good fortune: but there was no triumph of joy in his eyes. "If all goes as planned, the whole family will be permitted into America in six years time."

There was nothing to say. America was as good as closed to immigration. Britain was closed. Australia had actually suggested that the refugees were cowardly to want to come to their country at all rather than stand and fight, presumably with only their bare hands, against German tanks and artillery. The entire batch of fifteen thousand Palestine certificates that Britain promised to give out for the year had been issued by March. And as for the places you once thought you could buy your way into, well, the refugee centers were full of stories, experiences like that of the *St. Louis*. In 1939, nearly a thousand Jewish refugees with all their visas in order were refused permission to land by the Cubans and forced to return to Europe on what was called the "voyage of the damned." No matter what you paid, once the money changed hands there was absolutely no guarantee of getting anything in return.

Orliansky stared into his tea without seeing. Avram stared at the table. "What is going on at the Japanese Consulate?" he asked before they both suffocated from gloom.

"The consul there issued a transit visa to one fellow who had less than iron-clad permission to land in some Dutch colony on the other side of the world that would never in a million years let you

40

in. There's some diplomatic quirk that lets the Dutch stamp in your passport that you can go to this place without a visa. And on the basis of *that* you can get a transit visa that will let you stay a few weeks in Japan. And from Japan. . . ." Orliansky shrugged. "I don't know. Maybe from way over there things look better."

Avram's interest was aroused instantly, but so were his suspicions. "How are you going to get across Russia even to get to Japan?" he asked.

"That is another problem. But anyway, I don't really think that it is a problem I'll ever have to face. The Japanese consul, whose name I don't even know, has already been turned down once by his government when he asked permission to give out these visas. He said he was asking again, but I really don't see that anything can come of it." Orliansky shook his head slowly. He was willing to dream but reality was defeating him at every turn.

"Too bad, though," he went on. "Too bad it's all phony. I could really enjoy a life in some nice place just now."

Avram had given up dreaming entirely. But he had not given up his desire to escape this tiny piece of Europe before it, too, was crushed completely between fascism and communism. For a Jew, doomed to destruction by either equally, giving up on escape would be tantamount to suicide. That he could actually get to Japan, and be allowed entry to a country that was, after all, Germany's Axis ally, and that he could then go from Japan to any free country whatsoever, seemed to Avram almost impossibly unlikely. But only "almost." At any rate, this Dutch colony scheme was the first possibility of any sort that had opened up in five months.

"Tell me, Orliansky," he asked, "where is this Japanese consul whose name you don't know?"

Consul Sugihara sat at his desk, gazing out on a bright August morning. If he looked through the opposite window, he knew from the experience of the past five days that he would see a scattering of refugees still waiting for word of the visas. The view over the beginnings of his small Japanese rock garden he found more restful.

Sugihara himself did not understand a word of Yiddish, but he'd heard stories – horror stories about what was happening to the Jewish refugees. The more he heard, the more untenable Sugihara felt his position was. The refugees had nowhere to go. Their native land had already lost a war in which they themselves were considered one of the stakes: their very lives were merely the rightful spoils of war as far as the Nazis were concerned. Going home would be suicide – a suicide with no meaning and no purpose. Yet if they stayed here and the Russians annexed the Baltic states, which the consul had no doubt they would soon do, they would at best merely have put off the evil day. The Russian government said it accepted Jews on an equal footing with everyone else. But Sugihara had heard other opinions and other stories about how the Russians felt . . . and acted.

There were half a dozen of them still sitting on a bench across from his house; bearded old men in broad-brimmed black hats with locks of long, gray hair dangling in front of their ears. They were waiting, just waiting patiently, determined to be successful even if only a few visas were handed out. Ones like these would not have an easy time under Stalin either.

Clearly, the rest of the world had turned its back on the refugees. Grand international refugee conferences had been held in comfortable resort spots like Bermuda and southern France, but no country had done anything other than suggest that some other country take care of the problem. Well, the West had never had much sympathy for non-Westerners. It had been raping China and Indo-China for a century. It had tried to do the same to Japan, but Japan had been clever enough to maintain her independence. But were the Jews Westerners? If they had originally come from Palestine, Sugihara could see why England and France and America would not consider them so. And he himself had seen characteristics of his own grandmother in the faces of the old Jewish women.

What would happen to the refugees if Japan did not take them? Sugihara could see no answer but their destruction. But what would happen if Japan *did* open her doors to them? And what would happen to the professional diplomat Sugihara if *he* were to be the doorman?

For the ninetieth time in a day and a half, Sugihara read over the second cable he had received on the subject: CONCERNING TRANSIT VISAS REQUESTED PREVIOUSLY STOP ADVISE ABSOLUTELY NOT TO BE ISSUED ANY TRAVELER NOT HOLDING FIRM END VISA WITH GUARANTEED DEPARTURE EX JAPAN STOP NO EXCEPTIONS STOP NO FURTHER INQUIRIES EXPECTED STOP [SIGNED] K. TANAKA FOREIGN MINISTRY TOKYO. The Foreign Ministry had been true to its word: Sugihara's third and final cable had simply not been answered.

What would they do to him for acting on a humanitarian impulse? Traditionally, Japanese who objected to unjust governmental decrees were very highly praised for their courage . . . and very speedily executed. On the other hand, Japan had been a democracy for several decades now, and the militaristic bent of Japanese society did not prevent a civilian government from maintaining control. If it were only a question of an official rebuke, a demotion, possibly even a temporary suspension from the Foreign Service Corps, how could that balance out the lives of all those people? How could he, Senpo Sugihara, carry out his responsibility to the Emperor and maintain his honor as a Japanese if he turned his back on these unfortunates? Ever since he had first received a hint of the refugees' problems, he'd been haunted by the words of an old *samurai* maxim: "Even a hunter cannot kill a bird which flies to him for refuge."

The more Sugihara thought of the plight of the refugees, and of his capacity to alleviate that plight, the fewer options he seemed to have. Not reading them again, Sugihara took the two telegrams and filed them under "Cables Received." He combed his hair, straightened his tie and started for the front door, the official visa officer for the imperial Japanese government.

**3** IN AUGUST 1940, Japan was at the center of an unstable spider's web of international relationships. In Asia, she was officially at war – though for the time being only with China. It was a war Japan had purposely renewed in 1937, and it lasted much longer than its instigators had anticipated – a no-win, no-retreat situation that was costing far more than it was worth. Farther from home, with the changing balance of power in Europe, Japan was shifting gradually into the German camp. In 1936 she signed an anti-Communist treaty with the German foreign minister, von Ribbentrop. In 1938, she made a cultural agreement with Hitler. Political relations with Britain and the United States, on the other hand, were deteriorating rapidly. And the effects of these diplomatic problems were beginning to slip into the economic sphere, especially after America declared a "moral embargo" on the export of certain strategic goods. Finally, with the U.S.S.R., Japan was continuing in her centuries-old state of suspicious watch-fulness. There were even some among the Tokyo leaders who felt that Japan should unilaterally attack Russia before the Russians had a chance to attack first.

These were the publicly recognized ties that bound Japan to the rest of the world. Unknown to the public – in fact unknown to all but a handful of Japanese officials – the country had one more line out, a line which she hoped and believed could strengthen all the others. That was her tie with world Jewry.

Japan's recognition of Jews as a distinct group in the world of "foreigners" dated back less than forty years. Cut off from Europe first by geography and then, after a brief but burning experience with politically active Catholic missionaries, by law, for the two hundred and fifty years of the seventeenth, eighteenth and first half of the nineteenth centuries, Japan historically maintained an un-yielding aloofness. She forbade any foreigner to enter the country and refused reentry to any Japanese who managed to leave. This self-imposed isolation left Japan no insight into the ways of the changing Western world. Knowing little of Christianity, Japan knew nothing of its religious forebearer. Having no contact with Europeans, she learned nothing of the actuality of Jewish life or of the Jewish people. By 1853, when the American naval commodore, Matthew Perry, steamed into Tokyo Bay, demanding that Japan open her doors to intercourse with the world, so many Jews had become assimilated into the mainstream of secular Western life that the differences between Jew and Gentile were not readily apparent to the Japanese.

After a few years of domestic turbulence, Japan responded to Perry's demands with total energy and unique agility. By the turn of the century, she had adapted to her own national life many of the most significant elements of Western culture – and a good deal of its nonsense: telephones and tall silk hats; universal compulsory education and the drinking of whisky; local elections; a large, standing army; a steam-driven navy. . . . By the twentieth century, Japan felt so "modern," so much on an equal footing with the leading countries of the West, that she felt she too could improve her lot by military conquest. Her chosen victim was that perennial threat to her northern borders, Russia.

By waging war on Russia, Japan hoped to seize the tsar's vast, empty northeast region, Manchuria. This would, she hoped, become a sure source of raw materials for her ever-expanding industries. Simply being able to take and control such a large slice of territory beyond her borders would give Japan increased respect throughout the world. With an explosion of nationalistic fervor, Japan entered into battle in February 1904.

Almost immediately, she realized she had bitten off too much. Russia was an immense country with a huge army and virtually unlimited financial resources. By April, the vice-governor of the government-owned Bank of Japan, Baron Korekiyo Takahashi, was in London trying desperately to borrow money on the international market. But it was a miserable excursion. Even under the most humiliatingly restrictive terms, he could find no more than half the absolute minimum Japan needed to continue the war. With only a few days remaining before he was due to sail back to Japan, Baron Takahashi went to a formal dinner given by a fellow banker. Over dessert, Takahashi found himself explaining his sense of disappointment to a man who happened to be seated next to him. Japan will *surely* be defeated, he said bitterly. Tsar Nicholas II will have another

45

success under his imperial belt. Takahashi's dinner partner, a Mr. Jacob Schiff, seemed more interested than mere courtesy would call for. Schiff too, Takahasi learned, also hated Tsar Nicholas II, holding him personally responsible for a recent pogrom against the Jews of the Russian town of Kishinev. The conversation between the two men continued until the party broke up for brandy and coffee. Then Schiff wandered off and Takahashi forgot about him.

The next morning Baron Takahashi's aide awoke him with the news that a Mr. Schiff wanted to see him – to discuss a five million pound loan! Takahashi was dumbfounded. "Who is this Schiff?" he asked.

"A partner in the American investment bank of Kuhn-Loeb," the aide had learned, "a powerful force in the world money market, a major factor in international capital. Also, a Jew."

Intrigued, Takahashi met with Schiff immediately and began what would become a deep and life-long friendship with him. (Ultimately, the Japanese banker sent his daughter to New York to live with the Schiffs for three years.)

Over the next several months, Schiff arranged four further international loans, and cash in hand, Japan continued the war until she was in a position to sue for a victorious peace. In Japan, Jacob Schiff became a hero. National newspapers devoted page after page to his role in the victory. History books added whole chapters about him. Emperor Meiji, in an absolutely unprecedented act, invited Schiff, a commoner, to luncheon in the Imperial Palace. Without Schiff's help, there would have been no victory over the Russians. With Schiff's help, Japan had earned for herself new territories, new resources and greatly improved status in the eyes of the world. No honor was too great for this man.

Jacob Schiff was an American, but it wasn't as an American that he had undertaken to help the Japanese. And the nearly two hundred million dollars that he'd raised wasn't even predominantly American money. In this instance, Schiff had acted as a Jew. The fact was not lost on the Japanese. For the entire victorious populace of Japan, "Jew" became synonomous with access to, and control of, vast sums of money.

It was not until 1919, when Japanese soldiers were sent to Siberia to fight alongside White Russian soldiers in a losing battle against the Communists, that Japan was introduced to a less positive view of the Jews.

Few White Russians had any affection for "zhids." But the strongest anti-Semite of all was one of the leaders of the counter-revolutionary forces, General Gregorii Semenov. Along with the rifles and canteens, Semenov issued to each soldier a copy of *The Protocols of the Elders of Zion* – a virulently anti-Jewish book which was purported to be the minutes of a secret meeting held by Jewish leaders to plot the takeover of the entire world. In fact the book was fiction spun out of the imagination of the Russian secret police. But to the Russian soldiers, who blamed the Jews for the Bolshevik Revolution, and to the seventy-five thousand Japanese soldiers who were for the first time living and learning in a completely Western situation, *The Protocols* were to be taken literally, word for word.

Among the Japanese soldiers were two young officers impressionable enough to allow *The Protocols* to become a major influence in their lives – and ultimately in the lives of several thousand European Jews. One of the officers was Captain Norihiro Yasue, a thirty-three-year-old Russian-language specialist who was posted to General Semenov's own staff. Yasue was a clear-sighted positivist from a *samurai* family of northern Japan. He would have much preferred to teach history in a good Japanese university than be a career officer in the Imperial Japanese Army. The other was Koreshige Inuzuka, a naval officer from Tokyo who had spent World War I in the Mediterranean and who was stationed during the Siberian Expedition on a battleship just off Vladivostok. Ambitious, not yet thirty years old, Inuzuka was still seeking a particular area to dominate.

These two – and to a lesser extent a few dozen other Japanese – accepted the premise of *The Protocols*: the Jews, having no land of their own, had been conspiring for years to make the entire world theirs. To this end, they had disrupted the stability of society by "inducing immorality into the young" and creating general dissatisfaction among all classes. They had cornered the wheat market in order to starve the world. They had seized control of the capital of the world and insidiously persuaded the innocent industrialists, bankers and "millionaires" the world over to join cause with them. Having successfully completed the preliminaries, the Jews stood now "on the threshold of sovereignty over all the world."

Men like Yasue and Inuzuka had only to look at the world around them to see that something strange was going on. After generations in power, the governments of Austro-Hungary, China and even Russia had fallen within a decade. Youth, certainly in Japan and reportedly in many other countries, had definitely turned away from the traditional values of their fathers. The bankers, industrialists and millionaires were indeed dominating society with their crass, economically oriented values as never before. And one had to look no farther than Schiff to see what power Jews had over world capital!

"But is it really so serious? Is the Jewish takeover really imminent?" Yasue would ask of the Russians.

"*Imminent*? Look at what they are doing in our country *now*! You can see what chaos that Jew Karl Marx caused with his idiotic *Communist Manifesto*. That evil pamphlet was just one more step in their plot to take over the world. Don't you realize, can't you see it coming? *You* are next in line!"

"But what can we do?" Inuzuka might ask. "Japan has never heard about the Jewish conspiracy. How can we possibly stop it?"

"You have no choice. You *must* stop them, or you will lose your country and your national soul. Educate Japan about the Jews; educate yourselves about the Jews. Learn their tricks and protect yourselves from them!"

By 1922, the Japanese Siberian Expedition had returned home. For most of the soldiers, *The Protocols* – book and concepts – were forgotten. But Inuzuka, at the Tokyo naval headquarters, began collecting around him a coterie of sympathetic officers with whom he would discuss and examine the "Jewish conspiracy." And Yasue, in the Army Intelligence Bureau, began a Japanese translation of *The Protocols*.

As the years passed, the military clique of "Jewish experts" became larger and more outspoken. Articles began appearing in various departmental journals with titles like: "Studies in the International Conspiracy," "Jewish Information," and "Studies on the Jews." Supplementing these, informal lectures were given and discussion groups held. Lists of known Jews were drawn up and circulated: Jews in the West, in China, in Manchuria, and most often in Japan itself. (In Tokyo, it was learned with suspicion and dismay that the owner of Japan's most influential English-language newspaper, the *Japan Advertiser* was a Jew, Benjamin Fleisher!) The translation of *The Protocols of the Elders of Zion* was published and its contents studied at length. By the mid-twenties, Yasue and

Inuzuka had succeeded in getting the Foreign Ministry, the *Graimusho*, interested in "the Jew race." From their point of view, it seemed logical to study Jews in the closest thing they had to a native country. In 1926, they borrowed Yasue from the army and sent him off to the Middle East to investigate the Jews in Palestine. Yasue traversed the country, north and south, east and west, talking to political leaders (including Chaim Weizman and David Ben Gurion), farmers, shopkeepers and rabbis. He learned a great deal about the Jew's attachment to that particular piece of land. He noted with interest the emerging *kibbutz* concept which he was convinced the Jews would later use to colonize the countries they conquered. But, as he reported to the Foreign Ministry, the Jews were very tight-lipped about their plans to take over the world. No one so much as whispered a hint about the international conspiracy.

The intelligence section of the *Gaimusho* was disappointed but even more determined to learn as much as it could about the Jews. It sent a memorandum to every Japanese embassy and consulate around the world requesting information on Jews and Jewish activities in their areas – this was to be on a continuing basis. Immediately, paper began pouring in from everywhere: synagogue newsletters; reprints of rabbinic sermons; youth group activity programs; the anti-Semitic speeches of an Austrian house-painter and the ongoing effects of his rise to political power; the unsuccessful plan of certain Polish Jews to boycott Japanese goods; the percentage of Jews who voted for Franklin Roosevelt; the presence in China of a Jew called Two-Gun Cohen acting as Sun Yat-sen's financial and military adviser. . . . So much material came pouring in that a special office had to be set up just to handle it. This intelligence was gratifying in amount, but useless in content: the *Gaimusho* never could find any clear evidence of the worldwide Jewish conspiracy that it nevertheless remained convinced of.

The gradual expansion of the influence of the "Jewish experts" during the twenties and early thirties was made feasible by developments within Japan. The domestic turbulence and change ascribed by Yasue and Inuzuka and others to the "Jewish conspirators" continued to deepen. The old virtues of patience and respect and self-sacrifice were being overrun by new virtues: efficiency, productivity and materialism. The conservative young men who were attracted to the armed forces were more and more displeased by what they saw of "progress." The noble soul of Japan they saw as sullied by men who wanted only to line their pockets. The noble mind of their beloved emperor – from Christmas Day 1926, Meiji's grandson, Hirohito – was being clouded by greedy politicians. Internationally, Japan was not being accorded the respect she deserved. (The Exclusion Act of 1924 which barred Japanese immigrants from the United States was seen as a prime example.) And the quality of life at home could not be maintained in the face of an exploding birth rate.

Conflicting answers to Japan's problems were offered from every political viewpoint. By the late twenties, the strongest and most appealing voice was that of the Manchurian Faction which recommended a return to traditional ways and an expansion of Japan on mainland Asia, more precisely into Manchuria. The international economic collapse of 1929, and the ensuing worldwide depression, made Tokyo's planners yearn for Manchuria – with its wealth of raw materials, its vast arable fields and its emptiness just waiting to soak up Japan's excess millions. Furthermore, to a certain extent, Japan was already there. Since 1905, her Kwantung Army had been guarding the Manchurian railways which Japan had been awarded by the Treaty of Portsmouth ending the Russo-Japanese War.

The Manchurian Faction was led by two officers in the Kwantung Army, Colonel Seishiro Itagaki and Lieutenant Colonel Kanji Ishihara. By 1931, these two had persuaded their superiors that control of Manchuria was crucial to the salvation of Japan. In a matter of months, acting independently of the government in Tokyo, the army simply took command of the entire six hundred thousand square miles of the region and presented the world with "Manchukuo" – "the independent State of Manchu" – which would be "guided" by Japan.

From the beginning, all did not go as the Manchurian Faction had planned. The excess population of Japan could not be lured by any inducements into the Manchukuo wilderness. Though it was true that Manchukuo had vast reserves of coal, iron, timber and other raw materials, getting at those precious resources required vast amounts of capital. And, in the depression years, capital was as scarce in Japan as it was everywhere else in the world. Attempts were made to attract foreign investments, especially from America. But even America had little money to export. Moreover, the capital that might have been available was in the hands of men and corporations who did not at all approve of Japan's imperialistic designs on the rest of Asia. In part, this was a moral stance; but to a greater degree, it was economic self-interest: Japan was upsetting the region's stability. She was intruding on the Chinese business scene, and China was still considered a *Western* economic preserve. The era of not-so-good feeling between the two countries – an era which would be turned into war at Pearl Harbor – had begun. The Manchurian Faction – like those who were trying to protect Japan from the menace they saw in world Jewry – had been stymied by reality. But unknown to either side, the stage was being set for the uniting of the interests of the Manchurian Faction with those of the "Jewish experts." The union would be made not by a government official, nor by a militarist, but by a former ironmonger.

Gisuke Ayukawa was one of the leading industrialists in prewar Japan. Having learned the latest techniques of ironworking in the United States, he had returned to Japan to create a huge combine which would one day be known as Nissan Industries. In 1932, this powerful business leader was invited by the South Manchurian Railway – a quasi governmental organization which controlled most of Japan's industrial and mining ventures in the area – to advise it how to go about settling and developing this six-hundred-thousand-square-mile wilderness. Ayukawa accepted with enthusiasm. Consulting first with his long-time friend Baron Takahashi (the same Takahashi who had negotiated the huge loan from Jacob Schiff), Ayukawa then went on an extended study tour of Manchukuo. He spent many days talking to Yosuke Matsuoka, the railway president who would one day become foreign minister of Japan. He held long discussions with Colonel Ishihara and, by now, Army Chief-of-Staff Itagaki, about the plans of their Manchurian Faction – with which he was in complete sympathy. One contact led to another. Through Colonel Ishihara, Ayukawa met Yasue – the translator of *The Protocols of the Elders of Zion*, and by now considered one of Japan's leading "experts" on Jewish matters. He also met Yasue's fellow "experts" – the naval officer Inuzuka (a loyal supporter of Ishihara's Manchurian Faction from the beginning) and General Kiichiro Higuchi, another officer who had taken part in the Siberian Expedition and was now chief of the military mission in Manchukuo. The discussions among these men often turned to Jews. Ayukawa had a great deal of knowledge about, and a very high opinion of them, thanks to the influence of Baron Takahashi. Also, he had worked with Jewish iron-and-steel businessmen in America. Within a matter of months, Ayukawa's advice to the South Manchurian Railway began to focus on a new idea: why not use the Jews to help develop Manchukuo?

It was a radical and bold idea. Jewish settlers, if they could be brought from Europe, would provide the creative energy, the industrial skills, even the cultural finesse that Manchukuo needed to realize its potential. If Jews established settlements in Manchukuo, the American and British Jews who had a stranglehold on world capital would naturally become interested in investing there. Furthermore, to protect the interests of their co-religionists, the Jews who were secretly pulling the strings of the government of the United States would cease haranguing Japan for its "aggression," and there would be no more threat to boycott Japanese goods. This plan had its perils however. Despite the reams of information they had collected, the Japanese still considered Jews an unknown and suspicious quantity. However, as Ayukawa's discussions continued in Manchukuo and back in Tokyo, events in Europe seemed to be edging the Jews into a particularly tractable position. On January 30, 1933, Hitler took office as chancellor of Germany. On April 1, a German boycott of all Jewish businesses began. By October, Jews had been barred from all positions of authority in the government, the professions, and the social, cultural and educational institutions of Germany. Ayukawa decided to act. In 1934, he sent up a trial balloon in the form of a Foreign Ministry journal article entitled "A Plan to Invite Fifty Thousand German Jews to Manchukuo." The article was heavily publicized in the Japanese press and in Jewish journals. There were no negative repercussions.

The Manchurian Faction leaders were pleased; the "Jewish experts" were ecstatic. All their theoretical work and study now had a chance to pay off for the good of Japan, and the good of their careers. The potential was virtually unlimited. So was the danger. "This plan is," Captain Inuzuka remarked at an informal meeting of the 'Jewish experts', "very much like *fugu* [the Japanese blowfish whose deadly poison must be removed before it can be eaten]. If we are indeed skillful in preparing this dish – if we can remain ever-alert to the sly nature of the Jews, if we can continue to devote our constant attention to this enterprise lest the Jews, in their inherently clever manner, manage to turn the tables on us and begin to use us for their own ends – if we succeed in our undertaking, we will create for our nation and our beloved emperor the tastiest and most nutritious dish imaginable. But, if we make the slightest mistake, it will destroy us in the most horrible manner."

To serve *fugu*, however, one first must catch it. If Manchuria was to be the happy new home for thousands of Jews, it would have to regain the reputation that it once had before the Japanese took it over.

The Jewish population of Manchuria dated back to the last years of the nineteenth century when Tsar Nicholas II, anxious to "Russify" the region he had recently taken from the Chinese, declared that any Jews willing to settle in the "Manchurian paradise" would be allowed freedom of religion, unrestricted business rights and quota-free schools. With its seven-month winter, when the temperature reached forty degrees below zero, and hot dry summers, when the air was so heavy with flies you could scarcely breathe, Manchuria was not precisely "paradise." But the desire for a free life was so strong that by the mid-1920s, there were over thirteen thousand Russian Jews living in the major city of Harbin and in smaller communities in Hailar, Tsitsihar, Manchouli, Mukden and Dairen. The Harbin community, under the leader-ship of Dr. Abraham Kaufman and Rabbi Aaron Kiseleff, organized an entire Jewish social system: schools, a hospital, a bank, an old people's home and a cemetery; and its synagogue was the pride of Manchurian Jewry. In spite of the arrival in 1920 of hundreds of anti-Semitic White Russians, Harbin was indeed thought of as a paradise by Jews.

Then, in 1931, the Japanese came. The Manchurian Faction army leaders wanted to make a utopia of Manchukuo. But the civilians who followed on the heels of the army wanted only to get rich and get out, back again to "civilized" Japan. Businesses were taken over and houses and commercial buildings appropriated. Kidnapping for high ransom – up to four hundred thousand dollars – became common. (The Japanese did not single out the Jews for extortion, but the White Russians did, and the Japanese often worked with them – or, as police, approved of their activities.) Harbin, a paradise in the twenties, became a city of living death. And it all seemed to culminate in the kidnapping of Simon Kaspé.

Simon Kaspé's father Joseph had come to Harbin from Russia in 1907. By the early thirties, he was a very wealthy man. He owned the prestigious Hotel Moderne in the center of Harbin and most of the movie houses and theaters throughout Manchuria. Though originally considered stateless, Joseph Kaspé had gained French citizenship for himself and his family and proudly flew the bright French tri-color from the gray stone façade of the Hotel Moderne. Joseph's son Simon, an excellent pianist, had studied at the French Conservatory in Paris. It was while Simon was home on summer vacation, in August 1933, as he was returning from an outing with his girlfriend, that he was attacked from behind and rushed away to a hideout some thirty-six miles west of Harbin. The next morning, Joseph Kaspé received a note demanding one hundred thousand dollars ransom.

It was not a new story and, considering the usual stakes, the demanded ransom was not exhorbitant. But Joseph Kaspé was not a semistateless Jew: he was a citizen of France and went immediately to the French consul.

As far as the consul was concerned, the honor of France was at stake. He insisted that Joseph Kaspé would not pay the ransom: the consul, working with the Japanese police, would find Simon Kaspé.

After thirty days, half a bloody ear was sent to Joseph Kaspé, but the French consul assured him that the authorities were on the verge of finding the kidnappers. Joseph again agreed not to pay the ransom.

On December 3, 1933, ninety-five days after the seizure, Simon Kaspé was found by the police. He had been starved, beaten and tortured. The nails of the pianist's delicate fingers had been torn out. Both his ears had been cut off. He had been kept for weeks underground, in a pit of half-frozen earth with a lid over his head, while the temperature dropped to twenty-five and thirty degrees below zero. Before he was found, the kidnappers had performed their one act of mercy by putting a bullet through the boy's head.

In all Manchuria, there was never such a funeral as the funeral for Simon Kaspé. To prevent the gathering of a large crowd, Japanese authorities warned the mourners not to travel through the main streets but to go, instead, through the narrow alleys. Nevertheless, tens of thousands, including Chinese as well as Europeans, attended the funeral. All along the procession, the crowd shouted: "Death to the Japanese military! Death to the damn monkeys!"

Both the Harbin and the Shanghai Jewish communities protested to Japan's vice-foreign minister, Mamoru Shigemitsu about the

54

maltreatment of the Jews in Manchukuo, but to no avail. The kidnappers were found and although they were placed in jail, they were free to go home at night. After a long trial, to everyone's surprise, they were convicted. Two days later, the Japanese police arrested the Chinese judges and prosecuted them for treason. At a retrial, with Japanese judges, the kidnappers were given ten- to fifteen-year sentences . . . and freed under an amnesty one week later.

The Jewish community had had enough. At the same time that Yasue, Inuzuka and Ayukawa were thinking out the foundations of the *fugu* plan, thousands of Jews were leaving Harbin. Some went to the international settlement in Shanghai, some to other Chinese cities. A very few even preferred to return to the Soviet Union rather than remain in Japanese-held lands. By the mid-thirties, nearly seventy per cent of Harbin's Jews had fled. And as they fled, they spoke out about the conditions that were driving them out.

If the *fugu* plan were to work, its creators knew this exodus had to be stopped; once again the cities of Manchuria had to become a paradise for Jews. Yasue himself, now a colonel, was put in charge of making sure that just such a thing happened.

Yasue moved carefully and with discretion. He established a friendship with Abraham Kaufman, a physician who was the unofficial leader of the several thousand Jews holding on in Manchukuo. He showed a sincere personal interest in the activities of the community. He made repeated visits to Harbin to keep in touch with the situation there. But when it came to solving problems, Yasue always waited to act until he was asked for help. It was one of the major ploys of the "Jewish experts" that no one should ever think that Japan *needed* the Jews, or was purposely wooing them.

His tactic was effective. This gradualist approach seemed, to the Jews, to show a sincere change of heart on the part of the Japanese, rather than merely a short term change of policy. Some may have been completely taken in, while others played along with the Japanese to improve their situation. In either case, by 1937, the community, with Japanese encouragement, had asked for and received permission to form a representative body to speak on its behalf – the Far Eastern Jewish Council, headed by Dr. Kaufman. In December of that year, the first Conference of Jewish Communities in the Far East was held, with representatives coming to Harbin from as far away as Shanghai, China and Kobe, Japan. The

FEJ Conference at Joseph Kaspé's Hotel Moderne was also attended by over seven hundred Jewish delegates and spectators, as well as by Colonel Yasue and his fellow "Jewish expert," General Higuchi, who continued to hold a high position in the military administration of Manchukuo and Northern China. Each Japanese speaker expressed the hope that the conference delegates would make known to their fellow Jews around the world the good treatment they were receiving. "Do not let this become a dead statement!" Higuchi exclaimed, referring to his just-completed proclamation: "The Nipponese, having no racial prejudice, look with friendship toward the Jewish people and are ready to cooperate with the Jewish people . . . and maintain close business relations."

To the delight of the Japanese, the Jews responded, as hoped, with a resolution which was sent to every major Jewish organization in the world: "We Jews, attending this racial conference, hereby proclaim that we enjoy racial equality and racial justice under the national laws, and will cooperate with Japan and Manchukno in building a new order in Asia. We appeal to our co-religionists." Dr. Kaufman wrote to the World Jewish Congress, successfully applying for membership for the Far Eastern Jewish Council.

In 1938 yet another FEJ Conference took place in Harbin, with similar requests from General Higuchi and from Colonel Yasue who, by now, had been posted permanently to Dairen, in commuting range on a fast luxury train, of Harbin and his "good friend" Dr. Kaufman. But more important than the second FEJ Conference was a meeting called just a few weeks earlier in Tokyo – a top secret get-together of the entire Japanese cabinet.

It was called the Five Ministers' Conference; and it was never referred to by any other name in the hundreds of government memoranda based on it that circulated the length and breadth of the Japanese Empire throughout the next five years. The five ministers in attendance that December night were: Prime Minister Prince Fumimaro Konoye, Foreign Minister Hachiro Arita, Army Minister General Seishiro Itagaki, Naval Minister Admiral Mitsumasa Yonai and Seishin Ikeda who was then holding the portfolios of both the Finance Ministry and the Ministry of Commerce and Industry. These five, with the emperor himself, were the most important and most powerful men in all of Japan. All five had been kept abreast of Japanese interests in the worldwide Jewish community, and they knew of the major details and current progress of the plan to manipulate that community. Thus far, however, the plan had been only an expansion of Ayukawa's original trial balloon: the government and the country were not committed officially to anything. World events, though, and Japan's own political moves were once again forcing the country in the direction of doing *something* about the Jews.

The development of Manchuria had never gotten underway. After months and months of trying to entice American capital into the region, the industrialist Ayukawa had finally given up in the summer of 1938. Capital would have to be found through other sources. Moreover, economic relations in general with the United States were deteriorating. If nothing reversed the trend, the commercial treaty which had linked the two countries since 1911 would not last out the following year. The Jews, however, had once again shown their economic power. In response to the early November explosion of looting and destruction in Germany, called *Kristallnacht*, American Jewry had spearheaded a nationwide boycott of German goods. Japan was tremendously impressed by this remarkably successful endeavor. Like no other event in recent history, the boycott pointed up the economic power of the Jews. Japan actually benefited slightly, as Americans substituted Japanese products for the untouchable German ones. But the benefit threatened to be short-lived: Japan's increasingly close ties to Hitler were becoming a serious liability.

Out of enthusiasm for the cultural agreement established between Japan and Germany in November 1938, several Japanese institutions had dismissed Jewish staff members. The government, too, began to follow Germany's lead on Jewish matters. The most widely publicized incident involved an Austrian professor of music, J. Gustav Vogelfut who, although he held a signed employment agreement with the well-known Takarazuka Music School of central Japan, had been flatly refused an entrance visa by the Japanese Embassy in Vienna. Such an act could have tremendously negative repercussions. Clearly, December 1938 was a time of great potential for Japan in her dealings with world Jewry. But it was a time of even greater uncertainty.

The Five Ministers' Conference was held on December 5. Officially it was convened at the request of Army Minister General Itagaki who was having difficulty reconciling two administration factions: those in favor of promoting good relations with world

Jewry in hopes of turning them to Japan's profit, and those inclined to swallow the Nazi line and have nothing to do with Jews. These divergent opinions were reflected in the cabinet as a whole. The five leaders arrived at the secret meeting not at all in agreement on what to do with or about the Jews.

Foreign Minister Arita and a large section of army opinion were strongly against any official involvement with the Jews. Their spokesman was General Nobutaka Shioden, another participant in the Siberian Expedition who had, over the years, become fanatically pro-Nazi and anti-Semitic.

For years, Shioden said, many countries had tried to keep a large Jewish population under control – Spain, Portugal, Russia, Germany. . . . Always, in the end, the only forms of successful "control" were slaughter or exile. Wasn't it bad enough that Japan's mainland neighbor, Russia was so thoroughly controlled by Jewish Communists? It might be suicidal to put a Jewish state in the interior of Manchukuo. After all, the region of Russia which bordered Manchukuo was Birobidzhan, a state specifically established to be a homeland for Russia's Jews! And in Birobidzhan, a large-scale road-building program was already underway. Clearly, this was a militaristic activity. Should Japan really contemplate setting up a Jewish community so near an area which was known to be a staging ground for the Russia–Jewish takeover of Manchukuo and China?

The navy tried immediately to counter the argument with an idea that Inuzuka had been promoting for years. Naturally such a settlement should not be in Manchukuo, the naval spokesman said. Rather, it should be in the Shanghai area – in Hoto or Daido City or Minami. Probably it was not a coincidence that the Shanghai area was administered by the navy; Manchukuo was governed by the army.

Shioden's faction was opposed not only to locale but to policy. No matter where they were settled, the general insisted, the Jews would conspire in the ruination of Japan. Referring to *The Protocols of the Elders of Zion*, he reminded the meeting, "We have seen what they themselves say are their ambitions, their goals: nothing less than the disruption and ultimate takeover of the world. We Japanese should listen to people who have more experience in this matter. Germany and Russia know better than we do; we must follow their advice and opinion."

58

The countervailing side was led by Finance and Commerce Minister Ikeda, a supporter of Ayukawa and a disciple of Baron Takahashi. (The baron had been assasinated in his bed twenty months before by army radicals attempting to overthrow the government.) Ikeda, strongly supported by Army Minister Itagaki, the original leader of the Manchurian Faction, was equally vehement: "Of course Japan can control the Jews! No matter where we settle them, we will maintain control over all their dealings with the outside world. Their self-government will be only on a local level. After all, are we not at least as able as the Chinese? Hundreds of years ago, China permitted thousands of Jews to settle in the Kaifeng region. Did they take over? By no means! In time, China, having benefited from their cleverness and industry, calmly swallowed them up until today there is no such thing as a 'Chinese Jew.' Surely we Japanese, being even more conscious of the potential danger, can do as well.

"And dangerous or not, we *need* the Jews. The settlers themselves will be an asset to Manchukuo and to Japan. As Ayukawa-san has said, 'No Japanese has ever made a good pair of shoes. But the *Jewish* shoemakers. . . .' Even more important, their settlements will encourage other Jews to release the capital we can't get any other way. By simply welcoming these beleaguered Europeans, we will gain the affection of the American Jews who control the press, the broadcast media, the film industry . . . and possibly President Roosevelt himself. We cannot afford to alienate the Jews. If Japan imitates Germany's severe control of the Jews, discrimination will develop in connection with our foreign trade. On the other hand, if Japan goes in the opposite direction and befriends the Jews, entirely new economic possibilities will open up before us."

These were only the opening salvos. The Five Ministers' Conference was one of the longest and most complicated meetings held by that cabinet. Decision making in Japanese politics is a question of consensus. There is no such thing as a "rule of the majority." A discussion continues until all parties are willing to agree to a policy. Though the factions at this meeting were diametrically opposed and each was fanatically attached to its own reasoning, both agreed absolutely on one thing: the wrong step here could have very serious, even ruinous, consequences for the Japanese Empire. The term *fugu* was not used at the Five Ministers' Conference, as it was not used in any but the most informal of conversations. But to a man, the ministers would have agreed with the aptness of the plan's title.

With the ministers seated at a long wooden table, their assistants nearby, their tea cups even nearer, the entire array of Jewish–Japanese problems was examined, every detail, every foreseeable ramification. Could a closer relationship with the Jews improve Japan's relations with the United States? Did Japan really want to improve those relations, or would it be wiser simply to plan on war? What was the extent of Jewish influence over American public opinion? Over American banking? Over the American president? (And what of the rumors that Roosevelt himself was really a Jew who had changed his name from "Rosenfeld"?) Would the right Jews – the artists, the scientists, the industrialists, the intellectuals like Freud and Einstein – want to come and settle among the Japanese? Had the Japanese been successful in changing their image after the 1931–5 debacle in Manchukuo?

The faction favoring involvement with the Jews was extremely well prepared for the argument. It had collected intelligence reports on the so-called Jewish conspiracy, on the increasingly insecure position of Jews in almost every country in the world, even on the many divisions within the Jewish community. The very fact that these policy makers had done their homework with such impressive thoroughness angered some members of the opposing side. "You are merely creating jobs for yourselves!" they complained. "Your 'special missions' dealing with Jews will no longer be needed if we cease our relationship with them! You are thinking only of yourselves!" But on the whole, reasoned argument rather than heated name calling was the mood of the meeting.

The discussion continued late into the night; but eventually, the necessary consensus was reached. In typical Japanese fashion, it managed to speak for both sides. For the anti-Jewish faction: "Our diplomatic ties with Germany and Italy require that we avoid publicly embracing the Jewish people, in the light of their rejection by our allies. . . ." And for the backers of the *fugu* plan: ". . . but we should not reject them as they [our allies] do. . . . This is particularly true in light of our need for foreign capital and our desire not to alienate America."

Captain Inuzuka and Colonel Yasue, though not present at the meeting, were quickly informed of the resolution. Their energetic preparation had led to a significant measure of success! Now the question was to bring their scheme to life, to draw up plans for specific settlements and, even more crucial, to get the powerful Jews in America involved in its development. The *fugu* had been hooked and brought safely to the kitchen. Now was the time to apply the knife.

**4** Between the birth date of the *fugu* plan in 1934 and its coming-of-age at the 1938 Five Ministers' Conference, a new dimension was added to the Japanese–Jewish relationship, a result of the ongoing war with China. In July 1937, Japan had successfully attacked Shanghai. Japan's control of the city extended, however, only to its Chinese areas. There were two sectors of Shanghai which, though obviously very much in China, were legally considered to be "extra territorial." They were the International Settlement and the French Concession. These two areas contained roughly thirty-eight thousand foreign residents, including about four thousand seven hundred Jews, who had never been under the authority of the Chinese government and were definitely *not* under Japanese control. It was an unusual situation, but prewar Shanghai was an unusual place.

Sitting on the Whangpoo River, only a few miles from the mouth of the mighty Yangtze – the only feasible trade link between the vast interior of southern China and the sea – Shanghai is endowed with a tremendous commercial potential. This fact was not lost on the British who, in 1842, when they were enlarging their "sphere of influence" on the Asian mainland, made Shanghai one of their major bases in China. The security offered by the British stronghold soon attracted traders and fortune hunters from Europe, the Americas, and, from the end of the nineteenth century, Japan. The majority moved into the International Settlement. The smaller and commercially less important French Concession which adjoined the Settlement had a separate administration, but in both sectors foreigners lived and did business safe under the sheltering umbrella of a Western legal system and a liberal commercial code.

The international sector of Shanghai did not exist for any one nation's glory, for any one culture's pride, for any one religion's propagation: its sole *raison d'être* was business. And this was business in the form of capitalism hardly constrained by government edicts, and often not at all by the forces of morality. Such as

62

it was, the government of the International Settlement was administered by a municipal council which, by the 1930s, was made up of five British, five Chinese, two Americans and two Japanese. It provided little in the way of municipal services – schools and hospitals, for instance, had to be either privately or charitably supported – and it demanded equally little in return. For anyone of any nationality, the International Settlement meant the ultimate in freedom. Even after the United States had begun closing her doors to "the tired, the poor, the huddled masses," Shanghai remained open. No passport was asked for, no work permit was needed, either to manage vast enterprises in the magnificent offices lining the embankment, named the *Bund,* or to swelter in the tiny, one-roomed factories crammed into the tangle of dead-end lanes.

From the beginning, Shanghai was as open to Jews as to anyone else; and from the beginning, Jews came. One of the first Jewish companies to be established there as early as the 1840s, was David Sassoon and Sons, Ltd., which set up a Shanghai branch of its already successful Bombay trading and banking company. Sassoon who came originally from Iraq, was soon joined by other Sephardic (Middle Eastern) Jews – the Abrahams, the Hardoons, the Kadoories and others, and most of these families, in time, took British citizenship. In prewar Shanghai, the Sephardim represented wealth and power out of all proportion to their numbers. Silas Hardoon, for example, had the unique distinction of being appointed to both governing councils – the international and French – at the same time; the company run by Sir Victor Sassoon, a slim, graying, dignified millionaire known as "The J.P. Morgan of the Orient," owned Shanghai real estate valued at nearly nine million pounds sterling. The president and more than a third of the ninety-nine members of the Shanghai stock exchange were Sephardic Jews. Yet, in the thirties, there were in total no more than seven hundred Sephardim in Shanghai.

From around the turn of the century, an expanding community of Ashkenazic (European) Jews, mostly from Russia, joined the Sephardim. They came down to Shanghai in waves after each of the successive upheavals in the tsar's empire. The final contingent arrived from Manchuria in the early 1930s, driven out by the Japanese. Politically, the overwhelming majority of Ashkenazim were "stateless"; most had lost their Russian citizenship for their nonsupport of the Communist regime. By the time Japan took control of the Chinese areas of Shanghai in 1937, the Russian Ashkenazim numbered about four thousand. Socially and economically, they were a mixed lot. Some, particularly the earlier arrivals, had been successful. They, or their children, were now part of the comfortable middle-class foreign communities in the Settlement or the Concession. Others were still trying to pull themselves up from the bottom.

Almost invariably, the least affluent lived in an area of the International Settlement called Hongkew, a riverside section also heavily populated by Japanese. This was primarily a commercial area, not grand international commerce as on the *Bund*, but local trading: farmers' markets, hat shops, pickle shops, and Chinese and Japanese department stores. The cost of living in Hongkew was a third less than in other parts of the Settlement.

During the mid-1930s, the Ashkenazic community of Shanghai was swelled by increasing numbers of refugees from Germany and Austria. These early emigrés were, as a group, far more financially secure than those who fled later. They had had the time to organize their departure – either by ship or through northern China to Shanghai. Unlike those who followed later, these refugees, some fifteen hundred by the end of 1938, had been allowed to take a certain amount of money with them, and generally they had not been relieved of all their personal possessions at the German border. They were, therefore, better prepared economically and psychologically to survive the devastating change from Central Europe to the heart of the Orient. But both waves of refugees settled in Hongkew, at least at first.

The 1937 takeover of Shanghai presented the Japanese "Jewish experts" with exciting new possibilities. Although the international sectors remained nominally free, the Jews became unquestionably more vulnerable to Japanese influence. Even the wealthy Sephardim were approachable. Inuzuka began to spend more and more of his time in Shanghai, and he was assigned to the Naval Bureau there full-time in April 1939. Within months, the entire focus of the Jew-utilization plans began to shift away from Manchukuo. Meetings were no longer held in Dairen or Harbin but in Shanghai; and a new face began appearing at the meetings, that of the Japanese consul general, Shiro Ishiguro. Ishiguro was less a "Jewish expert" than a *Gaimusho* liaison delegated to keep track of the military's involvement in this aspect of foreign affairs. From the spring of 1939, three men – Captain Inuzuka, Colonel Yasue and to a lesser extent Consul General Ishiguro – assumed responsibility for executing the cabinet policy laid down at the lengthy December 5 meeting. They were the ones who had to decide precisely how the Jews were to be manipulated, how a refugee settlement scheme was to be initiated, how it was to be presented to those potentially able to finance it. Those three men now assumed the duty of preparing for their Emperor the tastiest and most nourishing dish imaginable, not a deadly poison.

Inuzuka, Yasue and Ishiguro met week after week in the Shanghai Consulate or, when special secrecy seemed called for, on the ten-thousand ton Japanese battleship *Izumo* which was moored within sight of the Consulate off the Shanghai *Bund*. To achieve success, they would need to walk a tightrope. If they tilted too far to one side, the Jews would see through their machinations, and their cause would be utterly lost. If they leaned too far in the other direction, those "most clever and tricky internationalists" would overwhelm the poor, innocent Japanese. In Yasue's words "We cannot develop northern China without the Jews; therefore it is proper to use them; but care should be taken . . . that we can properly defend ourselves from a potential enemy who may one day devour us." Inuzuka was less delicate: "Jews must be strangled by the throat if they do not cooperate with us."

As 1939 progressed, "the experts" began work on three fronts. Locally, Inuzuka laid the groundwork for a future appeal for the goodwill, and superb capital resources, of the Sephardim by developing relations with the Ashkenazic community. The Ashkenazim had already shown signs of cooperation with the Japanese. Suspicious of Japanese links with Germany, they nevertheless were realists. They had left Russia for good; they had no government to turn to. If Japan had truly reversed her anti-Semitic policy, as it appeared from the conferences and other activities in Manchukuo, what could they lose from responding to her overtures? It might help stabilize their position in the world. It could even improve the situation of their fellow Ashkenazim, the German and Austrian refugees who were by now pouring into Shanghai at a rate of nearly a thousand a month.

Inuzuka, with his fluency in English, Russian and French, was easy to talk to. And since he had, for years, been under general orders from the navy to "find out everything there is to know" about Jews, he was always interested in visiting schools and synagogues and discussing any problems the Jews might encounter.

By mid-1939, Inuzuka had been successful in converting good faith into cash: the Pacific Trading Company was formed with an initial capitalization from Japanese, Chinese, Ashkenazic and Sephardic sources of seven hundred thousand dollars. The mere existence of this company was more important than anything it might accomplish: it was a well-publicized demonstration that Japanese and Jew could work together for a common goal. At about the same time that the Pacific Trading Company got off the ground, Inuzuka achieved another long-sought goal: the elusive Sir Victor Sassoon finally afforded him the social and personal honor of accepting one of his dinner invitations.

Yasue, on the Manchurian front, also was stepping up his activities. Plans were proceeding for a third FEJ Conference the following December. More important, Yosuke Matsuoka, still president of the South Manchurian Railway, had hired into his public relations department the only Hebrew-speaking Japanese in the world – a Christian minister named Setsuzo Kotsuji. Kotsuji's particular field, the Bible, had led him to become proficient in classical Hebrew. He had, in fact, written a Hebrew grammar in Japanese. The book was hardly a bestseller, but it did qualify Kotsuji as a first-rate suitor to woo the Manchurian Jews.

As a further proof of the increasing goodwill of Japan, Yasue arranged for the Harbin Jewish leader, Dr. Abraham Kaufman, to be invited on an official visit to Tokyo. For the full month of May 1939, Kaufman went from ministry to ministry, and his reception at each was more gracious than the last. Not only was Kaufman given the opportunity of explaining the feelings of Manchurian Jewry in these high places, he was himself reassured everywhere he went that Japan did not believe in racism and other such forms of discrimination, and that the country had no reason to persecute the Jews. He heard time and again the answer Foreign Minister Arita had given to a question posed in the Japanese Diet the preceding February: "Japan has never made any discrimination against alien people either through legislation or as a matter of fact. In view of public attention attracted by an increasing number of Jews in the Far East since last autumn, the government has decided on a definite policy toward Jews. . . . This policy aims at no discrimination against Jews. Jewish residents in Japan shall be treated just as any other foreign residents, who are free." Before returning home, Dr. Kaufman was presented with an imperial award. Few ordinary citizens, and far fewer foreigners, had been so honored.

The third front to which the "Jewish experts" were devoting their attention was the creation of a more direct line of communication with the American Jewish community. Early in 1939, Inuzuka got in touch with an Osaka steel-container manufacturer, Mitsuzo Tamura, who had studied twenty years before at the Massachusetts Institute of Technology and was then traveling frequently to New York to purchase scrap metal. Tamura had Jewish business contacts and already, several months before, he had been exposed to his country's interests in American Jewry. The Japanese Embassy in Washington had asked him to evaluate the feelings of the American Jewish community toward Japan, and Tamura was complying with this request on a continuing basis when Captain Inuzuka reached him.

Inuzuka asked Tamura to speak with his Jewish contacts only in general terms to get their reaction to the possibility of Japan's offering to settle a number of refugees from Europe somewhere in Japanese-held Asia. As he had complied with his Embassy's request, Tamura agreed to assist Inuzuka. Three contacts he enlisted in New York in April, 1939, were Otto Gerson, Ernst Grunebaum and Franz Hirschland, all active in Jewish and communal self-help organizations including the Joint Distribution Committee. Hirschland was a close friend of Rabbi Stephen Wise, president of the American Jewish Congress. Grunebaum, Hirschland's brother-in-law, was on the board of directors of the World Jewish Congress. Whether by accident or design, Tamura had provided Inuzuka and his fellow "experts" with extremely useful contacts in the American Jewish community.

By mid-spring 1939, the Jewish "experts" in Shanghai felt they had done all they could to prepare for the serving of the *fugu*. A settlement scheme had been approved, in theory, by the five most powerful men in Japan – a settlement scheme that would provide a non-belligerent, strictly humanitarian framework for large-scale Jewish investment in the empire; an enterprise that would convince the Jewish opinion-makers in the New York press, the radio networks and movie studios, and hence the world, that Japan was a fine, generous and humane nation. But, so far, it was no more than an idea. What was lacking was a positive action. It had been policy throughout that the Japanese did not initiate favors toward the Jews. If only a Jew would initiate an actual settlement scheme. . . .

The Japanese did not have long to wait. In March 1939, apparently on his own initiative, a Jew obliged. Lew Zikman, a wealthy Manchurian concerned about the plight of European Jews, broached an idea to Inuzuka and his two cohorts. Would it be possible, Zikman asked, to settle two hundred leatherworkers, with their families, over six hundred people in all, on the outskirts of a town in Manchukuo? Zikman himself would put up some of the money necessary: an additional two hundred thousand dollars he would try to procure from the Americans, probably through the American Jewish Congress.

To the "Jewish experts" this was an answered prayer but it was limited. "Three thousand is a better figure," Inuzuka said. Zikman demurred; he thought it wiser to begin with a small number of settlers. But soon it no longer mattered what Zikman thought. The Jew had initiated the suggestion; from then on it was a Japanese affair.

The more frequent Shanghai meetings took on a new excitement as Inuzuka, Yasue and Consul General Ishiguro began to pull the threads together. By June, there was a formal report: "Concrete Measures to be Employed to Turn Friendly to Japan the Public Opinion Far East Diplomatic Policy Close Circle of President of USA by Manipulating Influential Jews in China." Within days this document was approved by the top Japanese brass of central China and Manchukuo and Inuzuka himself carried it to Tokyo. On July 7, it appeared as a confidential joint research report, somewhat more euphoniously titled, "The Study and Analysis of Introducing Jewish Capital."

The ninety-page document was not devoted entirely to the settlement scheme. It also covered measures for the attraction of capital investments by wealthy Shanghai Sephardim, not only for their intrinsic value but so that Jewish financiers in the West would be persuaded to follow suit. (It was a "well-known fact" that Jewish investors stuck together. Even back in 1903, hadn't Schiff-the-Jew received money from a Jew, Warburg, in Germany and another Jew, Cassel, in England?) Additionally, several pages of the confidential report were devoted to plans for swaying American public opinion. Jewish journalists (it was another "well-known fact" that

68

"eighty percent of American journalists are Jewish") would be invited to Japan to write glowing articles about the country. Hollywood movie producers (*"all* Hollywood movie producers are Jewish") would be asked to make movies in Shanghai about how nice the Japanese were to the refugees there.

An official delegation from Japan would be sent to the leading rabbis in the United States to explain how much Judaism and the Shinto religion had in common and to invite the American rabbis to Japan for the purpose of introducing Judaism to the Japanese people. But the heart of the report was the plan for creating a Jewish refugee settlement. In the words of the report, "a truly peaceful land so that the Jews may be comfortably settled to engage in business at ease for ever." In Yasue's words, this would be an "Israel in Asia."

The plan was at once detailed and flexible. Several sites were suggested as alternatives – areas in Manchukuo favored by Yasue, areas near Shanghai promoted by Inuzuka and Ishiguro. A variety of population levels were proposed, from eighteen thousand up to nine hundred thousand. Each projected population level was followed by a string of figures, determined "according to the standard planning of modern cities," to be the number of square meters needed per person, how much of the land would be used in common, how much reserved for private use and so on. Considered were all the necessities of daily life for up to almost a million refugees: elementary and high schools, synagogues, hospitals, sewer lines, industrial areas, parklands. . . .

All these things were put in the form of suggestions, recommendations. One aspect of the settlement plan, however, had been firmly decided: Jews would be allowed total religious, cultural and educational autonomy but otherwise, in all other matters, the settlement was to be ruled entirely by the Japanese. Colonel Yasue – throughout the development of the *fugu* plan, the most idealistic of the three and apparently the one most interested in the good of the refugees themselves – had argued long and hard for a truly autonomous area where, except for matters concerning external relations and defense, the Jews would be left on their own. But Yasue was overruled. "We have no objection," the commander of the Middle China Expeditionary Army wrote in his preliminary memo of approval, "to permitting residence of Jewish people under the appointed location and time if the Jewish plutocrats accept the construction of New-Town under our demands and conditions. However [the settlement's] aim is . . . to help the development of Japan and China. Therefore, details shall be studied sufficiently. And it is not good to permit an autonomous system for Jewish people." In the report, such recommendations became policy: "As for the administration of the Jewish section, which is to be made to appear autonomous, steps will be taken to place our authorities in a position to supervise and guide it behind the scenes."

"The Study and Analysis of Introducing Jewish Capital" was a proposal; it was not a blueprint laid out in detail down to the last roofing nail. To give reality to their plan, the "experts" suggested some figures. But they purposely left matters open. They themselves were only suggesting the tune. Paying the piper was to be left to the Jews themselves – not to the refugees, naturally, but to all those "members of the Jew race" who, the Japanese continued to believe, controlled so much of the world's capital. The Japanese did, however, suggest a possible round-figure price for the settlement of thirty thousand refugees: one hundred million dollars.

At that time, one hundred million dollars was roughly two hundred million yen, and this was, of course, much, much more than would be needed to settle thirty thousand people even in the most remote wilderness. In fact, the Japanese thought that the settlement itself would absorb only about twelve million yen. The remaining one hundred and eighty-eight million yen (ninety-four million dollars) it was suggested, could be in the form of credit extended to Japan to purchase various items from the United States.

Even in 1939, with the world still coming out of a universal economic depression, the Japanese did not consider one hundred million dollars outlandish, especially since it was simply an opening figure. Where else were the increasingly despised Jews of Europe to go? What other country was offering a refuge at any price at all? The Japanese believed they were making a reasonable offer. They believed they could expect a positive response from world Jewry. It stunned the Japanese planners, therefore, when, at just about the same time that they forwarded their "Study and Analysis," the very Jews that they already controlled, in Shanghai, began protesting about continued Jewish immigration to their areas. At the least, it became clear that very little of the resettlement capital would come from the foreign community there. With the Sephardim and

Ashkenazim well represented, a delegation actually pleaded with Captain Inuzuka to *stop* so many Jewish refugees from coming into the city. As the nominal authority in most of Shanghai, the foreigners asked, could the Japanese not persuade their allies Germany, and Italy, to prevent Jews embarking from Europe for Shanghai in the first place? And, failing success with Germany and Italy, couldn't Japan herself restrict the refugees' entrance into Shanghai?

Inuzuka and his cohorts were confounded – and suspicious. "This is a trap," they muttered among themselves. "These sneaky Jews are trying to manipulate us, trying to trick us into providing the fuel for more anti-Japanese editorials in the *New York Times*." Inuzuka held long discussions with Sir Victor Sassoon, Boris Topas, leader of the Ashkenazic community, and other prominent Shanghai Jews, trying to reconcile this strange request with the vaunted "Jewish brotherhood" that had been a key consideration in the development of the *fugu* plan. Through it all, the Jewish leaders held to their request. True, they felt a certain amount of responsibility for their European cousins, but things were not simple. By July 1939, there were more Jewish refugees in the city than there were Britons, Frenchmen and Americans combined. The city's economic base had been torn apart already by the Sino-Japanese War. They attempted to explain to Inuzuka and the others that Shanghai simply could not support any more people who could not support themselves. There had been anti-Semitic pogroms before in history. There was never any sense to them, never any but the most trumped-up reasons for the violence they wreaked on the Jewish communities, but this particular problem had *not*, thank God, broken out in Shanghai. So why should the Jews of Shanghai have to suffer so greatly the effects of it? Over the past months, the Shanghai community had willingly accepted the burden of thousands of charity cases laid on its shoulders. Enough was enough! "We have too many already! Let the rest go someplace else. Let someone else pay for them!" (In fairness, it should be mentioned that in 1939, Hitler's plans for annihilating all of European Jewry had not yet been learned of by the rest of the world.)

Tactically, the Japanese decided to placate the Sephardim who were in the forefront of those pleading for a surcease of refugees. Further, the Japanese knew that any restrictions they did lay down could easily be relaxed in an instant in the future. Ultimately,

Captain Inuzuka asked for, and received, a promise from the Jews of Shanghai that they would not protest about any restrictions. On August 9, 1939, repeating as often as possible that "this measure has been taken at the request of the Jewish Refugee Committee itself," Captain Inuzuka announced measures limiting further immigration into Shanghai from Europe or Manchukuo. Henceforth, a refugee would need either four hundred American dollars "guarantee money" or a contract for a job.

As intended, immigration virtually ceased. The Jews of Shanghai were pleased and grateful. The "Jewish experts" disappointed that this particular community did not possess any interest in rescuing European refugees, turned their attention to the Jewish community in the United States.

In New York, Tamura the steel container manufacturer, began speaking to his Jewish business contacts, Gerson, Grunebaum and Hirschland. They considered numbers, specific employment possibilities, specific settlement zones, and so forth. As the discussions deepened, the men met regularly at an office on the seventh floor of the Empire State Building. Gerson, Grunebaum and Hirschland responded with gratifying enthusiasm to the plans Tamura was proposing. But they were essentially businessmen. They could not speak for American Jewry. The one man who appeared to be a spokesman for the entire community of American Jews was the president of the World Jewish Congress, Rabbi Stephen S. Wise.

Sixty-six years old, Stephen Wise was one of the most respected men in America. Because of his close friendships with both Woodrow Wilson and Franklin Roosevelt, he was believed by Americans and foreigners alike to have considerable influence on American governmental decisions. As Inuzuka had written: "He goes anywhere the president goes as the shadow follows the form." Rabbi Wise was a liberal, politically as well as religiously. He was one of the leading spokesmen for both Reform Judaism and Zionism. He was involved with the labor movement, with the movement for world peace, with the struggle of all minorities for civil and political rights. He also staunchly opposed the Japanese. Since Japan's first incursions on the Asian mainland, in letters, articles and sermons Wise continually referred to the "criminal aggression" in China, and advocated that the United States take any action "short of war or what may lead to war that will make it impossible for Japan to continue its relentless and criminal war against China." Lew

Zikman, the Manchurian industrialist, wrote Wise in 1938, saying merely that the Japanese seemed to be treating Manchurian Jews rather fairly, and received this response:

> I think it is wholly vicious for Jews to give support to Japan, as truly Fascist a nation as Germany or Italy. I do not wish to discuss the matter any further and I deeply deplore whatever your reasons may be that you are trying to secure support for Japan from Jews. I promise you that everything I can do to thwart your plans, I will do. You are doing a great disservice to the Jewish people.
>
> I do not wish to discuss this with you further. I have no desire to speak with anyone who like you is prepared to give support to Japan for reasons which are invalid and without regard for the fact that Japan is like Germany, Italy, a nation that is bound to take an anti-Semitic attitude, and indeed has already done so.
>
> Faithfully,<br>Stephen S. Wise

This was the man Mitsuzo Tamura wanted to convince of the wisdom of settling hundreds of thousands of Jewish refugees in Japan's Chinese empire.

Tamura's meeting with Stephen Wise took place early in 1940 in Wise's office. Physically, it was Mutt and Jeff. Tamura was short, even for a Japanese. Wise was huge – six foot three, solid, an expansive man of broad gestures, a man who greeted even strangers with a warm handshake and an arm around the shoulders. And to Wise, Tamura was not a stranger. The rabbi had spoken often to Franz Hirschland about Tamura while Hirschland was trying to persuade him actually to meet with the man.

Thus, in spite of his feelings toward the Japanese, Wise felt he had no choice but to meet Tamura. He agreed to Hirschland's suggestion that Tamura come to his office.

Rabbi Wise's feelings, stated so bluntly in the 1938 letter to Lew Zikman, had never been conveyed directly to the Japanese. Nevertheless his negative attitude toward that nation's policies were as well known as the strength of his influence. From the moment in Shanghai that Inuzuka, Yasue and Ishiguro received word from New York that Tamura had been given an appointment with the Jewish leader they were on tenterhooks: this was the time for hooking the *fugu*.

Like the three in Shanghai, Tamura was aware that Wise was

*the* man. The enthusiasm of Gerson, Grunebaum and Hirschland was important only insofar as it was indicative of his response. If Stephen Wise was interested in the plan; if Stephen Wise began asking questions in his proverbially direct and highly perceptive manner; if Stephen Wise nodded, ran his hands through his wavy gray hair, developed a faraway look in his eyes; if he could be led to imagine that thousands of Jews could be rescued from the brutality and death they were now condemned to suffer in Europe . . . if all these responses, if any one of them came out of the meeting, then the bait had been taken and those who had had a hand in reeling the *fugu* in would receive their just rewards.

Wise's office was immense and practically monastic in its simplicity. Aside from a desk lamp that spread a wide circle of light in one corner of the office, all was in shadow. The two men greeted each other cordially. Tamura took the offered chair and after a few moments of introductory small talk, brought the conversation around to the purpose of the visit.

Throughout the brief meeting Tamura never discussed specifics. He spoke of the respect the Japanese people always held for the Jews; of the close and mutually successful business and cultural ties that had developed between Jews and Japanese from as early as the 1860s. He informed Wise that a Jew had played a crucial role in the writing of Japan's first constitution, and he referred to the fact that not only had the first English-language newspaper been founded by a Jew (Raphael Schoyer), but that the most influential present-day English newspaper, *The Japan Advertiser*, read even by the Emperor himself, was owned by a Jew. Tamura described the current position of Jews within the borders of Japan's authority. Jews were living in Kobe and Yokohama; and in Manchukuo and China there were communities in many of the more important commercial cities. All of these people lived in peace and security because, as Foreign Minister Hachiro Arita had stated on the floor of the Diet, Japan was not a racist country: she had a policy of treating Jews just as she treated all other foreigners. No doubt Rabbi Wise was familiar with the three conferences on Far Eastern Jews which had been convened strictly under the auspices of the Jews themselves during the past three years?

Wise nodded; he was indeed aware of the conferences, he had received memos of their discussions and copies of their closing resolutions.

Tamura continued. Japan, of course, is well aware of the difficult position in which many European Jews now find themselves. Would it not be mutually beneficial if a certain number of these European Jews – a certain sizable number, he said, without using any precise figure – were to emigrate to some prearranged settlement area in either Manchukuo or China?

Rabbi Wise did not run his hands through his hair, nor was there a faraway look in his eyes. He simply watched his visitor politely but steadily.

Japan would be honored, Tamura went on, to have such a settlement. It would, of course, entail some expense which Japan herself could not be expected to pay. However, beyond the basic cost of construction of housing, factories, roads, and other amenities, Japan would not be interested in cash as such but would be happy to accept trade arrangements with the United States for such items as industrial machinery, scrap metal and fuel.

Not authorized to discuss the plan in any greater detail than this, Tamura said little more and then waited for the response. From Rabbi Wise's lack of obvious enthusiasm, he didn't expect much. But even less did he expect the response he got.

"The Japanese authorities certainly seem to have persuaded a great many otherwise perceptive people that they have the interest of the Jewish people at heart," Wise said without hostility. "But I have noted, over the past several years, that the Japanese military . . . the military is, I believe the organization now in control in Japanese-occupied Manchuria and China?"

Tamura nodded noncommittally.

". . . The Japanese military have been excessively, if not in-humanely, harsh with *other* minorities who have come under their power. The Manchurians, for example, or the Koreans who loathe the Japanese as perhaps no other conquered peoples in the history of mankind have loathed their overlords. Certainly the Chinese, par-ticularly the residents of Nanking – excluding, naturally, the three hundred thousand civilians who were massacred *after* that city surrendered in 1937 – certainly the Chinese would have little cause to recommend living in Japanese-controlled lands."

Stephen Wise had not become a public spokesman for no reason. He spoke calmly, politely; his tone of voice was so reasonable as to be almost friendly.

Not knowing what to say, Tamura said nothing. "Do you represent the Japanese military government, Mr. Tamura?" Wise asked.
Tamura shook his head.

"Has this matter, this settlement plan, been discussed with our
State Department?" Wise asked.

"I believe it has not," Tamura replied with all the calm he could
muster. "It was felt, I believe, that the American Jewish community could deal with Japan directly. Or perhaps that the
American Jewish community could use its considerable influence as
a kind of 'power behind the throne', so to speak, to convince the
government to trust Japan in this – and perhaps in other matters."

"I see," Wise said, leaning back in his swivel chair as if weighing
several possibilities. Then he spoke.

"Let me say at the outset, Mr. Tamura, that I must correct one
false impression you seem to have. American Jews are far *far* from
being in any way what you referred to as a 'power behind the
throne.' Our influence is exactly the same as that of any small
minority in a democracy – no more and no less. Now, as to the question of America's exporting to Japan items such as fuel oil, heavy
machinery and scrap metal . . . . These are items which might possibly be considered war material and are at any rate very similar to,
if not identical to, the things covered by the 'moral embargo' which
the American government has had in effect for several months
now. Wouldn't you think, Mr. Tamura, that it might be a rather
unpatriotic thing for American Jews to do, even to discuss the future
export of these items to a non-allied country without consulting at
length with the State Department?"

The word "unpatriotic" rang a familiar bell. Hirschland had
mentioned to Tamura that Wise was a "super-patriot," that he felt
that the United States was the only really safe place for Jews these
days in the whole world, and that Jews and especially the Jewish
leaders ought to bend over backward not to show even a hint of
disloyalty to the policies of the American government. But the
question of whether he, Tamura, thought it would be unpatriotic
clearly had been rhetorical. The Jewish leader had risen from his
chair and was now towering over him, a friendly giant. Fearing the
meeting might end on this negative note, Tamura spoke quickly,
reluctantly rising from his chair.

"Dr. Wise, there is no way of really knowing a thing except by
seeing it first-hand. Please, come to Japan, to Manchukuo and

China, come and see for yourself how some Jews are now living in the Japanese Empire and how so many more could be settled there safely and happily. If you yourself can not come, send a delegate – anyone you can trust to report back honestly. We are completely open to investigation by anyone you send."

They had reached the door of the office. Rabbi Wise was silent for an instant, once more simply looking steadily at his visitor.

"It has been very interesting making your acquaintance, Mr. Tamura," he said courteously stretching out one hand to Tamura while opening the door with the other. "And I hope you have a good trip back to Japan."

With no alternative, Tamura shook the hand and passed through the open door. He recognized his failure; but did not know what to do next. Wanting only to retreat to the familiarity of his hotel room, he left the building directly. Had he not, he might have overheard Rabbi Stephen Wise exploding to one of his assistants "I have no time for this *nonsense*!"

In spite of the discouraging report Tamura sent back on his meeting with Wise, the clique in Shanghai continued to hope that something might come from it. Inuzuka even persuaded Ellis Hayim, a highly respected Sephardi in Shanghai, to send Wise the following cable: REFERRING YOUR DISCUSSION TAMURA REGARDING REFUGEE IMMIGRANTS BELIEVE JAPANESE GOVERNMENT FAVORABLE STOP PRESENCE YOUR DELEGATION ESSENTIAL STOP REPLY TAMURA [SIGNED] ELLIS HAYIM. And only a few days later, the American Jewish Congress received a copy of a confidential resolution passed by the third Conference of Far Eastern Jewish Communities held in Harbin on December 23–26, 1939:

> We are also grateful to Japan . . . for the kind treatment given the immigrants [refugees] as well as the Jewish residents. Jewish refugees are overflowing in some places in the Far East, particularly in Shanghai. Several thousand have no place in which to live and are being accommodated in school buildings and the like. We, the world Jewish community, will be much obliged to Japan if she offers to these refugees some place to live and settle comfortably in the Far East through imperial Japanese effort. In the case of Japanese compliance (i.e. if Japan offers some land) we shall be responsible for the construction of that settlement and hereby promise to cooperate in building a new Asia as much as we can.

But by the end of January, 1940, the "experts" were forced to face reality: there had been no immediate response; there would be no delayed reaction. There was no delegation planning on visiting Japan to investigate further. At their headquarters on the battleship *Izumo*, Inuzuka, Yasue and Ishiguro writhed in disappointment and frustration that their *fugu* plan had been rejected completely out of hand. What had gone wrong? they asked themselves again and again. Why does Stephen Wise not investigate the idea for himself? Just as there had been no spokesman for the Japanese who could convince Stephen Wise of the possibilities of the *fugu* plan, so there was no American Jew in Shanghai who could explain Wise's response to the Japanese.

Ironically, within months of his meeting with Tamura, Rabbi Wise began softening his animosity toward Japan. In July, 1940, he wrote to Dr. Karl Kindermann, a German Jew then residing in Tokyo:

> . . . any offer to settle Jewish refugees in Japan which would come from authoritative sources in Japan would certainly receive the fullest consideration of Jewish organizations. There will however, you will understand, be no need of persons who have authorizations neither from Jewish organizations nor from the Japanese government to initiate such negotiations.

Tamura, moreover, did not give up. He continued his discussions with Gerson, Grunebaum and Hirschland and also made an approach to the New York headquarters of the one organization that could move refugees, the Joint Distribution Committee. The JDC was a little more receptive to the idea than Wise had been. But when its officials contacted the Japanese Consulate to find out who this Tamura was, they were informed that he had no government standing whatever. Since the Japanese *Gaimusho* below the highest levels was strongly pro-Nazi, the explanation for this disowning of Tamura is not hard to find. The Nazis did have some success in fostering anti-Semitism in Japan, particularly where it mattered most – in the government bureaucracy and the military. A sizable segment of the Japanese leadership believed, in 1939, that "any use of Jews would destroy the significance of the holy war and leave the empire to the same bitter ordeal . . . as that of other countries with Jews." The influence of this view was to grow as war fever heightened. Time began to run out. In July 1940, Yosuke

Matsuoka, president of the South Manchurian Railway and ally of the industrialist Ayukawa in his scheme to settle Jews in the empire, left his railway post to become the foreign minister of Japan. In that position, however, he had greater things on his mind than a scheme to rescue Jews. On the contrary, by the end of the month, he led the government into a military alliance with Germany and Italy. This tripartite pact, would not be publically signed until September. However, even its initial negotiation signaled, for the time being, at least, the end of *fugu*. No matter what agreements were reached now with the Jewish powers, they would be totally negated when the military alliance between Japan and the Jews' arch-enemy was announced. There would be no Jewish investment. There would be no refugee settlement. There would be no Jewish-inspired shift in the anti-Japanese opinions of America's public. Six years of planning, bridge-building and fence-mending between the Japanese and the Jews would be consumed in the explosion of Jewish wrath at the Pact.

Yet it is central to Oriental philosophy that the only constant is change. The *fugu* plan, in the exact form which they had developed it, might be finished. But, after the inevitable furor caused by the announcement of the Tripartite Pact, there would still be Jews in the Japanese Empire. There would still be Jews controlling American public opinion. There would still be Jews who had the ear of the United States president. Could not some indirect use be made of these factors? Japan, after all, was not *required* by the Tripartite Pact to annihilate all the Jews within her borders. Might there not then be some way to keep the options open, something that could be salvaged from all these plans so carefully laid and bridges so carefully built?

Toward the middle of August 1940, the foreign minister learned that one of his low-level officers in Kovno, Lithuania, in complete disregard of orders, had issued transit visas to several thousand Jewish refugees, some of whom had highly suspect destination visas for Curaçao, some of whom had no destination visas at all. Logically, reasonably, the Foreign Ministry should have disavowed this entirely personal action on the part of the young consul and refused to honor the visas. Matsuoka's Ministry issued no disavowal. In Japan, as elsewhere, there is more than one way to skin a blowfish.

# 5

THERE WAS a chill in the air on September 1, 1940 as Consul Senpo Sugihara led his family to the Kovno railway station. The Russians had given him until that day to leave the country, and in the two months that had passed since they had annexed Lithuania, Sugihara had seen nothing to make him question their sincerity. It wasn't far from the Japanese Consulate to the station, but the departing diplomat had left plenty of time to cover the distance. He had no doubt his path would be jammed with Jewish refugees, striving even at this final moment to have the precious transit visa stamped on their papers. He was not mistaken. Sugihara did what he could – in the street, in the station, even through the window of the train car – until the moment the train actually began to pull away from the platform. Then he collapsed into his seat, drained and exhausted. During the past nineteen days, he had stamped and signed nearly six thousand visas entitling their bearers to remain in Japan for a maximum of twenty-one days while in transit between any two countries. Whether Tokyo would honor the visas, he did not know. Other than a cable ordering him temporarily to join the Embassy in Berlin, Sugihara had heard nothing from the *Gaimusho*. He had done all he could. Resting his feet on the seat opposite, he watched his six-year-old son staring entranced at the colorful landscape of Lithuania steadily disappearing to the north. Sugihara thanked his ancestors for having been born Japanese.

Behind the departing consul, in Kovno and Vilna and in several of the smaller towns of Lithuania, six thousand Jews privately pondered the strange new stamps that guaranteed nothing more nor less than the right to enter a land so far away and alien that it might as well not exist at all. Then they carefully put their papers away in safe places and began worrying about a more immediate problem. Having a place to go, even temporarily, was one thing. Getting there was another. The Soviets were creating Utopia in Lithuania. One didn't ask to leave Utopia. Anyone wanting to leave must either be mad – or "unredeemably bourgeois." For either condition, there were only two responses: internal exile to Siberia, or execution. Such harsh controls were common knowledge to the Lithuanians. Many of them had already "disappeared." Why should anyone think it would not happen to the refugees? A Japanese transit visa would turn out to be like an insurance policy, the cynics were saying: before you can cash in on it, you have to be a corpse! The pessimists agreed, recalling the fate of the Jews of Lemberg. In 1939, after Stalin had successfully laid claim to eastern Poland, the new Russian authorities had let it be known that anyone who wished to move west, out of the Russian-controlled zone, could simply petition for permission. A group of Jews from the small city of Lemberg had done exactly that, and soon afterwards were asked to gather their belongings and board a train. The train did, indeed, move them out, but not to the west; the Jews of Lemberg went east, straight to the labor camps of Siberia. Hearing the story of the Lemberg Jews, the holders of Japanese transit visas had no doubt that the most dangerous part of their exodus – asking leave of the Russian "pharaohs" – still lay ahead.

Every day that passed seemed to make their position more precarious. Hostilities were intensifying all over Europe. Even unfamiliar Asia – a continent of little previous concern to the refugees – was boiling with war. Indeed, they asked each other after the formation of the Axis alliance was announced, what hope was there that Japan, this new ally of Nazi Germany, might honor their transit visas? In every tiny apartment, in every Joint Distribution Committee boarding house and relief kitchen, the debate raged: how could a person best secure his own personal survival – by staying put or by trying to leave? Further north, in four small towns where the famous Mir Yeshiva had taken refuge, the debate had broader overtones. On the Mir's decision would rest the future of Jewish scholarship.

Jewish education in Europe was in a shambles. Scores of yeshivas – organized groups of men between about seventeen and twenty-five who devote seven days a week to studying the laws of the Torah and the voluminous commentaries on them – had been completely destroyed. To Orthodox Judaism, this destruction of scholarship was, itself, a catastrophe. Each Jew must lead his life according to the laws laid down by God in the Torah. Each adult must know the laws, must know how to interpret them, how to apply them, how to derive the most from each of them. Without this knowledge, Judaism would cease to exist. Yet inexorably, every one of the nerve centers of this crucial learning process was falling before the Nazi/ Soviet advance. Rabbis were being executed; their students were being scattered to starve, or imprisoned to be worked to death; libraries of ancient manuscripts and books were casually tossed into the fire like so much garbage. By as early as 1940 there remained in Europe – Germany, France, Poland, Rumania, the Baltic nations – only small pockets of traditional European Jewish learning: the straggling remnants of the famous schools of Tels, Lodz, Slobodka, Lublin, Radin. Only one of the major schools remained intact – the Yeshiva of Mir.

The three hundred rabbis and students of the Mir Yeshiva had started their race with annihilation in the month of *Marheshvan*, the year 5700 (October 1939) after their small town in northern Poland had been shelled and was beginning to be encircled by tanks. First, the entire yeshiva fled to Vilna. Six months later, to escape anti-Semites in Vilna, they moved on again to the small town of Kaidan. And not long thereafter, to escape the occupying Russians, the yeshiva split into quarters and settled in secret, in yet smaller towns – Crok, Schat, Ramigola and Krakinava – scattered across the countryside of northern Lithuania.

From these small towns, two representatives of the yeshiva, the principal's secretary and a student, Moishe Zupnik, had gone to Kovno to obtain three hundred of the precious Japanese transit visas from Consul Sugihara. After that, the young men went back to studying, praying, and worrying aloud.

Yankel Gilbewitz hunched tensely against the one wooden arm of the chair he was sitting in and followed, again, the arguments of his fellow students.

"With all respect to our principal, Rabbi Finkel," Zev Levy was saying, "it is impossible for me to believe that we can actually get to Palestine. The British are such angels? They are suddenly going to open up the door to us? 'Come, my children,' Britain is going to say. 'Come to Palestine.' I beg your pardon, I do *not* think Britain is going to say that. They don't want us there. They don't want us *anywhere*. *No* one wants us anywhere. Even America doesn't want us."

"There's still hope that America will take us, if we can just pry open the door," another student insisted, gesturing with his long fingers the forcing open of a door.

Levy harshly mimicked the gesture and the voice. "'If we can pry open the door.' What have Rabbi Kalmanowitz and the *Va'ad Hatzalah*, and all the other people and organizations dedicated to helping us been doing for all these months but trying to 'pry open the door.' And where are we still?"

Levy broke into the sing-song rhythm the students used while studying the Talmud. "We are here. . . . America is there. . . . The Russians are deporting hundreds of Lithuanian Jews every week. . . . And the only reason they haven't exiled us is . . . they haven't *found* us!"

He paused to let the words sink in.

"I'll tell you, I would go to Palestine tomorrow – tonight! – if I could. I would walk on my bare feet to Odessa and float on a raft to Haifa if I thought they would let us in. But they won't. And since they won't, I want to go to the only other place where someone might let us in."

"Japan," the other student said with mild disgust.

Levy threw up his hands as if at the end of his patience. "No, I don't *want* to go to Japan! I *want* to go to *America*. But I can't *get* to America from *here*. And maybe I *can* get to America from *there*!" Levy glared at his fellow students, partly angry but mostly dismayed at their lack of understanding.

Yankel Gilbewitz lifted his thin frame from the chair and wandered off alone into the cold, deserted kitchen. It was a large room, both kitchen and dining room for the twenty-two people packed into this borrowed house on the outskirts of Krakinava. Like fraternal twins, the kitchen area was divided into two similar but distinct halves. Each had a long tin counter holding a stack of clean dishes; each counter had a small washing sink; and, amazingly in this far-from-wealthy house, near each of the two counters was a separate cooking stove. In such a place, it was practically impossible to transgress the injunction against mixing milk and meat.

Heedless of the cold, Yankel went to the cracked window and looked through narrowed eyes onto the frozen night. Absently fingering the delicate white fringes of the *tallis katan* under his shirt, he thought about the leading proponent of action, the one who had gone to get the transit visas in the first place, Moishe Zupnik. Zupnik was no more learned than the other students, but he had lived closer to the secular world than most of them. He had grown up in Germany which in itself almost guaranteed a closer brush with the *goyim*. In spite of this, or because of it, Moishe Zupnik was totally involved with the school and its interests. Not only had he accompanied the yeshiva's secretary to the Japanese Consulate in Kovno, he also offered to stay in the Consulate to do the actual work of stamping all three hundred passports. Yankel did envy Moishe Zupnik his worldly wisdom. He did not envy him his total dedication to Jewish scholarship. That sort of thing was fine for show; but it could get in the way of a man's true goals.

To Yankel, born Yaacov ben Yitzhak seventeen years before, the Mir Yeshiva was an excellent sanctuary. Even in these diminished and insecure circumstances, it was a vastly superior way of life to that which seemed to have been his birthright. Sometimes his mind would focus for a moment on that fact and he would sigh with satisfaction. Thus far, he had accomplished the goal he had set as far back as he could remember – to escape from the confining *shtetl* world of poverty and exhaustion and mud. The Gilbewitz family – Mama, Papa and three daughters – had been wretchedly poor in their tiny village in north-central Poland. Too poor to have meat even on the Sabbath unless someone out of kindness left a package by the door of their decaying hovel. Too poor to own leather shoes, which meant walking to market on muddy or icy roads in awkward, sodden boots of cardboard and cloth. Too poor even to have hope of ever being otherwise, unless, *im yirzeh ha-Shem*, there was a miracle. Finally, there was Yankel, and *he* was the miracle. Inside Yankel's head was a memory that would have been called "photographic" if anyone in town had known what a photograph was. From the age of five when he began attending *cheder*, it was clear that whatever entered his mind through those plain brown eyes would never be lost. Months later Yankel could repeat word for word with unfailing accuracy a verse of Torah or a line of commentary he had noted if only once in passing. In a world of learning, where each new interpretation must take into account all arguments that have come before it, such skill is invaluable. Yankel's family saw it as a gift from God; Yankel, from an early age, saw it as a means of pulling himself up and out of a world of dirt, drudgery and denial.

The efficient working of his memory did not, however, provide Yankel with a brilliant intellect. Day and night he had to apply himself to his studies, sitting on a hard bench, forcing himself to try and grapple with the meaning and significance of the page he was able to memorize so easily. There was little pleasure or fun in his childhood. Studying furiously season after season, always making sure he was noticed, his genius and diligence appreciated, Yankel passed first through the little village *cheder*, then through a higher school in a larger town several miles away by foot. Finally, having gained the benefits of local Jewish education, he began to rest easier about his future. In a world that ranks the scholar just below the angels, a boy such as Yankel had no trouble slipping the confines of his family's poverty. With the help of a traditionally anonymous charitable donation, Yankel left the discomfort of home for good and went off to the illustrious Mir Yeshiva. His acceptance at Mir, in early 1938, had been a moment of unmitigated joy. A Jewish scholar never earned a *pfennig* from his studies. But to have a scholar for a son-in-law was such an honor that, with his entrance into Mir, Yankel was all but guaranteed a wife from a good family and a better life.

Of its own accord, Yankel's hand moved from the *tallis* fringe into the pocket that held a worn postcard. It had come – surprisingly, some mail did continue to flow across the border – three weeks before, from his sister. "Well, we are all alive, and are still eating, most of the time." His parents and sisters, and all their husbands were all well, thank God. "And such good news!" she said at the end. "In March, I will be having a baby! I pray for a boy and pray that he will be a fine scholar like his uncle."

Rereading the card without bothering to look at it, Yankel felt a twinge of regret. He had never, never wanted to share in the miserable life of his family. But he had always told himself he would someday share with them any material rewards his scholarly success might bring. Now that hope was gone – at least for the immediate future. One way or another he would have to leave this land, this increasingly threatening world of Central Europe. He had not worked this hard or come this far to be denied his rewards by some *goyish* soldier. Others could hide their heads beneath their prayer shawls and call on God to rescue the Jewish people. He, Yankel Gilbewitz, had long ago learned the efficacy of calling on his own resources to rescue himself.

Ever since his passport had been stamped with the bold transit visa, Yankel had spent his nights weighing the possibility of escaping on his own – sneaking across the border into Russia, somehow crossing Russia and getting to Japan. Exactly what Japan would be like or where he would go from there, he did not know. But Japan had to be different than his *shtetl* or Vilna or Krakinava. And at seventeen, Yankel was adventurous enough to believe that what was different would surely be better. Yet, lying in his bed, thinking of independent flight, he had to admit it would be foolish. If he had been a worldly wise fellow like Zupnik . . . if he had been Zupnik, he never would have returned from his initial visit to the Japanese consul. He would have taken his passport and disappeared. Let his fellow students get their own visas! He wasn't Moishe Zupnik and he didn't know enough about dealing with the world outside the yeshiva to be able to get by on his own. In these impossible times, who would look after one lone Jew, no matter how well educated? But as part of the illustrious Mir Yeshiva, he had friends all over, even in America where Rabbi Kalmanowitz, a former teacher in the yeshiva, and other members of the Va'ad Hatzalah, the "Committee of Rescue," were raising the money that the whole school had been living on for months. So, he would stay with the yeshiva – and ally himself with those encouraging it to leave.

Outside the kitchen window, nothing moved in the winter field. There was little snow; the rocks and frozen furrows cast sharp shadows in the moonlight. Convincing the leaders of the yeshiva to apply to the Russians for exit permits from Lithuania was no easy task. Yankel had heard Moishe Zupnik, Levy and some of the others try. The principal and the teachers were set against it. Terrified of calling attention to themselves, there was even a possibility that the Russians were so far unaware of the yeshiva's presence in the country, unwilling to be responsible for the retribution that might rain down on even smaller pockets of yeshiva students hiding in other small towns, poignantly mindful of the story of Lemberg, the Mir leaders so far had refused even to consider talking to the Russians. Their fears, Yankel recognized, were not unrealistic. Application had to be made to the Russian NKVD, that terrifying mystery of a police organization that held absolute power of life and death over everyone in Lithuania. Back in Vilna, a few brave souls had applied, and some had been granted the exit permit. But who knew where those had really gone? Was it all just a repetition of Lemberg? On the other hand, if they stayed holed up like scared rabbits in Krakinava, how safe were they? Just the day before yesterday, he had seen two soldiers walking slowly along the dirt street, looking curiously at the yeshiva's house . . . and then scarcely five minutes later, walking slowly back, again staring at the building as if sizing up its dimensions and, worse, its inhabitants. It was nothing, Yankel had reassured himself at the time; soldiers have a right to keep their eyes open. But the incident had not slipped from his mind, it had cut into his heart like a cold knife. Asking the Russians for permission to leave would be a gamble, but a person would have to be a fool to think the yeshiva was safe here.

Suddenly aware that the rattle of voices from the next room had ceased, he turned and saw Lev Levy leaning against the door jamb watching him. Levy didn't like him, Yankel had long since decided. Alone among the other students, Levy seemed able to see the sharpness that lay behind the screen of piety and studious diligence which Yankel kept drawn down over his eyes. Still, Levy needed allies in his effort to get the yeshiva to move to safety.

"*Bari, she-ma*," Yankel said quietly, Talmudic shorthand for "the definite versus the doubtful." "If we stay, we are doomed. If we apply to the NKVD, we may be able to get out."

Yankel had been correct: Levy did not like him, but the older boy did need him.

"Did you happen to see the two soldiers walk past the house day before yesterday?" Levy asked, already knowing the answer.

Yankel nodded.

"Then perhaps you might mention it to Rabbi Finkel," Levy suggested. "You're not the only one here who couldn't make it on his own."

Yankel turned his face back toward the window. "I'll do that," he said briefly. He did not appreciate having someone read his mind.

Avram Chesno settled familiarly, if not comfortably, into one of the straight-back bentwood chairs in the Strashun Library. It was snowing outside, and in the places where the holes in his boots overlapped with the holes in his socks his feet were freezing. He could not protect his body from this December cold, but within its shivering shell, Chesno was in better psychological shape than at any time since his wife's death.

Three months ago, while he and Orliansky were sitting around in the Club discussing nothing of importance, Orliansky's ten-year-old son, Mischa, had sat with them for a few minutes. For the few children refugees, life had many of the qualities of a vacation – the most important being that there was no school. Mischa spent hours exploring the broad streets and narrow cobblestone lanes of Vilna, standing on the bridge watching the boats pass underneath, investigating the nooks and crannies of Vilna's magnificent Great Synagogue. On this particular day, he had visited one of the relief agency headquarters where a handful of children's books, in Hebrew, had just been received. Mischa had borrowed one but, being off on some extremely important mission and not wanting to carry it around, had decided to drop it off with Papa.

As father chatted with son, Avram absently paged through the book – long since beyond embarrassment that an intelligent adult should have nothing better to do than look at pictures in a children's book, a book whose language he had completely forgotten. But as he slowly turned over the pages, his eyes began to catch first on letters, then on the words which flashed back into his consciousness after the twenty-nine years of hibernation since his *bar mitzvah*. By dinner time, with the amused assistance of Orliansky – and the aid of the pictures – Avram had read the entire book. He was tremendously proud of himself! The next morning he went to the relief agency to borrow another book (making sure the woman there thought it was for Mischa). By the third day, he was beginning to build a vocabulary, and for the first time since Ruth's death, he had something to look forward to when he woke up in the morning.

Now, nearly three months later, he was able to read, more or less, the occasional Hebrew newspaper from Palestine that made its way up to Vilna. More important, this new activity had sparked his psyche into a new mode of thinking. Bleak and problematic as it might be, there would be a future. Since he had already rejected suicide and was in reasonably good health, he would have to cope with alternatives. Staying in Vilna meant remaining a charity case indefinitely or finding work. The first was too unpalatable and the second, over the long haul, probably impossible. But even in the unlikely event that he did find a job, staying meant yoking his energy and future to the Soviet system . . . which he had seen more than enough of in Bialystok.

There was, of course, an alternative to staying – but it lay behind dreary brown cement walls, through a maze of dimly lit corridors, in a bare room furnished only with one desk, two hard chairs and the cold expressionless eyes of an NKVD officer. Avram was a sophisticated man, well-educated, accustomed to being in authority and dealing with authority. But the thought of confronting the NKVD made his blood as cold as the December wind made his feet. Just contemplating it, sitting there in the library reading room, he shook his head in resignation. For the moment, there was Hebrew and the story of Noah which he had set himself the task of deciphering by lunch time. A dictionary on his lap, Avram placed the Bible to catch the maximum window light on the tiny letters and settled down to work.

The Strashun Library was more than a free and public collection of religious books. Forming one side of the courtyard, facing the Great Synagogue and the site of the former residence of the illustrious eighteenth-century Rabbi Elijah ben Solomon Zalman, the eminent *Gaon*, the library was the headquarters of most of the community's religious and secular activities. Avram often spent three or four hours there, reading, studying or simply observing the flow of informal meetings and group discussions going on around him.

This morning, a trio of observant Jews, their curly earlocks wrapped conveniently around their ears, were volubly discussing the impropriety of the theory of evolution.

It was not until they had moved off that Avram noticed the scene that was taking place in one corner of the room. Its central figure was an old man, his magnificent soft white beard flowing down over his chest and onto his shoulders; a Hasidic rebbe, Avram thought from his manner as much as from his long black satin coat and broad-brimmed hat. A rebbe is a particularly warm, personal type of rabbi, one who always seems to be standing very close to his followers; involved with them; sharing their problems totally; never coldly aloof from anyone. The rebbe was standing, talking to a pitiful couple and a boy who could not have been more than six years old. The boy's father, though a little taller than the rebbe, was considerably younger, and stood half turned away from the old man as if unsure whether he could withstand a direct confrontation. Yet he had placed himself in front of his wife and son, so as to bear the brunt of the rebbe's argument. The old rebbe was speaking slowly, calmly, almost tenderly to the couple. The reading room was quiet; Avram could hear every word.

"You must listen to me," the rebbe was saying. "You must have faith in what I am telling you. It is not only you that have been singled out. *None* of us can stay here. What will happen in one month's time, two months' time? These Russians don't *like* Jews, Getzel. It is as simple as that. They won't have us. Already they have closed our schools. Already they have begun exiling our leaders. If we try to stay, do you think they will not ultimately do the same with *all* of us?"

The rebbe paused to let his rhetorical question make its impression. He had been presenting the same argument to individuals and small groups of people for the past six weeks: we must leave, we must seize this opportunity because another will not come; we must trust in God, and we must go.

"Stalin cannot accept the existence of the Jewish people," he went on quietly. "We do not fit into his new Utopia, and we never will. Ultimately, he will destroy us. It's not only for you I am telling you, it's for the boy. What will. . . ."

Avram now could hear only the sobs of the woman as he watched her bury her son in her ragged winter coat. By the time the mother had quietened, the rebbe had stopped talking but the father had begun speaking more forcefully than Avram would have expected from his stance.

". . . will kill us all anyway, rebbe, or exile us. And *then* what will happen to our son?"

The man sitting nearest Avram at the long library table was also aware of the conversation taking place across the room. "That's the Amshenover rebbe," he said to no one in particular.

Avram's ears perked up at the sound of the familiar name. He had heard that the Amshenover rebbe – his family name was Kalisch, though his followers, by tradition preferred to call him by the name of his birthplace – was a leader among the Hasidim. Not a genius – the Hasidim didn't particularly favor geniuses – but an open, humane man. He was a modern version of the good men of the old stories – the old *tzadikkim* who, if they somehow acquired two *pfennigs*, would immediately give away one, maybe both. Avram had never seen the man before, but he knew his story. In 1939, the Amshenover rebbe had made a valiant effort to talk the large Jewish population at Otwock, a health-spa town where he was living, into moving themselves out of the way of the advancing Nazis. In the end, he had failed. He, his wife and son, and a few other families had departed at the last moment for the safety of

Vilna. But the rest were still in Otwock, now with little hope and less future.

The rebbe's hat glimmered in the sunlight as he shook his head, disagreeing with the father.

"No, I am not a prophet, but I do not believe what you are saying. If we stay, then yes, they will kill us. If we stay, then yes, they will take our children away from us. But we do not have to stay! Are we citizens of this country? We do not belong here, and we have valid, legal papers permitting us to go somewhere else. All we must do is have the courage to ask."

"But, rebbe," the man countered, "even though we are foreigners here, at least we know where we are. This other place. . . . Who knows where Japan is! Here there are other Jews. In Japan, there are no Jews. They aren't even white men!"

"Getzel, you speak without knowing what you are saying," the rebbe said gently. "If you look on a map, you will see Japan very clearly. It is a place, a country. It is not a jungle, with savages. The Japanese don't have tails to swing from the trees!"

The little boy had extricated himself from his mother's grasp and was looking fixedly at the old man. But he didn't even begin to smile at the image of the Japanese not swinging from trees. His parents had been so worried, so nervous for so long now, he almost couldn't remember back to when things had been nice. Their fear had taken its toll of him: he hadn't laughed, had scarcely smiled, in the fifteen months since they had left Alexandrov.

"And there are," the rebbe continued, "Jews living in Japan. Not so many, but some; and they live there not by force but of their own accord. But what is Japan is not very important. Japan is not the destination: it is a place to change boats, a place to leave from – for America."

"We have tried and *tried*," the woman said over her tears, "to go to America already. Do you really think we can get visas for America in Japan?"

In the light streaming through the high windows of the reading room, the old rebbe looked at the little boy. He stroked his thin, little anxious face, patted his hair and said mildly, "I don't know, Mrs. Syrkin. But I do know we cannot get them here – not you, not me, not any of us anymore. And the United States, I think, is our only chance of continuing to live as Jews. If the Almighty wants me to die as a Jew, I am quite willing to abide by His wishes. But on the off chance that it is not His wish that I die, but only the dream of Stalin, then I want to do everything I can to continue to *live* as a Jew. I too have a son. If I do not do everything in my power to keep him alive and keep him a Jew – even if it means taking chances with my own life and even with his life – then I am failing him and failing my people."

He put his arm around Getzel's shoulders. "*Ka-asher avadeti, avadeti,*" he said softly.

Getzel nodded and nodded again and again until he seemed, almost in spite of himself, to be affirming something beyond the philosophic resignation of "if I die, I die."

"Then we should go there *now*," he said quietly but decisively, "to apply for the exit permits."

It was the rebbe's turn to nod, and the four of them walked past the long reading tables toward the front door.

Avram rocked slowly back and forth in his chair, in sympathy with the little *shtetl* family. It was a terrible decision to have to make. If you said: "yes, I will apply" and took your place in that silent line of Jews that stretched out from the Intourist travel office, the first step in the process that ultimately led to the NKVD, there was no changing your mind later on. Even before you reached the head of the line, (sometimes the wait was as long as twenty-six hours), you became a "renegade bourgeois" in the eyes of those whose job it was to keep track of these things. Thereafter, for as long as you remained in territory controlled by the Soviets, even if you had to live out the rest of your life there, you would never be able to get a job or go to school – from that moment on you were at best in limbo, at worst an enemy of the state.

Avram watched the library doors swing closed behind the Amshenover rebbe. Applying for an exit permit was very different from simply asking the Japanese consul in Kovno for a transit visa. There had been no risk in that. But *this* meant calling attention to yourself. It meant having to submit to an interview, in person, for clearance from the NKVD – a dreadful danger to contemplate: who did not have some slight indiscretion in his past which, if discovered, might instantly turn that interview into a trial for his very life? Who could know all the activities of one's friends, or the friends of one's friends? And who could guess when an NKVD question was a question or when it was a trick? Applying for an exit permit was the ultimate political statement: it was a signed confession that you were one who did not want to contribute to the glorious task of building another Communist–Socialist state. Even a country fellow like Syrkin would have heard of the Lemberg catastrophe. Where was the difference between Vilna and Lemberg? No wonder so few had yet had the temerity to apply for the permit. What of those who had? Did they ever get past Siberia? Avram had heard that there had been cables received from Japan saying that the trip was possible, that Japan was safe. But a cable was nothing. The Soviets fabricated cables as easily as they fabricated everything else.

Yet, as the Amshenover rebbe had been saying, and his words had been convincing more and more Jews as conditions grew worse, going east to Japan was their only hope of getting out. His overheard plea to the Syrkins had helped Avram reach his own decision. And like Getzel Syrkin, he, too, trembled that afternoon when he took his place in the line that led to the petition desk at Intourist.

**6** LEW ZIKMAN was a bewildered man. The wealthy Manchurian had watched in bewilderment as his proposal to resettle a few hundred Jewish refugees was expanded out of all proportion by the Japanese – and then, just as quickly, apparently abandoned altogether. Now, try as he might, he could not understand what the Japanese were up to. Five months ago, in July 1940, the super-nationalist Tojo had been made minister of war. Three months ago, the government had signed a military alliance with Germany and Italy. Two months ago, Colonel Yasue – the best friend the Jews had in Manchuria – had been summarily dismissed from his army and intelligence post in Manchukuo. Clearly, it all pointed to bad times ahead.

Yet only last month, in November, Captain Inuzuka had made a long and well-publicized broadcast on the government-controlled radio station assuring Jews, and everyone else who would listen, that it was official Japanese policy to treat Jews favorably, and that this would be continued in the future. More recently, Yasue (apparently still a spokesman for the government in spite of having been dismissed) had called to spend several hours encouraging him not to close down his business in Manchukuo, not to liquidate his considerable financial assets there; Manchukuo, he was told, would continue to be a fine place for him – and, by extension, all Jews – to do business in. Now, today, what should arrive but an invitation from the Japanese foreign minister, Yosuke Matsuoka himself, asking him to come for coffee at his home at 5:00 on December 31!

Zikman had never been so astonished by an invitation. Surely this was not something left over from his suggested plan to settle two hundred leatherworkers in Manchukuo. Yet if not that . . .

Zikman was staying in Tokyo at the Imperial Hotel, and the Frank Lloyd Wright designed building was bustling with preparations for the New Year's holiday. From his window, Zikman could see workmen decorating the hotel garden with pine and bamboo, the traditional symbols of a long life. He stared at them absentmindedly, pondering the details of Matsuoka's invitation. Even more extraordinary than the fact of the invitation at all, was the timing: five o'clock on December 31! New Year's Eve was strictly a family occasion in Japan. It was certainly not the moment a Japanese would arrange to chat with a foreigner. And in his *home*! The Japanese rarely invited even good friends to their homes. Zikman well remembered meeting Matsuoka before he had become foreign minister, when he was president of the South Manchurian Railway. They were acquaintances but by no means were they good friends. Japanese actions often seemed to make no sense, he thought; but this was more incomprehensible than most.

Zikman was, of course, exactly on time for the meeting. Matsuoka greeted him warmly at the door, led him past his home's Japanese rooms and into a Western-style parlor. Here Zikman could relax comfortably in a chair rather than having to sit back on his heels, Japanese style, on a soft *tatami* floor. The two men spent some time chatting pleasantly over tea and cakes. Gradually, the foreign minister swung the conversation around to the Tripartite Pact and began to speak in a serious tone:

"You should not be overly concerned about this. It is true that I concluded a treaty with Hitler. But I never promised him to be an anti-Semite." From the weight he was giving the words, it was obvious this was the point of the afternoon's get-together.

"I lived fifteen years in America and abroad," he continued, "and I know how unjust people are to the Jews. This is not only my personal opinion, it has been a principle of the entire Japanese Empire since the days of her foundation that all people should be treated with sympathy and justice."

There was a brief pause. Matsuoka had finished.

"I am sure my fellow Jews in Manchuria and elsewhere would be heartened to know what you have just said," Zikman replied. "May I repeat these words of yours to them? And to other Jews abroad?" Clearly, this was the response that the foreign minister was seeking.

"By all means!" Matsuoka said with enthusiasm. "Yes, you can; of course you can!"

The goodbyes and wishes for a happy new year followed. The meeting was over.

"Why me? And why now?" Zikman thought as he rode through the darkness on his way back to the hotel. He finally concluded that it was *him* because he happened to be here, and because he did have some standing in the community. "But why *now?* What is special about December 31, 1940?" To that, he had no answer.

Across the world, Chesno, the Syrkins, the Amshenover rebbe, the Katznelson children, the five Orlianskys, the three hundred members of the Mir Yeshiva and several hundred other Polish Jews knew nothing of Matsuoka, Inuzuka, Yasue, Zikman or even Tojo. If they had heard of the Tripartite Pact at all – and not many had – it was either too complicated to understand or was just one more element of insecurity in an already untenable situation. What the Japanese were up to they would worry about later, or maybe never. The immediate reality was the Soviet government and its continuing silence on the question of exit permits.

By the end of December 1940, nearly a thousand Jews had applied to Intourist for formal permission to leave Lithuania. One by one they would be called into the NKVD for the necessary police clearance. Sitting in a bare cell of an office, pinned down by the cold piercing stare of a hostile interrogator, a would-be emigrant had to cope with a hundred questions, even the most innocent of which could be a deathtrap. Questions of family, of religion, of recent or long-past personal experiences; questions of education, of job skills, of politics, of money. When to tell the truth? When to bend the facts a little? When to be sincere? When to ease around a point and glide quickly on to the next? How much did they know already? And how much could they read in your eyes? Finally the moment came when there were no more questions. Then the interview was finished and you left. Whether you passed or failed, you had no idea. That you would learn only from Intourist. And Intourist continued to say nothing.

The Soviet grip on Lithuania grew rougher and tighter. Jews, and Christians too, continued to be dragged from their beds at midnight, for reasons no one knew and to fates no one dared imagine. Deportations of "undesirables" continued – undesirable religious leaders, undesirable political figures, undesirable Zionists or capitalists or Trotskyites, or simply those who were not sufficiently enthusiastic in their willingness to build a glorious Soviet state. The refugee community grew quieter than ever. These were days of pessimism and prayer. In the synagogues, men chanted psalms, and prayers and meditated on the ways of their God and the possibilities of their deaths. There was nothing else they could do.

Consul Senpo Sugihara with his family outside the Japanese Consulate in Kovno and *right* Sugihara in 1973.

Nathan Gutwirth with his wife in 1945.

Gisuke Ayukawa, an early backer of the *fugu* plan.

Mitsuzo Tamura, the *fugu* plan's negotiator in New York in 1973.

Colonel Norihiro Yasue, one of the creators of the *fugu* plan.

The 1939 Conference of Jewish Communities in
the Far East. Dr. Abraham Kaufman is standing
in the center.

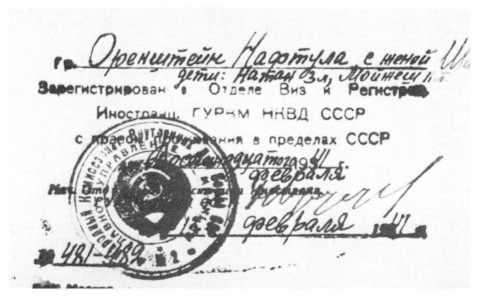

The Soviet exit permit which had to be obtained
by the refugees before they could leave Lithuania.

Refugees await Sugihara's decision outside the Japanese Consulate in Kovno.

The Amshenover Rebbe.

Members of the Mir Yeshiva arrive in Kobe, Japan.

Refugees soon after their arrival in Japan.

Inside the office of Kobe Jewcom.

The Kobe Jewcom Board of Directors: Anatole Ponve *fourth from left*, Alex Triguboff *third from right* and Leo Hanin *far right*.

Members of the Yeshiva studying in Kobe.

A group of refugees pose in front of the Kobe Jewcom
Headquarters.

Refugees outside the Kobe Jewcom office where they gathered daily to exchange news.

The day of the interrogation: *left to right* Rabbi Shlomo Shapiro, Dr Setsuzo Kotsuji, the Amshenover Rebbe, Rabbi Moses Shatzkes, Captain Yuzuru Fukamachi and Leo Hanin outside the Naval Officers Headquarters in Tokyo.

Moishe Katznelson did not run, he flew through the snowy streets to where Intourist had finally posted the lists of who could leave. It was a beautiful day – dry air, sun glistening on the white January snow. But Moishe was already late. By the time he arrived at the notice wall, the throng in front of it was solidly packed. Moishe squirmed and pushed and tried to worm his way forward, but at fourteen, he was too old to attract sympathy and too small to back up his determination with force. It was almost an hour before he got close enough to see. It was worth the wait! When his eyes lit on his own name, his heart threatened to fly away completely. He could leave! But wait! Where was Sophie's name? They had applied together, but they were two people; they needed two permits. Moishe's eyes raced up and down the columns. There were hundreds of names. But not hers. Over and over, he studied the list until those waiting behind shoved him away from the board. His anxiety mounting he began fighting to regain his place. But he soon gave it up. What was the point? Her name was not there and it would not appear magically just by his looking for it. Sophie could not leave, and without her, he could not leave. So long he had waited, so hard he had tried. With a groan, he collapsed on the sidewalk, sobbing, his whole body shuddering in inconsolable anguish, his head buried deep in his arms.

Heedless of him before, the crowd now broke around him, women kneeling on the cold sidewalk trying to comfort him, men reaching down to lift him up. But they soon yielded to a short old man with a long white beard. Though he had been immediately informed by one of his followers that his name and those of his wife and son were on the list, even the Amshenover rebbe was not immune to the excitement of confirming it for himself.

"It is not yet time to give up," the rebbe said loud enough to be heard over the boy's sobbing. "Come now, if one thing has failed, we will try something else."

Moishe was too upset to stop crying, but he recognized the familiar voice. He had heard it before, urging him and the others in the group he was staying with, to apply for the permits. His sobbing grew quieter.

The rebbe waited a moment, then said: "I am an old man, you know. It would be much easier if you would stand up so I wouldn't have to bend over."

Moishe raised his head and half a dozen hands instantly reached down to lift him to his feet.

"Now, what is it?" the rebbe said.

"My sister isn't on the list," he replied, too ashamed of his tears to look directly at the old man. "I am. But she isn't."

"Your parents are not there?"

"No," Moishe shook his head, clenching his teeth to hold back the sobs. "We have no family here."

"There are those who believe all Jews are a family," the rebbe murmured, though more to himself than to the boy. "At any rate we should do something about this. Come, we will go to Intourist and see what is the next step. Don't give up quite yet. You are not alone, you know. The lists often are separating families. They make no sense. Come now, let us see if we can make them make sense."

Moishe finally raised his head to look at the rebbe. He can speak to all of us, he thought. But who is he that he thinks he can change the mind of the Russian government? Yet the old man looked so completely calm, so confident, so unworried that Moishe began to feel just the slightest glimmer of hope.

The rebbe was relieved to see signs of the return of the boy's spirit. "Come," he said, suddenly turning in the direction of Intourist and beginning to walk very rapidly, not looking back. Moishe had no choice but to hurry after him. Maybe, *im yirzeh.* . . .

The moment one "insuperable" hurdle was cleared the refugees found another thrown up in their way. Yes, the government had given them permission to leave. But Intourist now demanded that payment for their trip across Russia to Japan be made in American dollars: two hundred apiece. Where was such a sum to come from? Even the pocketfuls of *zlotys* that some refugees had fled from Poland with were worthless currency now. The relief agencies – organizations that channeled the donations from the free world into food, shelter and clothing for the fifteen thousand Jewish refugees in Lithuania – were already outspending their incomes. There was no work to be had, and even if there had been, certainly there would not have been enough time to earn two hundred dollars. Nor were banks permitted to change local currency into American dollars. The exit permits had very definite limits – if you were still in the country after they had expired, you were subject to immediate deportations to Siberia.

In the days that followed the posting of the lists, a flood of cables went out from Vilna to HIAS, the Hebrew Immigrant Aid Society, to its European counterpart HICEM, to the Joint Distribution Committee and to hundreds of families, even second or third cousins whom no one had seen or spoken with in years: "Our hours are numbered. . . . Have pity on us. . . . Consider our lives. . . . Do not forget us now and even our grandchildren will never forget you. . . ."

But for some, there was simply no one to cable. For these, the only way to put together the sum was by selling every last thing of any value that they possessed on Vilna's black market. It meant they would be setting off on a journey half-way round the world, a journey that as yet did not even have a final destination, with absolutely nothing. And worse, as the refugees were warned by the red-haired manager of the Vilna Intourist bureau, "If you enter this office with American dollars, no one will ask you how or where you got them. But if you are caught with dollars on the streets, even just outside our door, you will be shot."

"It is some sort of game they are playing with us!" the refugees agonized among themselves. "It is all a trap. We are merely finding money to pay for our own exile!"

This new obstacle was not insurmountable, however. As a wave of cables had gone out, waves of dollars came back in – not in the perilous form of cash but as cables of certification from correspondent banks in New York, London, and elsewhere. They stated that the required amounts had been deposited on behalf of a particular individual or family. The Va'ad Hatzalah, the American organization dedicated to rescuing Jewry from the hell of Nazism, now made the Mir Yeshiva a top priority. Rabbi Kalmanowitz worked seven days a week – even on the Sabbath, which was forbidden in all but life-and-death situations – in pursuit of the fifty thousand dollars needed to move the whole yeshiva to Japan. That money, too, gradually came in.

By mid-January, the first refugees had passed safely through the system and were ready to depart. They had not had a pleasant few weeks. Several Jews caught selling their belongings to try to get the two hundred dollars locally had been executed to serve as an example to other potential black-marketeers. However, at least the police had not stationed themselves just outside the Intourist door, to catch "offenders" in their last few steps. And the tickets, hotel vouchers and itineraries distributed to each departing refugee appeared to be valid enough. Ironically, one of the first to receive its passage money from the Joint Distribution Committee and be cleared through the NKVD was the family of the reluctant to leave Getzel Syrkin. Early one morning, the three Syrkins stood on the Vilna railway platform – Getzel, with Cheya clutching his arm so tightly he thought the imprint of her fingers would probably become a permanent scar, and their son, Dovid, standing alone, though scarcely two feet away, his knees securely pressed against a rope-tied knapsack. Dovid's brown eyes were as big and bright as marbles as he looked at the convolutions of black metal rising up like a wall in front of him. He had never been so close to a locomotive in his life and could not imagine what it was going to be like to ride on the train.

He didn't have long to wonder. At the screech of a whistle, the train doors were opened and the passengers helped aboard. A second screech was followed by the clang of closing doors. Then there was a jerk forward. Dovid clutched tensely at the arms of his seat: but it wasn't the train that seemed to move – it was the platform. The very spot where, just a few minutes ago, he himself had been standing, was slipping away. The platform was followed by the entire station. Then, gradually picking up speed, the streets of the city began zipping off to some unknown destination. Dovid's hands hurt from holding on so tight. But why should he hang on if everything else was doing the moving? Trying to relax, he ordered himself to remember that he knew, after all, that it was the train that was moving. But his eyes – those most reliable sources of information – couldn't fit all that information in with the reality of the world passing by. Uncomfortable and a little frightened, the boy jerked his eyes away from the window to rest on the familiarity of his mother, sitting tense and straight, across from him. Of course, she was looking at him, – she was almost always looking at him. Seeing his excitement and feeling her own relief that they were now at least traveling away from the scene of a sixteen-month nightmare, Cheya Syrkin surprised her son with a tiny smile. For the first time in a long while, Dovid felt his stomach begin to unwind. Maybe the world was not, after all, completely without hope. He looked down at his feet which had grown uncomfortably big for his shoes. But he couldn't resist the lure of the window and the world moving past. Getzel shared neither his son's excitement nor his wife's sense of relief. Ever since that traumatic night in Alexandrov, he had felt himself poised on the brink of a bottomless pit. Only by a constant exercise of will could he prevent himself from toppling over the edge into nothingness. After sixteen months of this balancing act, he was exhausted – body, mind and spirit. And now what was confronting him? Now that he had managed to spirit himself and his family off to the temporary security of Vilna, now that he had forced himself to explore every conceivable avenue of legal and illegal flight from that insecure refuge and finally to seize this one final opportunity for escape . . . Even now, the nightmare was not over, but merely beginning a new, even more demanding phase. From now on there would be no more assistance from HIAS or the Joint Distribution Committee. In their place would be, at first, the alien, unsympathetic efficiency of Intourist and after that – if there would ever be an "after that," if they ever did get out of Russia – he would be at the mercy of the Japanese. Getzel had very little expectation that they would ever get to America through Japan. He had allowed himself to be persuaded by the Amshenover rebbe, but he had no faith in the so-called "Jewish community" in Japan. If such a group even existed – a question that had been raised by many of the refugees in Vilna – its members wouldn't be his kind of Jews, he would never feel at ease with them. They would be like the "Jews" who people said lived in China who were really Chinese or the "Jews" in Africa who were really black men. Japan wouldn't be home. Even America wouldn't be home. And home was the one thing, the *only* thing, that Getzel wanted.

Leaning his head back against the upholstered seat, he stared out into the darkness. The train clattered noisily across the flat plains of Lithuania and would soon be in Russia proper. Deeper and deeper he was going, like Jonah being sucked deeper and deeper into the cavernous mouth of the leviathan.

With a start, Getzel jerked his head forward, snapping himself back with difficulty to the sway of the train and started down the aisle for the toilet at the end of the car.

Cheya watched him stumbling from handhold to handhold. If only she knew what to do. How to comfort him, how to help him? She too had been terrified that night sixteen months ago. Who could not be? But a person had to cope, Dovid had to be cared for. Meals had to be prepared, clothes had to be washed and mended, *shabbos* candles had to be lit, even if all these things had to be done in strange and difficult surroundings. But Getzel wasn't able to occupy himself either at his religious studies, or even at his trade.

Cheya wondered if maybe that was a large part of his problem. If only they could get to America: if only, *im yirzeh ha-Shem*, Getzel could hold on till she could make him a new home in America.

Twenty-four hours after it left Vilna, the train pulled into Moscow. The refugees crowded the platform, wide-eyed and overwhelmed by the immensity of the station. They were met and conducted, in a group, out into the street. For the Syrkins, as for the hundreds of other refugees from the small towns and *shtetls* of Poland who would pass the same way, Moscow might well have been on another planet. Vilna had been huge – Moscow was infinite. Vilna had tall buildings and busy streets – in Moscow you could only imagine the tops of some of the buildings. And traffic! If it had not been for the traffic signals, no one could ever have crossed a street!

Once Intourist had been paid, it took care of virtually all travel arrangements. The refugees, dressed at best in old clothes, clumsily weighed down with bundles and small trunks, all they owned on earth, were led into the lobby of a fine hotel. There was clean, plush carpeting on the floor, and smooth round columns of polished marble stretched far overhead to support a carved and painted ceiling, gleaming bronze chandeliers brought daylight indoors. . . . The refugees merely stood with their mouths open, gaping in awe at the magnificence of it all, having to be reminded to follow the guide to the registration desk.

Though trains came in daily from the Baltics to Moscow, the great Trans-Siberian train left only every few days. Thus the refugees had at least twenty-four hours to rest up in finer beds, in finer rooms, in warmer baths and cleaner surroundings than most of them had ever experienced before. And beyond the rooms themselves, there were the telephones and the elevators! Few of the Jews had ever been in an elevator before. They rode up and down, up and down, going nowhere, savoring the mechanical magic. The equally unfamiliar telephones were also in constant use as grown men behaved like children, calling each other from room to room. The hotel was a toy for those who had grown up with hardly any play time. The constant fear and anxiety of the past several months was temporarily wiped away by the excitement of it all.

The one drawback to the arrangement was food. Intourist did not supply food, and having given their all to Intourist, few of the refugees had money left over to feed themselves. They could smell odors rising from the hotel kitchen or, on walks around Moscow, could watch through steamy restaurant windows as Russians ate their fill. Only a few, even of those refugees who were not concerned with the kosher status of their food, could afford restaurant prices, even for just a little black bread and cheese.

The Syrkins had nearly forty-eight hours to wait for their train. The first day was completely taken up with the hotel – the shining tiles in the bathroom, the delicacy of the net curtains, the wonders of the flush toilet. By the morning of the second day, the excitement had palled. Cheya, taking Dovid with her, joined half a dozen other refugees venturing out into the city streets to shop for provisions for the long train trip ahead.

Getzel remained alone in the room for a time, then went out himself to stretch his legs. He walked slowly along the broad avenue, block after block, not even noticing the crossing lights but letting the crowd around him indicate when to move and when to halt. It was cold but sunny, and when the throngs had thinned so much that Getzel had to begin looking out for himself, he found himself facing a broad open square where trolley cars turned around.

Entranced at the sight, Getzel leaned against the stone wall of a building and simply watched. Half a block down one of the deserted side streets that led into the open square, there was a brief commotion; two uniformed men were forcing a third to accompany them into a building. But Getzel paid no attention to that, preferring to lose himself entirely in the strange mechanical maneuverings before him. The brightly colored cars backed and turned, clanging and ringing as the conductors expertly pushed their levers this way and that, and fare boys shouted Russian words, that he couldn't understand. The trolleys made Getzel think of the tiny skatebugs that used to jerk across the surface of the ponds near Alexandrov, with their antennae sticking up like those things above the trolley cars. . . .

Suddenly, a dark shadow fell over him and, a quarter of a second later, a Russian voice cracked like a whip on his ears. Getzel looked up and froze: the man was dressed in the uniform of a policeman, buttons gleaming, his pistol black and tight against his hip, his eyes filled with suspicion. Getzel pressed himself closer to the cold stone wall and said nothing. Even if his throat hadn't been frozen with fear, he wouldn't have known what to say in response to the incomprehensible Russian.

Again, the voice, even louder this time. Obviously, the Russian was demanding some kind of an explanation but of what?

Quivering, gasping for every breath, Getzel shrank further into himself. With an imploring look and a nod that was half a bow, he slid out from under the policeman's eyes and started back in the direction he had come from. An arm like a length of steel grabbed him. Half fainting in fright, Getzel could only stumble along as the policeman dragged him down a side street toward an iron door. As they passed into the building, Getzel saw the same insignia on the walls that he had seen in Vilna, at the NKVD headquarters. That office had been quiet. Here there was noise coming from behind the closed doors – talking, crying, angry voices. Suddenly, coming from the innermost bowels of the building, a long, horrible scream of pain cut through all the other sounds. The policeman seemed to rise up to the ceiling as Getzel fell in a faint at his feet.

When he recovered, he nearly passed out again. He was alone in a tiny, one-bulb room, slumped as he had been thrown on a wooden chair. The door was closed tight, but only for a moment. As if they had been waiting for him to open his eyes, two men came in – the officer who had dragged him there, and another man in plain clothes.

"Do you speak Polish?" the second man asked, in Polish. Getzel stared at the man; but whatever hope might have begun to grow in his heart died quickly in the face of the man's iron expression. He barely nodded an answer to the question. The two policemen glanced at each other.

"What were you looking at so hard on the avenue?" the officer asked.

Getzel didn't know the answer he wanted. "The trolleys," he said softly.

Eyes narrowing in disbelief, the Polish-speaker took a sudden step forward and grabbed Getzel by his coat front. "Are you trying to fool us? What was so interesting about the trolleys? And the buildings around here have nothing to do with you. Why were you staring at them?"

His throat caught in his twisted coat, Getzel could scarcely breathe, let alone answer. His front teeth began to chatter softly.

Not letting go of the coat, the Polish-speaker said something to the other officer in Russian and got back an approval. Pushing Getzel down to his knees and standing over him, he said: "Listen, little *zhid*. We know what your kind is up to. We know how you crawled into this country, taking advantage of the generosity of the Soviet government. And we know how you'll worm your way into some other country, spreading your poison and trying to make trouble. Well, remember this. While you're here, we can do anything we like to you. The same thing that happened to that fellow out in the street – we know you were watching us when we picked him up – can happen to you, anytime, anywhere. And when you leave here, we can follow you to the ends of the earth. The arm of the Soviet Union reaches everywhere, so don't try anything *ever*, not here, not anywhere. Do you understand?"

With every emphasized word, the man shook Getzel till he thought his neck would snap.

"Do you *understand* me?" the man shouted in his face.

Getzel couldn't say a word.

"Now, whatever you were looking at out there, you forget it. What has happened in here you forget, too. Do you understand? Forget that you were ever in this building at all. If you ever tell anyone you were here – *anyone* – we will hear about it and we will find you . . . and you will wish you had never been born. Do you understand, Jew? Do you?"

His head aching as if it would split, his knees crushed against the hard floor, Getzel could only look imploringly at his interrogator. Finally, he managed a weak nod.

"Now, get out of here!" The officer jerked him up and released the front of his coat, only to grab him by the back of the neck and push him out into the corridor and down to the front door. Putting his foot against Getzel's backside, he simultaneously let go of his neck and kicked, sending Getzel flying headfirst down the shallow steps onto the sidewalk. The door slammed closed behind the policeman; then everything was still.

Getzel crawled whimpering to the side of the building and pulled himself to his feet. Slowly, clinging to the walls now deep in shadow, he made his way back to the hotel room. Cheya and Dovid were waiting, beside themselves with worry and fear of what might have happened to him. Getzel said not a word. He let Cheya wash his bloody face, but when she asked him what had happened, he merely shook his head back and forth, back and forth.

Their train left late that evening. As he sat in his assigned seat with the lights of Moscow disappearing behind him, Getzel was still shaking his head back and forth, as if to deny everything.

Cheya scarcely noticed the dark night rushing past. Staring at her husband, she had to bite her lip to keep from crying out so overwhelmed was she with concern about him. He had never been a strong man – neither bodily nor in his mind. From the first time the matchmaker had pointed him out, she had known she would be the stronger of the two. Yet she had never felt cause to complain. Getzel was a good man. He had always cared about her and doted on Dovid. He was an even-tempered, hard-working husband, a fine, competent human being. But what had happened to that man? What crucial aspect of him had been left behind in Moscow? Bad enough had been the shock of that September night, the nightmare of having been forcibly driven from their home. And now this. Getzel moved with the dull eyes, the exhausted gestures, the plodding movements of a man totally defeated.

Poor, unhappy Getzel. Whatever had happened to him back in Moscow? Clearly someone had beaten him up. But who and why? He looked so small and hurt, like a trapped animal sitting across from her, lost in his big overcoat. She wanted to take him in her arms and make all the problems and sadness go away. But he was a husband, not a child. He was a man. She needed him to be *her* man, to help her with whatever God had in store for them – and who knew what that was? Cheya was frightened to feel so alone. She was even more frightened at the thought that Getzel might disappear entirely – either that he might wander off again and never return or that his mind might simply stop functioning altogether.

"Take off your coat, Getzel. It's warm enough in here," she said quietly.

His shaking head stilled as he looked over to her. Such terror, such pain in those brown eyes! She rose and began helping him out of the mass of cloth, gently brushing his hair away from his eyes in passing. He winced as her fingers touched the spot that had hit the sidewalk hardest.

"Ahhh, Getzel'le, what have they done to you?" she whispered in anguish. Forgeting that they were in a public place with dozens of eyes watching them, she put her arms around his shoulders and held him against her heart.

"God, make him well," she prayed silently. "I am frightened of the Russians. About the Japanese, I don't even know. Our son needs him. I need him. Oh, God, I can't do this all alone."

For more than a week the great Trans-Siberian train moved eastward – through the Ural Mountains and out onto the vast, rimless plain of Siberia; it passed through Chelyabinsk and Omsk, crossed the great Yenisei River at Krasnoyarsk and made a long stop at the city of Irkutsk, capital of eastern Siberia. After seven days and three thousand miles, it skirted the edge of Lake Baikal, running along a narrow ledge blasted forty years before out of the lake's legendary vertical rock banks. And after eleven days, give or take a little, it plunged into Vladivostok – Russia's largest Pacific port. The very existence of the Trans-Siberian Railway was a feat of inestimable engineering determination. Its route was the finest way of taking the measure of Russia's scenic magnificence.

But to the Polish-Jewish refugees who cared not a bit for engineering feats or scenic grandeur, the trip was an extended practice in anxiety and anticipation. There was nothing, absolutely nothing, to prevent the Russians from marching onto the train, culling them out from among the other passengers and taking them off to be shot. There was no basis for hope that they would not be pulled off the train at any of the Siberian stops and marched to a labor camp, there to spend the brief remainder of their lives. With every mile that passed, the refugees were going deeper and deeper into enemy territory. Wanting to go west to America, they were going east into Russia. It seemed monumentally stupid, now that they were sitting on the train. But now that they were there, there was less than ever that they could do to control their destiny.

Life on the train was not uncomfortable. There was heat in the car and a constant supply of hot water for tea, from a samovar in the corner, even a courteous porter to pour it. The car was clean – in the beginning, at least – and the seats were upholstered. After the excitement of being underway passed off, though, the journey provided only one alternative to worry – boredom. People chatted and dozed, smoked and ate, sparingly, from the black bread and cheese and salami and, possibly, a spoonful of the chicken fat they had brought with them. Mix it with hot water and you had a reasonable chicken soup. But the anxiety never dissipated. Every time the train slowed, hearts began to beat faster. And after they crossed the Urals into Siberia itself, there was a terrifying portent. From time to time, they could never figure out why, the porters would come through the cars, courteously but firmly pulling down the blinds over the windows, leaving them to sit in the half-darkness and wonder what horrors were taking place outside that they were forbidden to see.

Omsk passed, and Krasnoyarsk and even Irkutsk – that city synonomous with exile and deportation – and all were still on board who wanted to be. Is it possible, the refugees began to mutter among themselves, that we are really going to get out? They were in Asia already. There had been no mistaking the dark yellow faces and slanted eyes of the Chinese crowd at Irkutsk. Would even the unpredictable Russians carry people four thousand miles in order to kill them?

Just before Vladivostok, the train pulled into a small station in the autonomous region of Birobidzhan. Standing at the door of the car, Dovid (the only refugee child aboard the train and excruciatingly bored) was amazed to see people that looked like Jews.

"Hello, you up there!" one of the men on the platform said in accented but informal, authentic Yiddish.

Taken aback at hearing his own language so far from home, Dovid said nothing.

"What's the matter," the farmer shouted good-naturedly. "Can't one Jew speak to another?"

"What are Jews doing *here*?" Dovid called back.

"Don't you know? This is Birobidzhan! This is 'our state' in the Union of Soviet Socialist States!"

The man laughed, though he didn't seem to be enjoying the joke much. "Never mind, ask your father. He can tell you about it."

Dovid thought of his father who scarcely said anything anymore, who only sat and stared at nothing, occasionally shaking his head back and forth. He would ask the Amshenover rebbe, if ever he saw him again. Or perhaps his mother who was then coming over to see who he was talking to.

"Where are you going to, *boychik*?" the man asked, nodding a polite greeting to Cheya.

"To Vladivostok and to Japan and then to America," Dovid replied, "*im yirzeh ha-Shem*," he added.

The Jewish farmer looked long and silently up at the young boy. Then sadly, shaking his head, he said to Cheya, "No one aboard here will ever leave the Soviet Union alive." As if saddened by the thought, the man turned away. Dovid pressed up against his mother, chilled to the bone by the words.

If they had been the only ones to hear such a thing, they might have kept the terror to themselves. But other Birobidzhan Jews had whispered similar things to a few of the refugees who had gotten off the train to purchase food at the station kiosk. The fear in their hearts blossomed as never before. Those outside had not been just Russians – they were Jews. And they weren't merely Jews, but Russian Jews. Who would know, who could possibly know, better than they what the Soviet government did with Jews?

Cheya sank back into the corner of her seat. Ever since Irkutsk, she hadn't been able to help thinking maybe, just maybe, they might reach Japan; and from Japan, of course, change boats for America. But it wouldn't happen; and God was punishing her, all of them, for even secretly beginning to think it might.

The afternoon sun swung round to the side as the train turned south for the final leg into Vladivostok. The few religious Jews aboard stood facing the sun, facing toward Jerusalem, and prayed. The rest, like Dovid, sat quite still, silent and miserable, no longer looking forward to the moment of arrival.

The train pulled slowly into the Vladivostok station and, with a tremendous exhalation of steam, announced it was home. The refugees who disembarked showed no such exuberance. Stiff and tired from eleven days of confinement, they had no idea what to expect – or how to cope with it when it came. Unlike Moscow no one seemed to be here to greet them. They stood in a group on the cold platform, forty-five ragamuffins in a sea of knapsacks and old suitcases. One of the station officials approached and said something in Russian, but they could merely frown and shrug their shoulders. The official, apparently unconcerned, had just turned away when a young man with the Intourist insignia on his hat came rushing up.

"I beg your pardon that I am late," he said, trying to catch his breath. "It took longer than I had thought. . . . Are you ready to go?"

The refugees stood, looking at him. No one but a Jew would speak Yiddish like that. But what would a Jew be doing working for the government here?

"What's the matter?" the young man said. "Come now, we can't stand here in the cold. We must go to the hotel!"

A hotel! Not a boat? They were supposed to take a boat from here for Japan. Was this the plan, the trick – a trick covered over by sending a Jew to lead them on? Though they were not beyond caring, they were far beyond coping. The refugees picked up their baggage and followed their leader outside.

The direct cold, after so long in the heated railroad cars, almost took their breath away and was in no way thwarted by their thin winter coats. For several blocks they trudged along snowy sidewalks until they arrived at a hotel. Vladivostock was not Moscow: no golden chandeliers, no elevators, no telephones. But also no barbed wire and no soldiers with dogs.

"How long will we be here?" one of the refugees asked the Intourist official.

"Regrettably, probably three or four days at least," he said. "The harbor is completely blocked with ice – it's been a terrible problem this winter. Probably three or four days till the ice-breakers can smash through."

"Will we be getting our tickets for the boat?" the refugee asked timidly.

The Intourist man stared at him for a moment. "You will get your tickets just before you are allowed on board the boat, and that is all," he said. "What's the matter with you? What are you so worried about? The ice will melt, you know. The ship will come in. You will leave. Believe me!"

Believe him? Or believe the Jews in Birobidzhan? Who knew? As again and again in the past, who could do anything about it anyway?

For three days, the refugees waited, cold and hungry and, in some ways, in a worse state psychologically than they had been before – now half believing they really could get away from Russia, but still half fearing to let their hopes reach too high.

Yet as they waited, another train was making the trans-Siberian journey, bringing another group of refugees to Vladivostok. On the third day, Dovid and his mother were sitting in the narrow hotel lobby when they spotted a familiar figure walking toward the front door.

"Rebbe!"

The old man from Amshenov turned at the sound of the word. "So far, so good, no?" he said, not remembering their names but recognizing them from Vilna. He smiled and continued on his way. The rebbe was not beyond feeling pleased with himself for having recommended what so far seemed to have been exactly the right course of action. It more than made up for the fact that he had been having stomach trouble ever since he had left Vilna.

Dovid was delighted to have seen the old man. If the rebbe was here, how could they *not* get away?

The next morning, the temperature rose and the icebreakers began clearing a way through the harbor. In less than a day, the now seventy-one-strong group of refugees filed into the one rough unheated cabin of the Japanese freighter *Harbin Maru*. The Soviet Union was behind them.

# 7

THE AIR OF THE TINY CABIN was close and heavy with the fetid odor of too many bodies having gone unwashed for too long. For nearly two days the overcrowded tramp freighter had been bucking and pitching through the Sea of Japan, groping through the winter mists toward the tiny Japanese port of Tsuruga. After the relative luxury of the rail journey to Vladivostok, the seventy-one passengers found themselves in steerage squalor. This ship – like the few that had preceded it and the dozens that would follow – had not been built for human cargo. The tiny box of a cabin, the decks, the holds, the entire boat, reeked of coal dust and the half-cured furs which it customarily carried. There was one washbasin, one toilet and, except for three or four small kerosene stoves, no heat against the bitter wind.

The Amshenover rebbe had not slept well since leaving Vilna. Awake now, before dawn, he rose carefully and, carrying his blanket, stepped over half a dozen sleeping bodies on his way to the door. The cold was intense, but the air on the windward deck was fresh and clean. He wrapped the blanket around his shoulders and watched as the stars were lost, one by one, to the gradual graying of day. He was thankful there were no clouds: rain would only make worse whatever was to come.

With the end so near – surely they would land today – the responsibility he had accepted seemed overwhelming. His mind had traveled repeatedly over the possibilities of the future. Could he be taking these people to something somehow even worse than the horrors of the Europe they had left behind? For all his words of encouragement, what did he know? He could advise that going to Japan was a positive step. He could *say* it would be easier to get to America from Japan. He could tell his people that the Japanese were kind, that they were trustworthy, that whatever happened, Jews would be safer in Japan than in the Europe that soon was to be. But what did he know? The rebbe was acutely aware, as he stared from the deck out over the dark water, that he was directing people on the basis of intuition, not knowledge. It was a very Hasidic trait. But if he was wrong. . . . If he was wrong, they were all in trouble. But they would all have been in trouble anyway. Better to die trying to live than to die not trying at all.

The sun, just now clearing the horizon on his left, lifted his spirits. Straight ahead was a dark band that was too long to be anything but the coast of Japan. Mesmerized by the actuality of it, the rebbe watched, totally engrossed, as the darkness was replaced by the green of pine-covered hills. Was this not the most beautiful sight he would ever see – this clear, calm, solitary dawn over Japan? Trembling, he whispered a prayer that was at once a thanksgiving and a plea – let this gentle beauty be a true reflection of what Japan holds in store for us.

He hurried inside to awaken the others.

"It's beautiful! It's so green, for February! It is so bright under the sun, and so fresh. . . ."

After two days at sea, any land would have looked good. With seventy-one people crowding the rail, the ship tipped slightly, but few were aware of it. As they steamed effortlessly toward it, the town of Tsuruga appeared like a beige splotch at the water's edge. With equal measures of hope and dread, they had waited in great anticipation of this moment. Now, for a short while, anxiety subsided as excitement was caught and passed on.

"How tiny it is. . . . So lonely, with no neighbors but the mountains. . . . But how clean and bright it looks, like a flower!"

"Where are the people? How can there be a town with no people?" "Only wait, we are still too far away. . . . Look! Those little dots are people!"

"If the dots are people, those little boxes must be houses. I thought they were chicken coops!"

As the town grew in size and detail, the voices grew quiet. Who had even heard of Japan before the past few months? Throughout the voyage, wild conjectures had filled the void of real knowledge. Now, that knowledge – good or bad – would be theirs.

Moishe Katznelson stood just behind his sister, his thin arms encircling her on the ship's railing. Leaning as far out toward the water as he could without crushing her, he examined the approaching town in detail. As everyone kept saying, it was as beautiful as a flower. But it wasn't Jewish. Non-Jewish places, he knew, were lumped categorically by the Talmud under the heading of "places of idolatry." Idolaters didn't know God or His ways of justice. Idolaters – like the Polish peasants who would sometimes run riot through the market at home – were famous for their cruelty. Perhaps all this was just a cruel trick – from the kindness of the Japanese consul through the patience of this ship captain. If it was a trick, they were all doomed. Even if it wasn't, he himself might never set foot on that beckoning shore. The unthinkable had happened: Moishe had lost his visa.

It had happened in Vladivostok. In the confusion, it had disappeared, simply disappeared. The one thing standing between himself and destruction had fallen out of his passport and disappeared. When he realized it, he had become a wild man, dashing back to all the places he had been, searching every nook and cranny of the dormitory-style room he had been assigned to. He combed through wastebaskets, questioned the other refugees, prayed to God that it would reappear. But all to no avail: the magic paper with the two-line Curaçao visa and the bright red Japanese transit visa was gone from his passport. He had thought, first, of asking the help of the Amshenover rebbe again. But he couldn't, simply *couldn't* admit to that wonderful old man what a stupid dolt he was. The otherwise pleasant city of Vladivostok became a nightmare.

Yet even in despair, Moishe found a sense of determination that he had never experienced before: he *would* get on that ship. Moishe did not in the least understand where that solid kernel of determination had come from. But at fourteen, without parents, with his sister to protect, Moishe had had to mature quickly. The lost visa was a problem; but it was *his* problem, not the rebbe's, and he would be the one to make it right, no matter *what* it took. He was ashamed even to confess it to Sophie. Common sense, however, finally overcame bravado: he did consult with the Japanese consul in Vladivostok. There had been difficulty with the language, of course, but once the consul was able to apprehend Moishe's problem, he had not been unsympathetic. "For my part," he had said, "if you have a ticket for the ship, I will not insist that you have the visa. But I cannot guarantee that the immigration officials in Japan will actually permit you to enter."

As the ship drew closer to shore, Moishe studied the layout of the town, visually experimenting with a variety of escape routes. As he had known he *would* board the *Harbin Maru*, one way or another, he *would* enter Japan.

Avram Chesno, leaning back against the cabin structure, alternately watched the approaching coast and the increasing excitement of his fellow passengers. His nerves, too, were on fire. Chesno knew little of Japan, but he did know something about the current political situation. The Axis agreement, the Tripartite Pact, was not a mere piece of paper. Japan had bought Hitler's line. And wasn't it true that "the enemy of my friend is also my enemy"? What was to prevent the Japanese from simply shooting them, one by one, as they stepped off the ship? They had paid all the fees; none of them had money to give the Japanese. Who would even find out? Who after all, was for Jews these days?

There was no logical pattern from which to reason. Just because the Japanese had been so accommodating up to now did not mean that they might not abruptly turn the tables. The ship slowed as it neared its landing point. The passengers, their trance broken, rushed about gathering together their meager belongings in preparation for disembarking.

With a creaking thump the ship nudged up against the dock and stopped. The refugees were breathless, motionless with anticipation. Only their eyes moved, darting everywhere, seeking hints as to what kind of welcome Japan had prepared for them. A handful of Japanese officials appeared, walking slowly in step from a wharfside shed toward the ship. The officials were in uniform and they were armed. But scarcely had they set foot on the dock than a well-fed European, well dressed in civilian clothes, dashed out of the same building and overtook them. Collectively, the refugees held their breath. A few words passed between the European and the Japanese – words impossible to hear from the ship. Suddenly, the Japanese broke into smiles. Bowing slightly, they gestured the European to proceed as he wished ahead of them. Within seconds, the European was aboard the *Harbin Maru*, greeting the passengers with a "good morning" and a "welcome to Japan" and "please listen to the following immigration procedures . . ." – all in familiar Yiddish!

The refugees exploded with relief. They were safe! This sparkling bright land was more than beautiful. It was beautiful in a way they had feared they might never experience again. Japan was *open* to them. There would be no firing squad. And to top it all off, the rumors they had discounted – that there were actually *Jews* in Japan – had been true.

The European's name was Alex Triguboff. He, and two others

waiting in the customs shed, would act as interpreters and help with any problems that arose. Then this afternoon, he explained, the refugees would go to the city of Kobe where clean beds and kosher food were waiting for them. The Jews looked at each other, looked at Triguboff, looked at the shore where the clean neat town of Tsuruga was spread out in the sunshine, and laughed. After six thousand miles and eighteen months of defeat and despair, here in this unknown country, they were welcomed.

Chesno was the first off the ship. The dock stretched out before him like a magic carpet. He shifted his sparsely filled suitcase to his left hand and started for shore, grinning to himself and to the world.

Much to Sophie's annoyance, Moishe was in no hurry to get off the ship. In spite of her encouragement he hung back, purposely it seemed, as if he wanted to be the last one processed through immigration. Such was exactly the case. If the line took long enough, Moishe was hoping, the ship would leave again for Vladivostok or wherever boats went from here. But it remained at the dock, stubbornly waiting to make sure there were no fools who had lost their visas and would have to be carried back to Russia. Well, he wasn't going back to Russia. But in the midst of the general excitement, he was miserable: he didn't know what he *was* going to do. Here, now, having disembarked at last, standing in the customs shed, he could see the folly even of thinking of running off into the countryside. But if they. . . .

"You're the last one, are you?"

Moishe looked up to see a smiling Alex Triguboff. He could not bring himself to return the joy.

"Are you feeling all right?" Triguboff asked. "There will be a doctor in Kobe if you're not."

As the man spoke, the person ahead of Moishe in line finished and a chasm of empty space opened up between him and the immigration desk. His best intentions failed, the words came out: "I don't know what to do. I lost my visa in Vladivostok . . ."

Sophie gasped: "Moishe! Oh, Moishe, how *could* you?" she began to cry.

Moishe could feel the curious stare of the immigration officer until Triguboff moved casually around, blocking him out of the officer's line of vision.

"Now, pull yourself together. You, stop crying. And *you*, don't start."

The very idea was enough to force Moishe to still his trembling lip instantly.

"This has happened before, you know," Triguboff added more gently. After a minute, he led them up to the immigration desk. Speaking in very basic Japanese, he explained the situation to the immigration official. Then he acted as interpreter.

"Where do you want to go to, from Japan?" the official asked.

"America," Moishe answered. Where he *wanted* to go was America, even though his visa had read "Curaçao."

The official looked helplessly at Triguboff. Triguboff looked meaningfully at Moishe. Sophie, for once, caught on faster than her brother.

"Kurasow, Moishe. Kurasow," she whispered loud enough to be heard all over the pier.

"Curaçao, I mean," he said quickly, nodding his head in nervous affirmation. "Definitely, Curaçao."

Instantly, the official slapped the orange-red stamps on Moishe's documents. His instructions were clear – to permit entry to any of these people who had a visa to another country or had the phrase concerning Curaçao in his passport. In all cases, his superior had informed him, consideration even to the extent of leniency was to be shown. "Leniency," the official decided, encompassed universal facts of life like young boys losing things. Besides, as he stated enthusiastically, "No visa to Curaçao is required!"

"*Kum gezundt,*" he added, handing Moishe and Sophie their passports. Though it was all the Yiddish he knew, he used it liberally among these poor people. It took so little to make them happy.

Bewildered, but relieved for the first time in four days, Moishe could say nothing but *"Danke shein, danke shein!"* Triguboff translated the thanks for the benefit of the other grinning Japanese officials and heard them recite the catchphrase that would welcome all the refugees who would follow them across the Sea of Japan. "Do not forget to tell your brothers in America how kind we are to you Jews!" Then he hurried both children off toward the waiting group.

In the forefront of the refugees, Avram Chesno walked slowly along the Tsuruga street, examining everything in as much detail as he could without appearing rudely inquisitive. That fellow on the ship hadn't been far wrong; even close up, the square wooden houses looked like chicken coops. The wide doors slid on tracks instead of opening on hinges. Most of the windows had paper panes rather than glass and many of them were fronted by narrow vertical wooden bars. The sewers were open, just cement ditches alongside the street, with little flat bridges crossing to the entrance of every house or shop.

Trudging away from the dock area, the group came to a narrow shopping street. Most of the shops were open to the street, with goods set out along the front. An old woman, bent over almost double, was sweeping the street with a short-handled broom, swirling up low clouds of dust in front of her flower shop. Avram smiled at a little boy in a fish store, and mortified, the small fellow immediately hid from sight behind a barrel brimming over with fish. A paper store, a cloth store, a tiny grocery store, a restaurant with strange foods set out in the window to whet your appetite. Avram's appetite needed little whetting, but the group kept moving.

Japan seemed so clean, especially after the stinking boat: clean, cloudless sky, clean street, clean shops, clean people. Glancing at his companions, he saw how unkempt the refugees looked. But also, he suddenly realized, how gigantic they were! The buildings were so tiny that these really rather average-height men were virtually at eye level with the eaves of the roofs! The group halted spontaneously at a fruit store – baskets of bright red apples, boxes of orange persimmons, the slightly flattened spheres of tangerines stacked five deep in little straw nets, and a strange curved yellow fruit no one had ever seen before. Triguboff bustled around his charges.

"Please don't stop here. Come. The same things are waiting for you on the train to Kobe. Please come. We don't want to miss the train. The yellow things? Banana . . . ba-na-na. Yes, very tasty, very good. Come now. . . ."

They went, turning right at the end of town, and came to an open railway station. It was 2:09 and far down the track a train was just coming into view.

Like the others, the Amshenover rebbe noted the approach of the train. He took Mr. Triguboff aside.

"What time does the sun set in Kobe?" he asked.

"At 5:23," Triguboff replied, already prepared for the question. Today was Friday: the twenty-five hour day of *shabbos* begins with the setting of the sun on Friday evening. No observant Jew – and the Amshenover rebbe was one of the most devoutly observant Jews in the world – would work, or buy or sell, or begin a journey or do many other things, from that moment till three stars had appeared in the Saturday night sky.

The rebbe thought only a second before firmly setting down his bundles, and declaring: "Today, we do not take this train. We will spend *shabbos* here and go to Kobe on Saturday night." Triguboff hastened to assure him. "Rebbe, you needn't worry about not being safely in Kobe by 5:23. Japanese trains are extremely punctual. We will arrive at 4:15, in plenty of time."

The old man had no experience with Japanese trains, but he had had a great deal of experience with Polish trains. They never went anywhere on time.

The previous *shabbos* he had spent on the Trans-Siberian train. But there had been no choice. It is axiomatic that one may forego Sabbath observance if it is a matter of life and death. Escaping from Europe surely was that. And traveling according to the Trans-Siberian schedule had been the only way to escape. But now the travel was no longer a question of life and death. The rebbe shook his head.

"We cannot begin our stay in this country by violating the Sabbath. It would be too much. We will wait here until Saturday night."

Seeing the rebbe refusing to board the train, the other refugees also remained on the platform.

Triguboff looked at the conductor who, in turn, was looking puzzled at the refugees. There were only four minutes till departure and the refugees looked as if they were determined to camp right here on the platform.

"Rebbe, I swear to you on my father's name, the train will arrive in Kobe at 4:15! By 5:23 everyone will be settled in clean houses, prepared to welcome in a peaceful and blessed Sabbath. Please get on board *now*. You must, really, or it will leave without us."

The rebbe was unmoved. He knew he couldn't trust any train to arrive promptly. And how could he trust the word of a man who didn't even keep his head covered?

The conductor blew his whistle.

"Rebbe, you see, it is 2:13. This train will definitely leave on time."

The rebbe looked at the big platform clock hanging overhead. It was indeed 2:13. He stroked his beard but held his ground.

"All right, if you want to stay all Friday night and Saturday here, on a freezing cold railway platform, if you want to subject your followers and fellows to *another* twenty-four hours of privation, that is your responsibility. I am going to get on this train, and in exactly two hours, I will step off the train in Kobe station and fifteen minutes later will be at the *shul*, waiting to greet the Sabbath. You and your fellows will be here, hungry, cold, tired. There is no hotel in Tsuruga and the people here speak only Japanese."

Triguboff boarded one of the three cars which had been added especially for the refugees. The conductor blew the warning whistle.

Chesno was distraught. He hadn't overheard the earlier parts of the conversation, but Triguboff's last words explained it all. Once even a casual observance of the Sabbath had been alien to him, but he had come this far with these people and would be living with them in Kobe for some time to come. He paced back and forth along the chilly platform, but made no move to board.

The rebbe looked at the clock. As the minute hand made its tiny mechanical hop to exactly 2:15, the train whistle sounded and the wheels began to move. It was cold. It would be colder. A *shabbos* of no food, no rest, no comfort did not fulfill the commandments of honoring the Sabbath with joy. With more hope in his heart than confidence, he stepped aboard the train as it inched forward.

As if suddenly released from an invisible force, the refugees raced for the train, jumping through the doors, scrambling through the windows, clinging to the railings as it slowly gathered momentum. By the time the final car had passed the end of the platform, even the slowest had managed to get aboard. The engineer shook his head in amazement at the customs of these strange foreigners and accelerated to normal departure speed.

Chesno, sorting himself out from the mass of humanity which had landed on top of him, also shook his head. But it didn't matter. Due to whatever powers that be – even, conceivably, God Himself – they were in Japan.

# Part Two

# JAPAN
# 1941

## Security
## in an
## Alien Land

**8** LAID OUT along the shallow indentation that forms the harbor, the port of Kobe looked as if a great tidal wave had washed in and deposited a thick mass of commercial buildings on the narrow strip of flat land that stretched inland for less than a quarter mile before rising abruptly into a ridge of hills, so steep, they could support only small shops and houses. In the upper reaches, high enough to catch a fresh breeze even during the stifling summer rainy season, were the Western-style houses of Kobe's foreign residents. Prewar Kobe was one of Japan's largest cities and, after Yokohama, its second busiest port. Since 1937, when the war with China began in earnest, Kobe had become a major military depot. Its docks were stacked with tarp-covered artillery pieces, camouflaged tanks and military-green bales and boxes. Soldiers and sailors filled the streets, ordered and purposeful by day, carousing at night. Commerce thrived on the war.

By 1940, there were approximately three thousand Occidental foreigners residing in Kobe, about one hundred of them Jews. Most of the aliens were engaged in some aspect of the import-export business. For them, the Sino-Japanese War trade helped make up for the normal trans-Pacific shipping which had been curtailed by America's "moral embargo" on trade with Japan. And even beyond the realm of business, prewar Kobe was a comfortable place to live. For all its commercial importance, it had a very different air to it than the other two cities that had foreign populations of any size: Tokyo and Yokohama, the latter situated so close to the capital as to be practically an extension of it. Not a political center, Kobe was out of the international limelight. Let the capital worry about how its local actions were viewed by the rest of the world, Kobe had no such problems. Since the city owed much of its development to Western interests and enthusiasm, there was traditionally a warm feeling of mutuality and cooperation between the Japanese and the foreigners, the *gaijin* – a feeling which continued undiminished into early 1941. For foreign residents, Jews and non-Jews alike, provided they had reasonable incomes and did not feel totally at odds with the sea of Japanese around them, life in Kobe was comfortable, cosmopolitan and relatively secure.

The Jews who lived in Kobe during the 1930s and 1940s were predominantly Russians who had emigrated to Manchuria in the early twentieth century when the building of the Trans-Siberian Railway had opened up that vast, empty land. During the world-wide economic reorganization of the thirties, Manchurian businesses began to pay more commercial attention to Japan – all the more so after the two countries became politically enmeshed in 1932. Textile firms, tea firms, silk, cotton and fur traders began sending representatives to Kobe to promote their interests there.

One of these representatives was Anatole Ponevejsky who had, as a child, emigrated with his parents from Irkutsk to Harbin. In 1937 he moved again, this time with his own wife and children, to Kobe to look after the Japanese branch of the family textile business. On the occasion of that move, he had shortened his name to Ponve.

Ponve was a very warm, kind person, continually and deeply involved with his fellow men. Though not religiously observant, he was very much committed to maintaining and furthering Jewish ideals. Thus, in 1937, shortly after his arrival, he founded the Jewish community (Ashkenazim) of Kobe, and became overseer of its community center – a cluster of rooms in a narrow lane at the foot of the steep hills.

The community of Kobe was, of course, very much aware of Japan's professed friendship for Jews. Its delegates to the 1937, 1938 and 1939 conferences of Far Eastern Jewry in Harbin had heard General Higuchi proclaim Japan's sympathy for the Jews. It had seen the honor accorded the delegates to the conference by Colonel Yasue. They had been deeply moved by the short speech delivered by Dr. Kotsuji – impressed less by its simple content than by the fact that it was written and spoken by a Japanese in excellent Hebrew. There had been fears in November 1938, at the signing of the cultural agreement between Germany and Japan, but the Jews of Kobe were reassured by the normality of their day-to-day dealings with the Japanese, who remained as friendly after that date as before.

With their own apparent security, however, they contrasted the increasingly perilous position of their fellow Jews in Europe. Thus, in June of 1940, the community responded immediately and enthusiastically to a cable from Lithuania asking help for a few refugees. The request was a simple one: Would Ponve, on behalf of the community, simply write a letter to the Japanese government guaranteeing support for seven people while they were in transit through Japan on their way to America? Ponve spent the afternoon, a Sunday, writing the letter, and the next day submitted it to the several government offices that would have to approve the arrangement. Then he sent a confirmation back to Vilna. Two days later came another request, then another . . . until three or four were arriving daily. In early July, Ponve called a meeting of the twenty-five member families of the community.

There was never any question but that they would accept as many refugees as could possibly reach Japan. Dealing with transient refugees on a large scale, however, required more organization than the community possessed. The result of the July meeting was a total mobilization: Committees were put together to cope with immigration procedures, temporary housing, local travel, onward travel, visa problems, and so on. A request for funds was cabled to the Joint Distribution Committee in New York. The reply read simply: SAVE JEWS MONEY NO OBJECT. The name "Kobe Jewcom," from the cable address, was adopted. In the space of a long evening, twenty-five families in Kobe had been brought out of their comfortable routines and into an international spotlight.

Officially, the first several hundred East European Jews to pass through Kobe – unlike those who came later courtesy of Consul Sugihara and the Curaçao visa – were not "refugees" in the strictest sense of the word. Each had a valid destination visa in hand for somewhere in North or South America. Theoretically, as far as these first transients were concerned, Kobe should have been only a way station en route from the landing at Tsuruga to a re-embarkation at Yokohama. If any help had been required, the Yokohama Jewish community might normally have been expected to handle the last-minute problems. But the Yokohama community consisted of only eight families and these were primarily German Jews. Historically, there is something of a split in the European Jewish world: the Russian and East European Jews tend to have an affinity for each other; and the Western European Jews (German and Austrian) work more easily together. Consequently, when the Western European Jews began leaving the Continent as early as 1934, they turned to the predominantly German community in Yokohama. The East European Jews (predominantly from Poland) reached out to the Russian Jews of Kobe.

The Jews of Yokohama were as generous with their time and energy and kindness as those in Kobe. The situation that they had had to respond to, however, was quite different. The earlier German and Austrian refugees had been permitted to take with them only a little in the way of personal belongings, but they all had legitimate passports and visas. And, thanks to the efficiency of the Hebrew Immigrant Aid Society in Berlin, and because there was usually enough time to make arrangements ahead, most of those refugees had precise travel schedules and some knowledge of the lands and conditions through which they would be traveling.

In the case of the East European Jewish refugees, however, after the emotional upheaval of having been driven from their homes and having to seek uncertain shelter in a land of which they knew nothing, and after grueling physical hardships which culminated in a long trek across Siberia, they were in no state to continue on to anywhere immediately. Exhausted, undernourished often to the point of illness, and economically destitute, they were physically and emotionally incapable of coping immediately with the intricacies of normal Japanese immigration and travel procedures and the last minute snags that often arose in working out final visa and travel arrangements. Thus, it quickly became apparent to Kobe Jewcom that its most serious problem was the lack of time allowed the refugees in Japan.

The standard Japanese transit visa was good for only twenty-one days. Even a simple problem, if it had to be solved by sending a letter across the ocean to the United States, would take longer than three weeks to straighten out. And the problems of the East European refugees were rarely *simple*. The strict time limit naturally made the refugees anxious and made Kobe Jewcom's problems all the harder. On one or two occasions during June and July, 1940, transit visas were extended on an emergency basis. But what was needed was a general, across-the-board extension that would relieve some of the pressure from both the refugees and Kobe Jewcom.

With this problem preying on his mind, Ponve heard with great interest the news that Dr. Kotsuji had returned to Japan and was now living in the city of Kamakura, not far from Tokyo. Kotsuji, the Hebrew-speaking Christian minister who had been the senior adviser on Jewish policy for the South Manchurian Railway, was in an excellent position to help Jewcom. Though he had no official standing in the Japanese government, he did have the ear of one of the top men in the cabinet – his former supervisor at the railway, now foreign minister, Yosuke Matsuoka. On behalf of Kobe Jewcom, Ponve went up to Kamakura, and by the time he left, Kotsuji had agreed to do whatever he could about the visa problem.

Kotsuji spent days plodding through the normal lower echelons of the bureaucracy, arguing that, in the name of humanity, the soon-lapsing transit visas should be extended. Having no success whatsoever, Kotsuji realized he had to play his trump card. He would see Matsuoka in Tokyo.

Kotsuji arranged to meet the foreign minister in his office at the *Gaimusho*. Once there, he outlined the problem: the transit visas of many of the refugees would soon expire. If they could not be extended or renewed, these Jews, having no destination before them, would have to return where they had come from. And that meant sure death. Kotsuji knew well enough that Matsuoka's experiences, both in the United States where he had studied and in Manchukuo, had convinced him that far from being the "scum of the earth," Jews were people who tended to have skills and connections that could be highly beneficial to Japan. In fact, Kotsuji knew that while he was in Manchukuo, Matsuoka had been working on a plan to have Jews actually settle in the region, a plan he occasionally referred to as the *fugu* plan – though what its precise details were and what had come of it, Kotsuji had no idea.

No matter how Matsuoka might feel personally about Jews, however, he was surrounded by some strong political realities. In the autumn of 1940, the military was solidifying its hold on the Japanese government. The Tripartite Pact, which Matsuoka himself had signed in September, had pledged military unity between Japan and Germany. Already, the Nazis were expressing their displeasure at the presence of so many Jews in Japan. Clearly, Matsuoka was in a difficult situation and nervous about even discussing such a controversial subject. Eventually, the minister suggested they take a walk.

The two men left the eight-story, dark brick *Gaimusho* and walked in silence the brief distance to the ancient wooden Cherry Blossom Gate which led into the Imperial Palace grounds. Turning right, they strolled along beside the peaceful palace moat.

"Quite clearly, the international situation and our military alliances make it absolutely impossible for the government to make any official statement or take any official action favorable to the Jews," Matsuoka said as they walked unheard beneath the bare branches of the willows that lined the moat. "Moreover, there is no precedent for extending the transit visas of foreigners in Japan. If we were to do so, particularly on a mass scale and specifically for Jews, the repercussions from Germany would be overwhelming."

That much, Kotsuji thought, he could have told me in his office. He waited for the minister to continue.

"You are well aware that I have expressed, in the past, a belief that Japan might benefit greatly, at some time in the future, if we could in some way manage to help Jews now. I still hold that view. But it is my personal view and must not be repeated. You would not, of course, repeat it," he said, looking straight at Kotsuji. The latter quickly shook his head.

The two men spent nearly an hour discussing this problem as they had discussed similar ones during the nine months they had worked together in Manchukuo. Over lunch, far from the restaurants frequented by *Gaimusho* officials, Matsuoka arrived at a solution.

"Kobe is not Tokyo. If the local authorities were to extend the visas, acting on their own, without informing the Tokyo authorities of what they were doing, we would probably never even know about it. Can you lead them to understand that?"

Yes, Kotsuji thought he could.

"Good. Now you must understand our official position with no doubt: If Kobe ever asks the government's opinion concerning visa extensions of any sort, we will insist on a strict application of the law. But as long as everything is achieved on the local level. . . . Even better," he continued, refining the idea as he went along, "Jews themselves are efficient. Let them handle the details of the visa extensions. Yes. Explain that to the authorities there. And you yourself, since you're so close with them, you oversee Jewcom's activities. That also will be the perfect way for us to be kept informed, unofficially of course, of everything that is going on there."

Matsuoka was pleased with his solution. Kotsuji was ecstatic. He went straight from Tokyo to Kobe, not even stopping off at Kamakura, and got in touch with the municipal officials in charge of transit visas.

Kotsuji's subsequent local negotiations were typically Japanese in indirectness. On two evenings, separated by a few days for recuperation, he entertained local officials lavishly. He had borrowed three hundred yen (about one hundred and fifty dollars), from his brother-in-law to provide gargantuan feasts, complete with samisen players, geishas and endless *sake*, at Kobe's best restaurant. But aside from a brief mention of the fact that he was concerned for the plight of the refugees and a quiet allusion to his friendship with Matsuoka, absolutely nothing was said about extending visas. Not until the third party did Kotsuji casually bring up the problem of the visas. The official in charge nodded his understanding. He also, he said, had been concerned about this problem. Could they, perhaps, work something out?

Within a few days, extension forms had been turned over to Kobe Jewcom. Any refugee in need of a fifteen-day extension filled out the form at Jewcom, and from there it was forwarded to the local government office for validation. From then on, Kotsuji was a gratefully-welcomed member of Jewcom, kept up-to-date on the details of everything that the Jews – refugees and residents alike – were doing.

On par with the problem of extending the visas was the question of finding accommodation for the refugees. The first few arrivals had been welcomed into the homes of the community members themselves, but before long the refugees began, literally, to pile up. By mid-July, a broader solution had been devised: Jewcom went into the real estate business. The Housing Committee rented a number of small buildings in its neighborhood, rearranged them dormitory-style and provided them, free, to the refugees. After all they had been through, the refugees were only slightly surprised to find themselves sleeping Japanese style between the soft *tatami* straw floor and a warm, fluffy, bright-colored *futon* quilt. The *heime*, as the dormitories were called in Yiddish, might have been communal, but, under the supervision of the Ladies Committee they were clean, secure and well managed. There were few complaints, even from those who ultimately lived there for seven or eight months.

Physical support – housing in the *heime* and a cash allotment of one-and-a-half yen (seventy-five cents) per person per day for food – was the most straightforward of the continuing challenges confronting Jewcom and the refugees. By transferring money through American banks to Jewcom Kobe, the Joint Distribution Committee paid the bills; and once the system was set up, administering it was merely a matter of bookkeeping. Serious illnesses were also less of a problem than anticipated.

Japanese doctors were more than generous in giving time, skill and medication, charging either minimal fees or waiving them entirely. (In fact, Kobe's entire Japanese population tended to respond to the refugees with one sympathetic word: *kawaiso*, "poor unfortunates.") But for Jewcom and the refugees, there was an endless stream of other difficulties. Relatives had to be tracked down in destination countries, usually on the basis of nothing more than a name and partial address, like "Samuel Cohen, Brooklyn." Money had to be found for the trans-Pacific passage. Wherever possible, money would be borrowed from relatives – often very distant family members. Otherwise, funds might come through one of the many religious or communal organizations to which a refugee might belong.

Jewcom also had to provide for the Orthodox religious practices of many refugees. Kosher wine and matzah had to be imported from the United States for Passover. Schedules had to be made to avoid travel on Saturday, a normal working day in prewar Japan. (One group of arrivals did, indeed, spend the Sabbath on the Tsuruga dock. Arriving after sundown on Friday, its leader agreed to disembark – lest they all be taken back to Russia – but refused to go further till after sundown on Saturday.) Whenever chicken could be afforded, arrangements had to be made for kosher slaughtering. Most important, Jewcom continually had to be the intermediary between the very Oriental minds of the Japanese bureaucrats and the very Jewish presumptions and methods of the refugees. And sometimes, it seemed that nothing short of a miracle was needed to rescue a group of refugees from a particular catastrophe.

Early in 1941, a ship landed at Tsuruga counting among its passengers seventy-two Jews who had no destination visas whatsoever, not even the Curaçao stamp. These seventy-two people were not frightened children, like Moishe Katznelson, who had lost their visas. They were adults to whom Consul Sugihara had issued Japanese transit visas which were conditional upon their getting some sort of destination visa. This, these particular refugees had not been able to do. Sadly, but implacably, Japanese immigration officials refused to let them into the country.

The ensuing dockside scene was not unlike those already being played over and over at concentration camps throughout Europe. Amid screaming and wailing, some passengers were allowed to turn toward the life, the hope, the future that Japan offered; others were forced away, compelled to remain on a ship that would only take them back to Russia and certain doom. Frantically, Kobe Jewcom contacted Japanese authorities in Kobe, Yokohama and Tokyo. They could do nothing. Cables were sent to government offices in Washington, New York, London, all over the world: Please save these people! No help came. Inexorably, the departure time came, and the ship, with its seventy-two desperate, desolate passengers, began steaming back toward Vladivostok.

Kobe Jewcom was not a place where secrets were well kept. One of those who heard of the plight of the seventy-two refugees was Nathan Gutwirth, the same shy young man who had first approached the Dutch ambassador in Riga. Again, he sought the help of his government, this time going to the home of the Dutch consul, N.A.G.de Voogd, in Kobe. De Voogd immediately asked the shipping line to radio its captain instructions not to offload the passengers at Vladivostok if, at any time before reaching the Russian port, he received another cable that visas were waiting for them in Japan. Then the Dutch consul began stamping out an official declaration that "No visa to Curaçao is required" in the name of each of the seventy-two refugees. The second cable reached the captain just as the coast of Russia appeared on the horizon: Seventy-two properly typed, stamped and endorsed visas had now been approved by the Japanese immigration officials. The refugees were *safe*. Cruelly, however, the captain kept this news from the passengers.

For their part, the terrified Jews had already decided that not only would they refuse to leave the ship voluntarily in Russia, they would not even appear to be on board. As the ship cruised into Vladivostok's Golden Horn Harbor, seventy-two bodies lay motionless as corpses, flat on the floor in the ship's hold. Minutes passed, then hours. The terrified refugees could not comprehend why they had not been roused at bayonet point and harried off to a Russian police station. Finally the ship's engines began rumbling to life, and one of the men could no longer stand not knowing. Cautiously, he peered out of the hold, only to find the captain grinning down at him.

"We are going back to Japan," the officer announced cheerfully. "You do have visas for Curaçao after all!"

As a joke, it was sick – but the refugees were too jubilant over their reprieve to care. In Kobe, meanwhile, Consul de Voogd dropped off a stack of signed and stamped Curaçao visa forms at Jewcom headquarters. Never again would that particular catastrophe loom so near.

Kobe Jewcom solved the problems as they arose – and those that could not be satisfactorily solved, they made the best of, always with patience and compassion. But there was one problem that remained insoluble. As 1941 progressed, it became unmistakably obvious that fewer refugees were leaving Japan than were coming in. The doors of the world, which had never been opened very wide for them, were closing even further. Immigration visas, acquired in good faith, suddenly were no longer valid. Guarantees evaporated; documents were declared insufficient or unacceptable. Already, by the end of January, there were two hundred and seventy refugees held over in Kobe. Where these, and subsequent arrivals holding the worthless Curaçao visa stamp would go, was absolutely unknown.

Avram Chesno sat on a concrete bench in one of Kobe's small hillside municipal parks and stared out over the scene below. It was a typical winter day – cold, dry, the air brilliant with sunshine. Camelia bushes along the park paths were budding; a few of the Japanese plum trees had already broken out in spherical splotches of red and white. Just down the hill in a schoolyard, uniformed elementary school boys were engaged in their compulsory daily military exercises, marching around with stick-guns held stiffly against their shoulders. And far below, over the rippling red and blue tile roofs of the tiny hillside houses, past the open cut of the busy railroad right-of-way, and through the plain gray cement blocks that were the waterside office buildings, there was the harbor. Dotted with ships, civilian and military, of every conceivable shape and size, the water was sparkling blue. It was a beautiful day, the kind that would make anyone glad he was alive just to see it. But the brighter the sun shone, the more depressed Avram became.

The night before, he had heard a translation of the latest news of Warsaw. Food rations for Jews, already barely sufficient to keep one alive, had been cut in half. There was no meat, except horsemeat, anyway. The average daily ration now provided scarcely a thousand calories against the bitter winter cold and the constant physical struggle merely to stay alive. There was so little coal that it was being called "black pearls." And over the past two months, the Germans had systematically confiscated every fur coat, fur lining, even fur collar and cuff in the ghetto.

After the broadcast, he couldn't sleep. Lying under a warm *futon*, the aftertaste of his dinner still apparent, Chesno had felt repelled from his past as if pushed away by the force of a reversed magnet. Europe was no longer a place to return to, not even in one's imagination. They had destroyed his Europe. They had taken a rich, full world of joy and possibility and life, and were savagely battering it into an agonizing, unrelieved day-and-night struggle simply to exist. Their bombs had made rubble of the buildings and their sadistic decrees were grinding out the life of the people. His early life – his education, even the culturally Jewish atmosphere he had grown up in – had created in him a passion for living. Hadn't the simple toast, *l'chaim* (to life), been the crowning moment at every occasion? But with his ears still hearing the statistics of suffering, his mind projecting the images of starvation and pain that constituted "life" for those who had not escaped, Avram could not help but feel that he was glad his Ruthie was already safely out of it.

Looking out into the clear air, he felt no nostalgia for his old life. It was finished. When Ruth had died, his central place in it had been swallowed up. Now, even the peripheral aspects of it were being destroyed. That world and his life in it had bequeathed to him nothing but the age-old role of wandering Jew. As the old rebbe had kept murmuring in a sing-song melody on the train and boat:

> Fun danen treibt men uns arois
> Und dorten losst men nit arein
> Zog shoin Tatenyu
> *Vee lang vet dos zein*
> From here we are driven out
> And there we may not enter
> Tell us, dear Father,
> How long will this go on?

Avram felt his eyes burning, whether from sunshine or tears he didn't know. If only he had made Ruth come with him. If only she were here now.

"Excuse, please . . . Jewish?"

Chesno sprang from the bench and spun around so quickly that the small Japanese man who had posed the question in limited English was nearly knocked over backward. He was a fragile man in a shapeless business suit, carrying a bulky briefcase. The Japanese recovered his balance and smiled hesitantly: "Excuse . . . Jewish?"

Chesno was mindful of the petty indignities – the slapping, the shoving, the spitting – that had usually followed such a question in Europe. He merely nodded.

"Ah!" The Japanese was delighted. Setting his briefcase on the bench, he reached in and took out a very large, highly polished red apple. Bowing deeply, he handed it to Avram. Yet, the Japanese acted as if *he* were the recipient.

"Thank you, thank you!" he said. "Good luck – *gombate!*" Still smiling, the man closed his briefcase. "*Sayonara, sayonara. Gombate,*" he said, bobbing his head on every word. Then he walked away and disappeared down the park path.

Chesno stared after the departing man, then looked at the fruit, completely bewildered. It was awfully small to be a disguised bomb. He held it gingerly up to his nose. It didn't look or smell, he thought, as if it had been treated with deadly poison. In fact, it looked absolutely delicious and was beginning to make his mouth water. (If it was, in fact, an apple, at least he knew how to deal with it. When he had first confronted the "ba-na-na," he had been horrified by the taste, until someone explained that it had to be peeled first.) But who was the Japanese man? And why did Avram's Jewishness entitle him to an apple?

The immediacy of the encounter and the question of the apple cleared his mind of its depression. Chesno stared back along the path, out the gate of the park and down the steep hill. Jewcom's headquarters were in a not very fashionable section of town, at Ikuta 4–2. If there was any place where he could find out whether an apple given by a Japanese to a Jew was fit to be eaten it was there.

Sam Evans was a short, broad-shouldered man with a remarkably easy manner. One of the foremost citizens of Kobe, and its senior Jewish resident, he had lived there since 1919 when, as Evanskoffsky, he had picked up a job with a ship-chandlering company during a one-day stopover of the ship on which he had planned to travel to America. Evans had done well as a ship chandler and over the years had acquired a good deal of real estate. Along the way, he had also gained the respect and friendship of many members of the local governmental bureaucracy, a significant asset in solving Jewcom's refugee problems. Sam had been the honorary president of the Kobe Jewish community from the day of its founding. But the lofty sounding title was misleading; actually he was very much involved with the day to day affairs of Jewcom. On this particular Monday, he was in its office putting a week's worth of refugee statistics into sensible order for the edification of the *Gaimusho*.

Avram knocked politely on the side of the door but walked in without waiting for a reply. Since his arrival nine days before, he had spent a good deal of time at Jewcom and had never heard any answer other than "Come in."

The organization in charge of the present lives and uncertain futures of hundreds of refugees had to make do with a very small office. Metal file cabinets stuck out from one wall, bookshelves stuffed with green and white file binders lined another. The sun streamed in through deep windows onto two battered wooden desks.

Evans looked up from his figures and smiled as Avram told him how he had come by the apple he was holding in his hand.

"Sit down, sit down," Evans said, pushing aside the statistics. Heedless of the tri-lingual "No Smoking" sign on the wall, he offered Avram a cigarette.

"It was probably one of the boys from the Holiness Church," he guessed. "They're a Christian sect who believe in something they call the 'common origin theory' – that the Japanese are descendants of the so-called ten lost tribes who somehow made their way here after they were driven out of Israel. The society prays three times a day for the survival of the Jews and for our return to Palestine. In fact, they're such Zionists, they've lost the support of the Christian missionaries around here. The precise logic of it all eludes me; but they are very nice. About a month ago, we had a bunch leaving for Palestine. Who should turn up at the train station but Bishop Nakada – he's the leader – and about a hundred of his followers, waving little Zionist flags and shouting '*Banzai!*' And as our boys were boarding the train, they started singing the *Hatikvah*. It was a little strange, but very, very moving. They are remarkable people, the Japanese. I've lived here twenty-two years and I'm still never sure which way they're going to jump. . . . Yes, go ahead, eat it. Looks delicious! No, thanks. I don't . . . well, yes, but a *small* piece. . . ."

When a man with nothing suddenly has something, you don't refuse him the satisfaction of sharing it.

The two men spoke briefly of Chesno's visa status. He had once again filled out the lengthy applications for entry into the United States, as well as Canada and Australia. Contrary to his hopes in Vilna, though, it did not seem any easier to be admitted to any country from Japan than it had been from Lithuania. He had already been rejected – thanks to his old soccer injury – for a place in the Polish army in exile that was being formed in Canada. His request for one of the much-prized Palestine certificates, British permission to enter that disputed land, had been turned down too. That, though, had scarcely come as a surprise. For the past several months, only the highest-ranking members of Zionist organizations had been selected for the few remaining places on the British quota. So many countries in the world, he had thought, and so few that would even consider taking in a refugee.

"How long can we keep extending our transit visas?" Avram asked, slipping unconsciously into the security of the group point of view. "If the unthinkable should happen and some of us should not manage to be accepted somewhere. . . ."

Avram didn't finish the sentence and Evans didn't rush in to fill the void. He simply did not know. The refugees could not stay in Japan indefinitely. Cooperative as the Japanese were now, the political and international situation was changing daily and in the wrong direction. There was no way of knowing how long it would be until something happened somewhere that would make it politically impossible for Japan to continue its hospitality to this growing number of destitute Jews. Day to day, matters were going smoothly. But if the crunch came and the Jews had to leave? Eighteen months ago, when the world situation was better in all respects, the ship, *St. Louis*, had only barely been accepted in Belgium after sailing halfway round the world seeking refuge for the nine hundred and thirty-seven European Jews on board. Evans didn't want to think about what might happen if such a ship had to set out now from Japan.

"We're working on the problem," Evans said, then eased into another subject.

"You came in with that rebbe from Amshenov, didn't you?"

"The sweet old man with the long white beard? Yes, right, straight through from Vilna. Why? Has he gotten worse? He was sick for most of the trip, I think."

"No, actually he's better, which may turn out to be worse for *us*. This morning he sent a cable, in Hebrew, to Vilna that has absolutely thrown the censors into a state of confusion. They can cope with a lot of languages, but not Hebrew. The *kempeitai* is suspicious enough of foreigners without something like this coming up. Hanin – you know him? – he's down at the telegraph office now, translating."

Avram sat back comfortably in his chair. It was a treat for him just to sit in this office and talk to this man. Comfortable and safe as Kobe was, it was just as boring as Vilna had been. Nothing to do all day but walk the narrow streets which, after only a short time seemed to repeat themselves in tedious lines of low wooden houses and shops. What had been fascinating in Tsuruga quickly became overly familiar. Yet at the same time, in spite of individual acts of kindness, like the gift of the apple, he felt very cut off from the Japanese. Any understanding of Japan was unreachable, cut off by the wall of language, a form of speech unlike anything Avram had ever before encountered. In Kobe, even more than in Vilna, the refugees were forced by circumstances to associate only with themselves. And among the refugees, simple relaxed, intelligent conversation on impersonal subjects was at a premium. All day and into the night, they talked only about visas and money, about the interminable paperwork or, at best, about local living conditions and how best to spend one's one-and-a-half-yen daily stipend.

In the Jewcom office, Sam Evans sensed his visitor's need to talk and accepted it as more important than the paperwork awaiting him. The two men talked for half an hour or so before the return of tall, wavy-haired Leo Hanin, whom Chesno recognized as one of the Jewcom members who had picked them up at Tsuruga.

"That cable the rebbe sent," Hanin reported. "SHISHA MISKADSHIM BETALLIS ECHAD. That's what it said: 'Six can be married under one prayer shawl,' and it was signed 'Kalisch.' "

Avram and Sam Evans were bewildered. "A response to a religious question?" Evans suggested.

"That's what I told the censors and that satisfied them. But it didn't satisfy *me*, so I tracked down the rebbe for an explanation."

Hanin moved closer to the tiny kerosene heater which was providing the only warmth in the room.

"It seems the rebbe discovered, while going through immigration, that a visa is valid not only for one person but for one family. In other words, if it looks like a family, up to six people can come in on one visa. So why waste visas? he thought. Arrange for groups of six people to come as 'families.' Not so dumb, no? He was quite pleased with himself."

"More work for you," Avram suggested, "if you get six times as many of us."

Evans looked out the window at the dozens of refugees crowded, as always, around the message board. "Better here than there," he said. "We can handle almost any number, somehow or other, if they can just get here."

"Speaking of which," Hanin said, "while I was at the telegraph office, I picked up a cable from Vladivostok listing the names of the passengers who just embarked. Should we include them in the statistics you're putting together for Inuzuka?"

Evans glanced at the paper held out to him and nodded. "What I wish someone would tell me is why Inuzuka, who is a navy man stationed in Shanghai, should be so interested in Jewish refugees coming into Kobe."

"I don't know. Maybe Inuzuka thinks that how we handle things here is how he might handle refugees in Shanghai. But, if statistics make the Japanese happy, statistics they shall have. God knows, they've been cooperative and helpful so far."

"We've got a couple of children coming this time," Hanin went on.

Probably it was the engaging conversation plus the mention of children that made Avram suddenly think of the son of Orliansky in Vilna. Pondering the fate of this family was not a pleasant thought. Orliansky had seemed such a *mensch* when he'd gotten to know him. A kind of friendly fellow, caught as they all were in circumstances not of their own making, but trying his best to get himself and his family through it all. But when the lists had been posted of those who would get exit permits, the Orliansky name had not been on them. Not on the long major list put up first, nor on any of the subsequent shorter lists of additions and corrections. Not his name or his wife's, or even his children's. At first, Orliansky seemed unable to believe it. Avram would see him daily in the Club, sitting on a sticky chair, staring, uncomprehending, into the middle distance. Gradually, after appeals to Intourist had had no effect, Orliansky's mood had grown blacker. His expression changed from uncomprehending to vindictive. When Avram tried to speak with him, he was unpleasant, curt, biting off his words almost before they were out of his mouth. And then he disappeared. Mischa, his son, still turned up occasionally, looking both better dressed and better fed than he had before. But the boy would only say vaguely that his father was "doing things" in another part of the city. Anxious to put Lithuania behind him at the earliest possible moment, Avram had more to worry about than the fate of his former acquaintance. But soon, Avram began to hear stories circulating through the club, stories about a big friendly bear of a man – a Jew – who was preying on the unsophisticated *shtetl* Jews who didn't know the ways of the world.

"Are you leaving for Japan soon?" the big friendly one would ask. "Are you one of the lucky ones whose name appeared on the lists?"

"Yes, I am," his mark would reply.

"I congratulate you and think you very fortunate," the friendly one would say. "But I must warn you of a fact that has recently come to my ears. The Russians – God curse their souls – won't let you take anything of value out of the country. No, absolutely *nothing*. No money, no jewelry, no gold, no stamps. What's more, you can't *sell* anything valuable within Russia. You can't barter it away: you can't dispose of it in any fashion whatsoever! And if they catch you trying to do so. . . ." The unstated threat was quite terrifying enough.

The victim would be astonished. He had no idea the Russians would be interested in, say, his grandmother Esther's one silver candlestick which he had carefully hoarded all this time.

"Well, no matter," he would reply. "If I should have something of value, I will simply sew it into the lining of my coat. The Russians will never find it."

"Never *find* it!? Why, don't you know, my friend? They have a special machine, which they have only recently invented that can actually see into things. They'll look into the lining of your coat as easily as you look into a Torah scroll on a Saturday morning!"

Now the victim would begin to be frightened. That one silver candlestick was his security, his savings account, his cushion to fall back on if the charity ever ran out.

"Well . . . but, what shall I do, if I should have something of value?"

The solution to the problem was always the same. Fortunately, the big friendly bear of a man happened to need one silver candlestick, or whatever it was that his mark possessed. Mind you, he couldn't pay much, certainly not what such a beautiful piece must be worth. But . . . better to get some money for it now than to get a death sentence for it in Vladivostok.

The story had upset Avram, and upset him even more when the descriptions given by the victims all pointed to Orliansky.

"Aren't they doing enough to us, without our doing such things to ourselves?" he asked himself. "Why is a Jew preying on another Jew?"

But he had not had to dwell long on this latest of the terrible stories. He had known the thrill of seeing his name on that list. Whatever was in store, at least he was getting away from here. And Orliansky wasn't. Who was he, Avram Chesno, to blame such an unfortunate man for thinking he had a right, in some small way, to even the score with the "lucky ones?"

The thought of Orliansky took a little of the edge off the pleasantness of the afternoon he had just spent with Evans and the savor of the apple he had eaten down to the seeds. The daylight was fading, and the two Jewcom men had wives and homes waiting for them. Avram said goodbye and went outside. With the sun down, the cold seeped through his old coat as he began the short walk back toward the *heim*. As he passed the synagogue, he could hear the enthusiastic responses of the evening prayer service: the yeshiva boys had already set up study rooms at the center and were hard at work, learning and praying fourteen hours a day.

Yosuke Matsuoka was a busy man. As foreign minister of a country trying to upgrade itself to empire status he had to contend with half the world including the United States, which opposed his efforts to dominate the sixth of the world that was China. Matsuoka was also, by nature, something of an eccentric – bright and shrewd, but inconsistent. And his habit of at least appearing to change directions in midstream made his working pace even more frenetic.

Dr. Kotsuji was well aware of all these sides to Matsuoka. He was also aware that on March 12, 1941, the foreign minister would be departing for face-to-face meetings with Hitler in Berlin and Stalin in Moscow. That had long since been announced in the press. So, all in all, Dr. Kotsuji was surprised to receive word not long before that date that the very busy official wanted to see *him* in Tokyo as soon as possible.

As he had during their last get-together a few months before, Matsuoka suggested that they go for a walk, this time nearby, in the open air of Hibiya Park.

"We are running headlong into some problems with your refugees," the foreign minister said after disposing quickly of the civilities.

Kotsuji had never thought of the Jews as *his* refugees; but he was quite aware of Matsuoka's position, and it didn't occur to him to quibble.

"I had anticipated some trouble with the Germans by letting these people pass through Japan at all. But now. . . . Do you know there are *hundreds* of Jews coming in every week, a torrent, a flood! And what is leaving? Virtually nothing! This was *not* my plan."

"Didn't you think that so many would come?" Kotsuji ventured.

"No, I didn't think 'so many would come!' And I certainly thought more would leave. They really have no sense of practicality, these Jews – no sense of what is proper. They come and come and come. . . . Surely word gets back that there is as little hope for them getting into America from here as from Lithuania or from the Soviet Union!"

"Perhaps they feel their lives are endangered where they are."

"I really don't care so much for 'their lives'!"

The two men stepped across a small cement bridge fashioned to look like wood.

"Don't misunderstand my meaning, Kotsuji-san: I do not wish to see Jews die. But I do wish to see Japan prosper. This to me is infinitely more important than the fate of those thousands of over-grown students and old men. We must consider our own situation. I never thought so many would come. Even when I heard about that youngster in Kovno. . . . What was his name? Sugihara. . . . Even when I learned he was issuing transit visas literally in batches of a thousand, I never thought they would *all* come. And you know, more are coming than have any legal right to come. So many, it seems, are taking advantage of our generosity by forging the transit visa themselves into their own passports."

"Perhaps if the immigration officials were told to prevent those with improper visas. . . ."

"No! That has nothing to do with it!" Matsuoka dismissed this with a wave of his hand. "The problem is, the Germans are getting very unpleasant about it. They are pleased with the books and articles they have seen – those of Hokoshi and Utsunomiya . . . and even those by Asahina," Matsuoka said, grinning slyly at his walking companion.

Kotsuji smiled slightly: under that name, he had written several articles which might be considered anti-Jewish. He had done so partly in order to keep the *kempeitai* from becoming suspicious of his activities on behalf of the Jews, and partly because he also, just occasionally, found himself worried about the potential of Jewish power.

There was no lack of anti-Semitism in any of the bureaus of the Japanese government. However, this prejudice was not of the same order as traditional European-Christian anti-Semitism. In Japan, Jews were not hated simply because they were Jews. Rather, some Japanese feared Jews because they equated Jewishness with Communism (and simultaneously, if irrationally, with the excesses of capitalism) and because they believed Jews to be the cause – through the "3-S tactic" of sports, screen and sex – of the breakdown of Japanese traditions. Throughout the late thirties and early forties, government and military leaders at all levels had been exposed to hundreds of articles bearing such titles as: "Jewish Power, Basis of Evil," "What Is the Jewish Plot?," "Russia under a Jewish Government," "The Jewish Commercial Movement" and so forth. The bulk of this nonsense appeared in the monthly journal; *Kokusai Hinmitsu Ryoku No Kenkyu (Studies in the International Conspiracy)*, which was funded by the *Gaimusho* and the German Embassy. All the "Jewish experts" were, under discreet pen names, heavy contributors to the KHR: Yasue, Inuzuka, General Shioden, Shogun Sakai (who had accompanied Yasue on his 1926 trip to Palestine), General Higuchi (who attended all the conferences of Far Eastern Jews) and a naval officer named Tsutomu Kubota who would one day be the director of refugee affairs in Shanghai.

Kotsuji knew he was in very good company writing for the KHR and other lesser journals, and he had made sure that the *kempeitai* knew that he was the man behind the name "Asahina." But he had not been aware that this information had gone all the way up to Matsuoka.

"Hokoshi is still writing?" he asked after they had walked a few moments in silence.

Hokoshi – known more widely as Colonel Yasue – had been one of the first casualties of the Tripartite Pact signing in September 1940. Too visibly identified with the pro-Jewish faction, he had been dismissed the following month by the war minister, General Hideki Tojo. Yasue had immediately flown from Dairen to Tokyo, not to protest his dismissal but to urge the War Department and by extension the whole Japanese government, not to let outsiders, even allies, dictate Japanese policy. Tojo had listened to him fully and with respect, then offered him reinstatement. Yasue had refused. His pride had been deeply wounded by his dismissal, but his protest had been voiced not on his own behalf but on behalf of his country. So now Yasue was no longer an official part of the army, though with his extensive knowledge of Manchuria, he was still an unofficial adviser and consultant for the Japanese government in Manchukuo. And apparently he had become sincerely pro-Jewish. Yasue had not always been a friend of the Jews. Kotsuji well remembered that he was also the man who had translated *The Protocols of the Elders of Zion* into Japanese. This was, however, not an accomplishment that Yasue now wished to have known. Once, in Kamakura, in 1939, when Kotsuji had mentioned it, Yasue, standing not two feet away, had jammed the point of his saber right into the wooden floor and screamed: "Don't you realize I can have you killed?" Fortunately, Yasue had calmed down almost immediately and apologized. But Kotsuji was just as glad not to have him around anymore.

"No," Matsuoka said, absently, "Hokoshi is no longer writing. But the important thing is, what to do with these refugees. I do not want to be sitting across the conference table from Hitler while yet another horde of destitute refugees is being off-loaded into the security of Japan! On the other hand even if the *fugu* plan isn't working out there is no point in creating an international incident. Or even in making it appear that Japan is being told what do do by the Germans. Especially, I don't want the Germans themselves thinking they can dictate our policy. I was being absolutely sincere last December, you know, when I saw that Jew from Manchukuo, Zikman. The reason I spoke to him at all was to send a message to the World Jewish Congress in America. But I was sincere in saying Japan is not an anti-Semitic country and that I had never promised Hitler we would become one. We have no need for that business: it would completely block off one potentially very lucrative category of options. And that is what I *don't* want to do.

Not for nothing had Matsuoka been nicknamed "the Talking Machine." Kotsuji said nothing, merely measured his stride against the minister's as they crunched along the gravel path.

"But there must be something we can do with those Jews, either to move them out faster or turn off the inflow." Matsuoka stopped and turned to Kotsuji: "You've been working with them for several months now. What ideas do you have?"

Actually, Kotsuji had himself been concerned about this "inflow" since the early weeks of February when a huge increase in arrivals had decidedly not been matched by an increase in departures. Such a situation could not continue, yet the refugees were still coming, and it was already well into March. But politics and international diplomacy were not Kotsuji's strong suits. He simply didn't have anything to suggest, which was what he said.

"Well, I am sorry to hear that," Matsuoka said after a short pause. "I really think you know Jews better than anyone else in Japan, Kotsuji-san – even better than me, in fact. But if you have no ideas, I will consult with my staff.

"We must find some way, you know," he added, almost off-handedly. "A simple, legal, sure-fire way to cut down on the numbers coming in. And it would be best, of course, if it could be timed for exactly when it will do us the most good with our friend, the Führer."

"What sort of thing will you do?" Kotsuji asked, a little alarmed.

"I don't really have any idea," Matsuoka replied, candidly. "But I, or someone, will think something up."

Matsuoka then turned decisively to the right and began walking down a narrow park path that would lead most directly back to the *Gaimusho*. The consultation was over.

**9** YANKEL GILBEWITZ awoke with the dawn, before any of the other boys who shared the large *tatami*-mat room in the yeshiva's *heim*. Quietly whispering the prayer of thanks that God had restored his soul to him after the night, he slid back the *shoji* door that led to the corridor. A few remaining nocturnal bugs skittered out of his way as he washed in the long communal tin sink. Donning the black pants, tie and jacket, the white shirt and narrow-brimmed black hat customarily worn at the yeshiva, he slipped into his slightly damp overcoat, took his prayer book and a small embroidered bag containing the leather phylacteries needed for morning prayers and stepped through another sliding door into the narrow street.

Yesterday, the weather had been absolutely foul. A freezing rain had fallen practically all day, not only coming down, but seeming to creep up from below as well. Until two weeks ago Yankel would have been quite content to stay indoors wrestling with Talmudic intricacies and arguing philosophical convolutions with his study partner. But, intrigued by what he'd seen of Kobe and anxious to see more, Yankel had volunteered to walk the few blocks from the yeshiva's newly established *heim* to Jewcom to pick up the bread ration for his section. The consequences of the simple act of volunteering turned out to be not insignificant.

The second day he made the trip, Yankel was returning to the yeshiva *heim* by a roundabout route when he passed a particularly well-stocked fruit stand. He had smiled shyly at the storekeeper – a magnificently wrinkled old lady dressed in a traditional long-sleeved white apron – and, in a moment of enthusiasm, exclaimed with gestures over the magnificence of all her produce. She had grinned – gold false teeth gleaming in the sunlight – and bowed in appreciation of his interest. The next day, Yankel found himself taking the same route, with a strange idea working its way through his mind. Finding the old lady alone, he tentatively broke off a chunk of one of the loaves he had under his arm and offered it to her. Surprised but pleased, she in turn offered him an apple. Yankel ate it on the way home and told his classmates he himself had eaten the bread. The principle having been established, it was a short step to a steady barter arrangement: every day Yankel offered the lady a loaf of bread – two if he thought it wouldn't be missed – and she gave him in return half a kilo of apples, half a dozen of a heart-shaped very sweet orange fruit she called a *kaki*, or whatever he liked. This was not, however, anything he wished to share with his schoolfellows, so Yankel would leave his gains in the back corner of the store to be collected later.

It was, he thought, a fine arrangement: the old woman was happy, his yeshiva section never seemed to miss the extra bread and, best of all, the fruit not only added an extra dimension to his daily menu, it could also, he discovered, be bartered among the other refugees. Yankel had made only one exchange so far: he had arrived in Kobe with one white shirt and now had two. The trade had been done so easily, however, that he was already asking if anyone had an extra pair of socks. It was very exciting, trading what you had for what you wanted. It was a totally new world!

As a child, he had had absolutely nothing but his mental agility to trade on. The yeshiva in Poland had been a completely closed world with virtually no opportunities for self-improvement in a material sense. And in Lithuania, Yankel, like all of them, had been too frightened to venture out of the house. Kobe, however, was different. The Japanese, so accommodating, always smiling, always bowing, weren't at all frightening. In spite of its different customs, Japan seemed almost to be inviting a previously very sheltered young man to step out into the secular world and see how it worked. Yankel accepted the invitation. Of necessity, he attended to his studies and maintained the appearance of full commitment. But in his mind, he was being pulled away from the yeshiva, out into the big world. There were moments, many moments, when this worried him. Never before had there been a conflict between his improving his place in the world and his improving himself as a Jew. Now there was. The simple bread-for-fruit exchange was the basis of all his dealings – those accomplished and many he had planned for the future. Simple or not, though, it was wrong. His fellow students might not know what they were missing; but he, Yankel Gilbewitz, knew he was stealing from them. He didn't like his new self image of thief. He didn't like to think of it. But he did like his new purchasing power. He continued to look out for someone with extra socks.

Yankel walked down the quiet alley where the yeshiva *heim* was located and turned left into a broader street. As if to make up for the unpleasantness of the freezing rain, yesterday's bread run had brought him the bonus of finding an old friend, Gershon Cohen. Yankel had known Gershon in Vilna during the two months that the Mir Yeshiva shared the living quarters of the Ramailes Yeshiva. Gershon, and a very few of the other Ramailes students had arrived in Kobe on Consul Sugihara's visa only two days before. The two friends had agreed to meet this morning, near the fruit stand. "Gershon," Yankel had promised the other youth, "believe it or not, I'll take you to a mountaintop to say the morning prayers."

As he had planned, Yankel reached the meeting place first. Nodding good morning to its owner, he retrieved yesterday's gain of two red-net packages of tangerines, then stood waiting for Gershon, casually watching the early morning scene.

Like most Japanese streets, it had a curiously intimate feeling. Zoning was unknown in Japan. So quite nice houses sat side by side with small factories, office buildings and shops. Each of the residences maintained its privacy inside a high wall enclosing itself and its garden. The walls – light colored masonry or dark, weathered board – lent an air of privacy as well to the street, as if whatever took place there was also a family matter. Off the main thoroughfares, there was little mechanized traffic. Motorcycles outnumbered cars and trucks; bicycles surpassed all three. Occasionally, a rickshaw man trundled his fare through the street. But mostly, there were pedestrians. Men in khaki pants and jackets – the officially sanctioned uniform for civilians wishing to show enthusiasm for Japan's war effort – strode briskly toward their offices. Many wore little square masks of white gauze over their faces, believing erroneously that this was a protection against contagious sicknesses. Women, more of them dressed in informal kimonos than in Western dress, walked more slowly. Many were bent almost double under the weight of children strapped to their backs. Youngsters were carried this way till they were quite large – three years old or so. One overcoat went around both mother and child, giving the women the unfortunate appearance of hunchbacks. Still they smiled and bowed continually as they passed among their acquaintances seemingly unaware of any awkwardness. The children rarely cried.

Even without the sounds of traffic, the street was noisy. The wooden sandals, *geta*, worn by many of the women and almost all the tradespeople, constantly clattered against the street. Shopkeepers greeted customers with rhythmic shouts of welcome and encouragements to buy. Bicycle bells rang continually as delivery boys wove expertly through the throngs. Radios blared the martial music that had been in vogue since the beginning of the war. Yankel leaned against one of the wooden poles that supported a web of electric and telephone lines overhead, and watched the day get underway. It was so different from Europe. No one seemed angry. No one seemed suspicious. The vegetables, flowers, sacks of rice, barrels of fish, stacks of china, everything sat out for all to touch – or take; but shopkeepers often turned their backs to the street, apparently oblivious of any danger of pilferage by passersby.

"You too haven't said the morning prayers!" Yankel turned to the familiar voice. Gershon Gohen in rumpled black jacket and pants, his hat pushed back on his head, appeared from around the corner. He gestured toward the embroidered bag containing Yankel's phylacteries.

"Where do we go and pray?" he asked.

"As I promised, I will take you up to the top of a mountain," Yankel said, happy to see his friend again. He directed Gershon down one of the intersecting streets. "Of course, it is a mountain in the form of a department store. But it is eight stories tall."

"And then," he added, holding up the tangerines, "I will treat you to breakfast!"

Gershon's mouth hung open in amazement. "Are those fruit? How did you get so many?"

Yankel only smiled – right now the joy of having enough to share with his friend was more than sufficient to offset the gnawings of his conscience.

"I still cannot believe I am here," Gershon was saying, talking fast but walking slowly as he peered curiously into every store. "I was so frightened when I landed because I didn't have a real visa. I had the visa for Curaçao, but not for Japan because that Japanese fellow had disappeared before I got to him. Where did he go? He was like an angel, like a gift from God. He appears. For no reason, he appears. And then, also for no reason, he disappears! But in the meantime, I didn't get a visa."

"So how did you get in?" Yankel asked.

"Ah! I copied the real one from a friend's passport. I copied it over and over again until I thought I had it down perfectly. Then I spent an exorbitant amount of money on a little bit of red ink and I made a copy of the visa in my own passport. What else could I do? But still it didn't look kosher. Everyone else's was a kind of red-orange and mine was more red-red. I was astonished it passed the Russians at all, but I knew it would never get past the Japanese. . . . Do they really *eat* these things?"

The boys had stopped outside a small shop. Oddly shaped, murky colored vegetables were packed in tubs of what appeared to be sawdust.

"I suppose so," Yankel said, having just two days before traded an apple for what he later learned was a pickle. "They taste horrible. What happened with the visa?"

Gershon shook his head in wonder at the diversity of the world and turned away from the pickle shop.

"What happened? Absolutely nothing! It was the biggest anti-climax of my life! I'm terrified. My legs are like rubber. My ankles barely support my weight. I stumble up to that little desk in the shed, you know? I hand over my passport. The immigration official looks at the Curaçao visa: fine. Then he looks at the Japanese visa. I can't watch anymore. But nothing happens. So I can't *not* watch any more. I glance at him out of the corner of my eye . . . and he's *grinning*! Laughing at the visa! That fellow, Triguboff, told me on the train later that not only had I used the wrong ink but I had copied it so badly the immigration fellow said his seven-year-old daughter could have done it better."

Yankel laughed out loud, but Geshon just smiled and shrugged. "Never mind! They are very nice, the Japanese. They let me in, as you can see. Where is this mountain? I'm getting hungry."

Yankel directed him toward a major intersection, the site of the eight-story Kobe Daimaru Department Store.

The two youths stepped out of the elevator at the roof level. They had tried to be casual about stepping *into* the elevator in the first place. But this was only Gerson's second ride in an elevator. The two youths grinned nervously and clutched the hand rail as the uniformed woman operator took the car up apparently without paying them any attention.

A typical Japanese department store, Daimaru had installed swings and slides up on the roof where children could play while their parents were shopping in the store below. But at this early hour, the play area was deserted. Self-consciously, Yankel introduced his friend to the fine and hitherto unknown joys of swinging on a swing and sliding down a slide. Childhood had never been like this! But gradually, as the elevator brought up a steady flow of young children, the boys began to feel their age. Standing off by themselves in a corner of the roof, Yankel pointed out the few landmarks that he knew: the main railway station, the big shopping area called Motomachi and the general area of Jewcom Headquarters, though the building itself was much too small to be picked out from this distance. Then, quietly, they began the rhythmic wrapping-on of the long leather phylactery straps which would hold in place two small leather boxes – one at the forehead, one on the inside of the left arm – which are worn during the recitation of morning prayers. The elevator came and went, the children played, the sun streamed down; and two young Jews praised God for having made the world and put them in it.

Twenty-five minutes later they were under arrest, behind locked doors at a police station.

When Michael Ionis arrived, summoned from Jewcom Headquarters by the police, he found Yankel and Gershon, pale with fear, seated motionless on hard wooden chairs, not comprehending any of the rapid Japanese exchanged by the policemen surrounding them and also bewildered by the English, which the sergeant in charge had been trying to speak. Ionis scarcely looked at them before asking the sergeant what the problem was.

"They were up on the roof of Daimaru Department Store this morning, police sergeant Okuda reported, taking pictures of the dock area and the railway lines with some kind of a camera on their foreheads. We think they also had a secret radio transmitter."

Ionis was relieved at the note of doubt in the voice of the sergeant. Obviously there was something in this that Okuda and the Japanese police didn't understand either. Ionis could not imagine yeshiva boys engaging in anything so worldly as military espionage. However, the truth would have to be brought to light very carefully to keep the sergeant, and by extension, the whole Kobe police force, from losing face.

"I see," he said, nodding gravely. "You have taken from them, of course, these, well, cameras and transmitters.

"Of course, Ionis-san." Okuda pointed to a table a few feet away. There were the embroidered bags, the *tefillin* (could anyone have mistaken the straps for antennae? Ionis wondered), two small prayer books (that apparently had been taken for the transmitters), two handkerchiefs and two nets of tangerines. "You realize, I am sure, that spying is a very serious business," the sergeant said.

"I *do* understand of course. If any of our people do any such thing, you are quite right to put them under arrest." He was silent for an instant, so as not even to seem to be taking charge, then said: "Perhaps if we merely asked the two young men about the camera and the transmitter. . . ?"

"Please do so, Ionis-san. We have been unable to question them at all."

For the first time, Ionis turned to the two prisoners. He took care to speak calmly and carefully, in Yiddish. "This situation is, potentially, very serious. I want you to answer me calmly, with no hysterics, no gestures, just spoken words as I am speaking to you now. Do you understand? . . . Good. Now, they think you were spying from the roof of Daimaru Department Store."

Yankel let out a small cry. People were executed for spying. Without doubt, they would be sent out of the country, back to Russia, for spying. He wasn't guilty of spying! But maybe this was God's way of punishing him for deeds he definitely *was* guilty of. Why had he done it? Why had he stolen from his friends? *Lo tignov!* Thou shalt not steal! Why had he tempted God by not obeying the commandment?

"Were you spying?" Ionis asked as Yankel began trembling almost uncontrollably.

"No, no!"

Behind Ionis, the police sergeant, comprehending the negative answer, pointed toward a table where the youths' phylacteries lay. "Just a second," the Jewcom official said in Japanese. Then, turning back to the two students, he asked, in Yiddish again, "What were you doing on the roof, then?"

"I didn't know it was . . . restricted," Yankel said, trying to keep his voice from trembling away entirely. "I took Gershon there for morning prayers and to show him the view . . . and to show him the swings. There are no signs. No one stopped us."

"No, it's not a restricted area. But the police say you were observed with a camera and a radio transmitter. Do you have such things?"

Yankel looked at Gershon who could not restrain himself from declaiming the impossibility of it all, from trying to show that his pockets were too small to contain anything as large as those objects. When Gershon stood up, several of the Japanese policemen started toward him. Terrified, Yankel grabbed his friend by the jacket, roughly pulling him back onto the chair.

"Shush, shaa, Gershon! Don't get *them* excited!"

Gershon retreated. "We have no radio," he said, and was quiet.

Ionis nodded and turned to Okuda. "Please excuse his outburst. They say they were not spying. They say they went up to the roof to pray – they wanted to be closer to God, just as *Shinto* shrines are so often on top of hills to be closer to heaven."

Ionis knew the analogy was not entirely accurate. But it seemed to have the desired effect on Okuda who seemed willing at least to listen to an explanation.

"Sergeant, these boys are country boys. They don't know anything about cameras or radio transmitters. Perhaps there may possibly have been . . . ummm, some confusion in this matter."

"What are those?" Okuda asked, pointing to but not touching the phylacteries.

Ionis picked up one of the leather boxes, explaining how it was placed on the head and the arm, explaining that it was definitely not a mechanical device of any kind. Okuda took it gingerly, shook it, and signaled to one of his men to bring tools to open it with. When the officer returned with a hammer and a chisel, both the students started to protest. A gesture from Ionis silenced them. Better to lose the phylacteries than their lives.

After Okuda had satisfied himself that, as Ionis had said, the leather boxes contained only inscribed parchment, he stood in silence for a moment.

No one said a word. The two boys looked cautiously at each other. Yankel silently vowed if he ever got out of this, he would never again venture further than the front door of the yeshiva.

"Who was it who observed these boys on the roof?" Ionis asked.

"The elevator operator," the sergeant replied. "A Japanese lady."

The emphasis on "Japanese" confirmed Ionis's understanding of the nature of the problem. A Japanese would not be wrong when making an accusation against a foreigner. If it should turn out that the foreigner was in the right, Japan would lose face. The overwhelming nationalism that had been growing since the early thirties had infected even small encounters like this. It was utter nonsense. But this was no time to discuss reality.

"Certainly a Japanese lady would never wrongly accuse anyone," Ionis said. "Could it be, Okuda-san, that perhaps she had never before seen someone wearing these leather boxes and long straps? No doubt, they do look a bit strange. And she would have been quite right in calling it to the attention of the police . . . just to *investigate* even if not actually to accuse anyone of spying."

Okuda's eyes narrowed with suspicion, but Ionis continued.

"Of course, it is we ourselves who have made the mistake. We have brought these people here without sufficient introduction to the people of Kobe. Do you think we could rectify this mistake by explaining who these people are and explaining that they have come to Japan because Japan has been the only country in the world humane and kind enough to let them come?" Okuda crossed his arms over his chest. Ionis did have a point. Japan *was* indeed the most humane country in the world. But she might not appear so if he clapped these two in jail without being able to prove they were spying. Foreigners were nothing but trouble. He had been specifically ordered on the one hand to look out for spies, but on the other hand word had come down, all the way from *Gaimusho* he had heard, to treat them with respect and understanding and even some latitude as far as applying the precise letter of the law to every small infraction.

At least, he thought, this foreigner was wise enough to take the responsibility for the mistake.

"All right," he decided. "Do that – do a better job of telling people who these visitors are. Japanese are very patriotic, Ionis-san. If they see anything strange from a foreigner, they will definitely report it to us."

Having ended comfortably with a threat, Okuda felt free to dismiss all three of them. At a gesture, one of the guards unlocked the door. Ionis bowed, Okuda nodded in return. Gershon and Yankel fairly flew from the police station. No one said a word till they had returned to the Jewcom office. Then both boys exploded in loud, tension-releasing expositions of their absolute innocence in the entire matter while Ionis recounted the story to Ponve.

Jewcom's president leaned back in the chair. He had been sick enough to be in the hospital until just a few days before and was glad not even to have heard about this latest problem till it was solved.

"You did a good job, Michael. Proof or no proof, that sergeant could have tossed these two into jail just on suspicion for days and days. Does it sometimes seem to you that we are being treated exceptionally well? I'll grant you that the Japanese in certain circumstances can be very kind and humane. I've seen it long before this situation began. But in the past, say, six or seven months, since business began to pick-up, so to speak, there have been so many courtesies. For example, this new business of delivering everyone's bread ration here so that the refugees don't have to stand in line . . . and before, when they *did* have to stand in line, the officials took care to make sure nobody pushed ahead of them. And the farmers sending in boxes of apples and tangerines and eggs for the children. And those times in the bathhouse when our newcomers couldn't help but stare at all the naked Japanese. . . ."

Yankel and Gershon had, by this time, calmed down. However, the mention of "naked bodies in bathhouses" brought them back into the conversation.

"Baths with Japanese? Naked?" Both boys spoke at the same time. Gershon was scandalized; Yankel was intrigued.

"Of course, naked, how ever do people bathe?" Ionis asked, amused. "And yes, with Japanese. Do you have a bathtub in your *heim*? Or did you perhaps think that the bathhouse you use was built especially for you?"

Both boys shook their heads – they hadn't thought about it at all.

"Bathing is a very friendly, communal thing here, you know. The women are all together on one side of the curtain and the men together on the other. . . ."

"Except when a woman comes into the men's section to wash her husband's back," Ponve mentioned.

Gershon's eyes practically bulged from his head.

"Well, before the Japanese officials kindly set aside a few bathhouses for us," Ionis continued, "people had no choice but to bathe with the Japanese – or go dirty. The Japanese weren't used to having foreigners in their bath. But when our boys, just off the boat, walked naked out of the locker rooms into their bath they were thunderstruck. Dozens of naked men and women, all in the room together; they couldn't get used to it. The story even got into the newspaper. 'The refugees,' it complained, 'seemed to be doing more gazing than bathing!' True enough, they all ran out – none even got wet.''

The two boys looked away, grinning self-consciously and then, after a few more minutes of thanks to Ionis for having rescued them from the police, they hurried back to their yeshiva. The two officials stared after them, lost for a moment in thought, and then Ionis returned to Ponve's original question about a reason for all the recent courtesies to Jewcom.

"I agree with you absolutely," he said. "The Japanese *have* been kind. And Okuda *could* have thrown away the key on these two. But to tell you the truth, Anatole, I don't know why it should be so. Maybe they really do feel sorry for us because of the mess in Europe. Maybe they like the way it looks – Jews fleeing Europe and seeking refuge in Japan. That was what I said to him, and maybe it's not such an inaccurate way of putting it. In fact, doing some kind of public relations on that theme might be a good idea. Some explanation of the background of the refugees – especially the religious boys. . . . If I saw someone putting on *tefillin* without knowing what they were, like that poor little elevator operator, I'd think it a little strange, too, to say the least!''

The phone rang and Ponve picked it up. "Hello? Ah hello, Dr. Kotsuji!" he said, smiling. Abruptly, however his smile disappeared. Barely audibly, he asked a few questions into the phone, then quietly hung up.

"Who was that?" Ionis asked.

Ponve replied without changing expression. "The Japanese Embassy in Moscow has stopped issuing transit visas."

Ionis was stunned. "Why? When? Is he sure?" he asked exactly the same questions Ponve himself had asked not two seconds before. "As of today. The official reason is, there is a bottleneck in Vladivostok – too many refugees, not enough ships to carry them to Japan, and the ones already here don't seem to be going on very fast. Kotsuji was absolutely sure the announcement said 'stopped' – not 'temporarily suspended' or 'commenced for a period of moratorium' or anything of that sort. Stopped. The end. Finished.''

Until now, there had been a tiny patch of hope, a skin-tight narrow way out for all the Polish refugees in the Russian-dominated Baltic states. Even after the departure of Sugihara from Kovno, the so-called "Curaçao visa" had been continued to save lives. With the tacit consent of the Dutch, more than one of these rubber stamps was still circulating among the refugee communities. And if one were adventurous enough, daring enough, to go to Moscow, one could, usually, on the basis of the Curaçao stamp, get a transit visa from the Japanese Embassy there. The Moscow visa officer was not Sugihara; he did not issue visas wholesale *only* on the basis of the Curaçao visa. But if one could talk a good story, if one seemed to have a firm final destination, or if one happened to catch one of the clerks on a particularly good day, a transit visa could sometimes be had.

At first, only a few had been brave enough to venture even deeper into the den of the Russian bear. It meant leaving the poor, but at least familiar, security of the refugee community in Lithuania, going to a strange embassy in a strange city, and finally applying for the exit permit in Moscow. And all along, during the minimum of three weeks it would take for the process to work itself through, how did one live? How did one eat? And how could one defend himself if picked up by the omnipresent NKVD?

As the situation in Vilna grew worse, however, increasing numbers of the refugees had decided to take this one last chance. In mid-February, 1941, the occupying Soviets had forced the universal registration of all refugees. Any found not to be engaged in "productive work" were to be shipped to the one place where workers were always needed – Siberia. By mid-March scores of refugees were lining up every morning in Moscow at the Japanese Embassy in Moscow. Everyone had a destination visa – almost all of them for Curaçao. Everyone needed only a Japanese transit visa, and a little luck with the NKVD which had continued to let out of the country most of those who had the required documents.

"You think the jam-up in Vladivostok is the real reason?" Ionis asked.

"No. That situation has been worse before than it is now." Ponve shook his head slowly back and forth. "I don't know the reason. I have never understood why the Japanese let any refugees in, and I don't understand now why they are stopping them. The Japanese are like God – totally unpredictable. How many Jews do you suppose there are now in Moscow? How many who have already burned their bridges behind them in going there in the first place? Who need only the transit visa to be saved?"

"I don't know."

The gloom in the sun-filled room was overwhelming. The natural reaction – "I'm sorry for them but thank God it's not me" – had long since been washed away by identification on the part of both men. The door that had been slammed in the faces of the refugees lined up outside the Japanese Embassy in Moscow, had been just as brusquely slammed in their own faces. The noose was growing tighter, and the victims still didn't know the reason for the judgment.

Foreign Minister Matsuoka received the news that the deed had been done while he was resting in his Berlin hotel room. He nodded without speaking and gently ran his finger across his short black moustache: truly, it was a masterful stroke of diplomacy.

# 10

ZORACH WARHAFTIG, one of the pioneers among the Polish refugees, had left Vilna, crossed Russia and arrived in Kobe in October 1940. Warhaftig, however, was quite unlike the bulk of those who had come later. A young, talented, Warsaw lawyer, and a devoutly religious man, he had close, high-level ties with the leading world-wide Jewish organizations: he had been a member of the executive board of the World Jewish Congress in Warsaw and he also had influence with the Joint Distribution Committee, the Jewish Agency in New York, the *Va'ad Hatzalah* and the Union of Orthodox Rabbis which was particularly concerned about the fate of the yeshiva scholars. Moreover, for the six months since his arrival in Japan, Warhaftig had been acting on behalf of the principal religious Zionist organizations, watching over the passage of those fortunate enough to have destination visas to the other side of the Pacific or to Palestine.

From his temporary home in Yokohama, the lawyer Warhaftig had devised several very creative schemes for saving the lives of his fellow refugees. During the winter of 1940–1 alone, he had been able to help hundreds of refugees get transit visas by guaranteeing the Japanese Embassy in Moscow that the Palestine Committee, of which he was the head, had firm destination visas just waiting for them in Japan. This approach foundered only when someone in the *Gaimusho* investigated and reported that the Japanese branch of the Palestine Committee consisted only of Warhaftig and two assistants . . . and, unlike the Central Palestine Committee in Palestine itself, had no access whatsoever to visas. But the things that Warhaftig had been able to accomplish up to now were mere drops in a bucket compared to the potential of the plans he devised after the cut-off of the Japanese transit visas.

"As you are well aware," Warhaftig outlined his proposal to a small group of men at the Yokohama headquarters of the Nippon Yusen Kaisha steamship company, "there are several thousand

Polish-Jewish refugees both in Lithuania and already in Moscow. Without exception, these people wish fervently to emigrate to the United States or Canada or Palestine. In these times, virtually the only way to leave Europe is to sail from Vladivostok to Japan. And from here, to go on to whatever final destination one choses."

In a sense, this mid-March meeting was a formality: Warhaftig's assistant had already met with low-level managers of the shipping firm to ensure that both sides were in agreement. Now that they were secure in their knowledge that both sides were already in agreement, the powerful and influential Japanese businessmen before him were willing to discuss its details with Warhaftig.

"Now, what I am proposing is simply this, that every one of those *tens of thousands* of refugees travel from Japan to their destinations exclusively in NYK ships. *Exclusively.* They will pay full fare. They will pay in cash. They will all leave from Japanese ports with destination visas in hand. Many will be crossing the Pacific to the United States or Australia; others will be going all the way to Palestine. A few perhaps will go only to Shanghai. But wherever they go, they will travel with NYK and *only* with NYK. We will guarantee this. We will even deposit money for the tickets in an escrow account here in Japan. Thousands of passengers, hundreds of thousands of dollars guaranteed.

The firm's two directors were definitely interested. Warhaftig would not be here if they were not. Now, as he outlined his proposal himself, it seemed even more alluring . . . and one of them admitted as much. "However," he concluded, "I believe this is only part of the proposal?"

"Quite right. There is one problem which must be solved before we will actually be able to provide you with these passengers. Japan stands between Vladivostok and America, and the Japanese Embassy in Moscow has stopped issuing transit visas. What we would ask you to do is to suggest to your government that it would benefit all of Japan – particularly NYK, but also Japan's image in the eyes of the Western world – if she began again to issue the visas."

The directors nodded, and one spoke: "But let me ask you, Mr. Warhaftig. America has not been so . . . shall we say, *prepared* to welcome refugees during the past several months. I believe there have also been some restrictions placed on Jewish people entering Palestine. Are you *sure* those conditions will change?"

That was, at the least, a polite understatement of the situation, but Warhaftig's reassurance seemed one hundred percent sincere.

"Absolutely. I am completely certain that America will change her policy and will welcome these refugees – as she has so many times in the past welcomed refugees from world catastrophes. As for Palestine, as you know, I personally represent the Palestine Committee here in Japan."

He said no more, trusting in the implications of the statement. The two directors looked closely at the young man seated across from them. He was *so* young. But most of the prime-movers among the foreigners seemed so young. NYK was well aware of the European refugee situation and well aware that there were reasons beyond the overcrowded conditions in Vladivostok that had blocked the transit visas. They had already investigated Warhaftig thoroughly enough to know that he was, indeed, the executive officer of the Palestine Committee, and that he had considerable connections to the Jewish leadership in the United States. There were, however, two points on which they would have to reassure themselves: the minor question of whether Warhaftig really could convince American Jews to deposit a sizable amount of money in an escrow account in Japan (a minor question because there seemed little doubt that he could), and the major question of whether the destination countries really would accept sizable numbers of refugees. The immigration policies of America, for one, seemed to be growing more, rather than less, strict. NYK knew well that the Japanese government thought there were already far too many hopeless refugees in Japan.

But if this scheme could be made to work, it would be a great boon to NYK. Its passenger business had come to a virtual standstill with the unsettled conditions in the world. Here was a man known to be in constant touch with the top Jewish leaders, and, by extension, with all the important people in the American government, assuring them there was absolutely no question but that the United States would be changing its immigration policy. The NYK directors also remembered another occasion when their firm had passed up a similar proposal. Twenty-one years before, in 1919 when Yokohama had been the temporary home of over seventeen hundred Jewish refugees from the Bolshevik Revolution, NYK had *not* had the foresight to arrange for that chunk of business, and eventually lost it to a more aggressive competitor. At that time, in spite of its apparently strict immigration policies, the United States had ultimately let in all those refugees. Jews were powerful in the United States, no question about it. NYK was powerful in Japan. Powerful enough, perhaps, to be able to secure the transit visas. And when two strong forces act in concert . . . a great deal of money can often be made.

The directors nodded and smiled; Warhaftig knew he had been successful. The details of the proposals were smoothed out; a preliminary number of two thousand refugees was decided upon for the first shipment. NYK would get back to him within a few days, confirming its belief that the Japanese government would go along with the idea. Then Warhaftig's problem would be explaining the details to the World Jewish Congress, the most likely source to guarantee the money.

With the dignity befitting the chief executive officer of the Palestine Committee, Warhaftig left NYK and returned to the office of the Yokohama Relief Committee. Once there, he exploded with enthusiasm to the delighted committee members: "They accepted! They will speak for us to the *Gaimusho*! They are sure they will be successful! I am sure they will be successful! Imagine it – hundreds of thousands of Jews rescued from the hell of Europe! They can come! Saved, for the price of a steamship ticket!"

All the accomplishments of his thirty-odd years were as nothing compared to this. Three days later, he had confirmation from NYK: the transit visas would begin flowing again as soon as the agreed-upon amount of money had been guaranteed. Warhaftig immediately sent his cable to the World Jewish Congress.

A week later, Warhaftig was sitting in Ponve's comfortable living room, shaking his head, still not comprehending what had gone wrong. The WJC had cabled back an astonishingly brief refusal. "This is not the way to handle matters," the reply had said. "You are putting the cart before the horse. First the refugees go to Japan. Then, of course, and without a moment's hesitation, we will provide money for their onward journey – on NYK or whichever line or lines you wish to deal with. The money is not the problem. But we cannot supply it until we know that the refugees are in a position to use it."

At his wit's end, Warhaftig had appealed to another executive officer of the World Jewish Congress and to the Joint Distribution Committee. "It is not a backward way of handling it," he tried to explain, "for the Japanese it is the *only* way." But to no avail. The

Americans were suspicious and simply would not consider tying up tens of thousands of dollars on what appeared to be a plan with no reality to it. The Americans were organization people: nothing was too ambitious to attempt so long as they knew exactly what they were doing. In this case they were being asked to have blind faith in another culture's *modus operandi*, but when they could not be certain of what their money was really going for, they simply could not bring themselves to act.

With tears in his eyes, Warhaftig glanced through the desperate yellow cablegrams that had been coming into Jewcom ever since the issuing of Japanese transit visas had been stopped. Half a dozen consisted only of a single word: HATZILU! (Save us!) But there was no way. Those who had secured their visas before March 17 would, no doubt, be permitted to leave Russia and enter Japan. Those who had not were lost.

"Why don't you come out with us, Getzel? The weather is fine. It would be good for you to take a walk. . . . Don't you think so? Getzel?"

Cheya Syrkin stood near the door of their clean airy *tatami*-floored room in the *heim*. Already Dovid was in the tiny, stone-floored entryway that adjoined their room, putting on the shoes that could never be worn within the room itself – they would have wrecked the *tatami* straw floor in half a day. Within the room, Getzel lay on the floor, a pillow under his head, a book he had long since finished lying open on his chest.

"I may go to Jewcom a little later," he said without spirit.

"You were there just this morning," she reminded him. "Come with us instead to the park. It will be so pretty. Mrs. Evans said this is the week the cherry blossoms are at their very best."

"Perhaps later." Getzel was not looking at her.

Always the same, she sighed to herself; always a "later" that never came. All day long her husband would either lie here in their room or walk the same five blocks to Jewcom and simply sit – not talking, maybe not even listening, just existing in the Yiddish environment, the last link to his memories of the *shul* at Alexandrov. Ever since Moscow Cheya had been the one who had to deal with all the details. Yet, "my husband would like to know – my husband requested that I ask . . . my husband feels . . ." always prefaced each of her questions – an attempt (usually unsuccessful) to keep up the appearance that he was in command of his family. It was an extremely awkward situation: her husband, after all, was there in person at Jewcom every day. Why wasn't he able to ask the questions for himself? Nonetheless, they were all kind – the Evanses, the Ponves, the Hanins, all of them, so very unexpectedly understanding and sympathetic. Not only did they never give the impression they felt anything was wrong with the Syrkin family arrangement, they had gone out of their way to make everything easier right from the beginning. No sooner had the Syrkins arrived and been settled by the Ladies Committee in their *heim* than Mrs. Hanin herself had come. Cheya had been flustered. Mrs. Hanin was a wealthy woman! She had a house with two servants; she had a motorcar. Yet, this same Mrs. Hanin took the time to show Cheya where and how to buy food from the Japanese, and where the ritual bath, the *mikveh*, was located. Moreover, in Dovid, Mrs. Hanin took a special interest: buying him apples, finding him an extra sweater, introducing him to other children – taking him out for walks sometimes with little Sophie Katznelson – and to his everlasting delight, even taking him for a ride in her motorcar!

"I'm ready, Mama," Dovid said, standing up in the little entry-way down one high step from their private room. Cheya sat on the step and pulled on her own cracked black shoes.

"We will buy a fish for dinner," she called back to Getzel who had not moved.

"Is it Friday?" he asked with mild surprise.

"It's Tuesday. But if we have another meal of eggs, we are going to turn into chickens!"

Like most of the refugees who followed the strict Jewish dietary laws, the Syrkins existed on a regimen of the rationed bread plus egg, fish, fruit, and vegetables which Cheya bought daily in the little neighborhood stores and cooked in the rudimentary kitchen of the *heim*. Chicken had to be specially slaughtered and inspected before it could be eaten which made it hard to come by.

Sighing once more over Getzel's state of mind, Cheya took Dovid by the hand and slid open the door. Her son, at least, would get out to the park.

The cherry trees in the little park a few blocks from the *heim* were, indeed, at the peak of their brief mid-March perfection. Clouds of pale pink and white blossoms crowned every tree, shimmering in a gentle breeze or cascading down like a rain of silk to settle softly on the clusters of people sitting on the ground beneath the branches. A few men were carousing with tiny cups of *sake*, fulfilling the Japanese custom of toasting the fleeting beauty of the cherry blossoms. From these, Cheya kept her distance, walking instead toward a small playground in the opposite corner of the park.

"Do you want to swing, Dovid'l" she asked, knowing what the answer would be. From the moment he had first spotted the swings in this playground so near their *heim* there had never been any question of where Dovid wanted to spend every waking hour.

Smiling shyly at the Japanese mothers who were there as always, watching over their own little round-faced black-haired children, Cheya watched Dovid climb onto the swing. "I'm flying," he called out, his legs stuck out stiff in front of him, his body tense with pleasure at the wonderful sensation. Cheya took as much pleasure from his enjoyment of it as Dovid did from the swing.

After a few moments, though, she was surprised to hear one of the Japanese women standing nearby speak in German. "He is a fine-looking boy," the lady said.

Cheya turned. To her utter astonishment, it appeared that the woman had been speaking to *her*. Always, she had smiled at these other mothers, even nodded in return to their little bows of greeting. But it had never occurred to her that actually there could be any communication in words with a Japanese.

"Do you speak German?" the woman spoke again, hesitantly, as if she feared she had made a mistake.

Now there was no doubt that this woman, this Japanese woman dressed like all the others in a gray kimono wrapped at the middle with a long soft sash, had actually spoken to *her*.

"Yes, a little," Cheya said in Yiddish. "I understand a little."

To be precise, she understood only those German words and constructions that were the same in Yiddish – but the two languages were closely related.

"I have seen you here before," the woman said, carefully pronouncing each word as if she had previously worked out the sentence and was now reciting it from memory. "I hoped I could speak to you. I have brought a little gift for your son. May I give it to him?"

Dovid's swing by now had slowed to a gentle rock. Though he could catch only a word or two, "gift" was one of them. Cheya looked over to see his brown eyes, staring at the Japanese lady.

"Yes . . . I'm . . . of course. . . ." Unaccustomed to receiving gifts at all, and especially from strangers, Cheya mumbled nervously as she watched the woman go off toward the benches alongside the swing area. From the periphery of her awareness, she heard responding giggles from half a dozen other mothers who had been watching the encounter intently – not understanding the foreign words but sensing the mood of them. Bright-eyed, they held their hands over their mouths, as if to hide their laughter. But behind their laughter, Cheya sensed not ridicule but only embarrassment like her own.

The German-speaking woman returned, now holding a small, square, colorfully wrapped box. "May I give it to him?" she asked again.

"I am sure he will be quite happy to receive it," Cheya replied, having recovered her dignity. "Dovid," she spoke more quickly, "get down off the swing and come here. This fine lady has something for you!"

If anything, Dovid was even less accustomed to receiving bright colored boxes than his mother. He, however, was not at all nervous. Considering the wrapping paper an integral part of the gift, he took his time carefully folding it back. Then he opened the box to find a beautiful red and yellow rubber ball, brand new and shiny, just waiting to be bounced.

"For me?" he whispered.

"For you," his mother said softly, her voice catching in her throat. "Say thank you."

"Thank you," he repeated, looking straight into the woman's gentle black eyes. Then he grabbed the ball out of the box and began bouncing it on the hard earth. It was magnificent, jumping high over his head with every bounce, a really *good* ball, just the right size for his hands.

"You are very kind," Cheya said to the woman. "It is very special for him to have such a thing."

"I wanted him to have it. I feel . . . *we* feel. . . ." The woman hesitated, not knowing how to say whatever it was she – and the others – felt toward these foreigners who had suddenly appeared in their neighborhood. She shook her head in frustration, muttering something in Japanese. But the translation eluded her.

"We want for you, good luck," she finally said simply.

"I thank you, all of you, for your kindness," Cheya said softly.

From that day on, Cheya looked forward almost as much as

Dovid to their trips to the playground. There were so few other women among the refugees in Kobe. And even among those there were great social and religious differences. They were all either, like the Amshenover rebbe's wife, so far removed from a little *shtetl* tailor's wife as to be totally unapproachable, or so *frum*, so strictly orthodox in their practice of Judaism, that they scarcely ventured out of their rooms lest they come in contact with too worldly a situation. The Japanese woman's German, Cheya eventually learned, had been taught to her in high school. Limited by the language and separated by an ocean of cultural differences the two women could never, Cheya realized, become true friends. But simply this much of a tentative contact, seeing and speaking to another woman, another mother, almost every day made Cheya feel more at home in this alien world where, in spite of the kindnesses of Jewcom, she was, to all intents and purposes alone.

Clusters of pink azaleas were already beginning to come into bloom as Captain Inuzuka passed through Yokohama in late April on one of his frequent trips back from Shanghai. Time consuming as the voyage was, he was never sorry when ordered to attend naval conference meetings in Tokyo. He enjoyed the brief sea voyage; but more important, he felt more secure when he was at the center of what was happening. As was his custom, he went directly to his home in suburban O-mori, just south of Tokyo, where his wife lay ill with the tuberculosis that had kept her from moving to Shanghai with him. Also at his home, Inuzuka kept a second office, and it was to there that Kobe Jewcom mailed its statistics each week, keeping him up to date on refugee immigration. The base figures were in the arrivals column: December 1940 – 198; January 1941 – 356; February – 969; March – 805. And that last figure was in spite of the fact that there had been no more transit visas issued after the middle of the month! But the figures that told a more significant story were the monthly departure totals: December 1940 – 91; January 1941 – 236; February – 147; March – 182. They came nowhere near balancing, or even keeping pace with the increases in the arrivals. No wonder the government felt it had to put an end to the influx. The figures for April already reflected the halt in transit visa issuance. Arrivals for the first half of the month were only a third of the comparable figure for March and less than a quarter of February's. As requested, Jewcom had also provided a running breakdown of the total refugee population as to sex and age (month-by-month, there were always three or four times as many males of military age) and as to country of origin and occupation. Inuzuka winced every time he noted this last column. Those Jews – financial wizards, invisible powers behind so many thrones, controllers of vast networks of influence! But forty-six percent of those who had come to Japan had absolutely no occupation at all!

Inuzuka spent long enough with the statistics to feel sure he knew whatever they could tell him. Then, passing through a sliding door into a small garden, he returned to the subject that had preoccupied him for the past several days.

The Germans were becoming impossible: simultaneously they were deeply suspicious of Matsuoka's recent signing of a neutrality pact with Russia and bursting with inflated confidence over their military invincibility. (With some justification, he had to admit – their military had just taken only a week to conquer all of Yugoslavia.) The combination of suspicion and arrogance was not a pleasant one, but that it should be causing strained feelings at the top of the Axis alliance was of only academic interest to Inuzuka. What he had to deal with on a practical day-to-day basis was the increasing pressure he himself faced from German sources over Japan's official treatment of the Jewish refugees.

"Why are you being so *nice* to the Jews?" he had heard more often than he cared to recall. "We Germans do everything in our power to wipe this plague off the earth and you, our allies, do everything you can to *help* them. You give them cement for their useless synagogues – cement *needed* by Japanese soldiers! You actually permit them to import strange food for their so-called Passover festival! And didn't Japan almost go back on her word to stop issuing transit visas in Moscow when some Japanese shipping company realized there was money to be made in transporting Jews? Everything you do is to *help* the Jews! This is no way for a sincere ally to act!"

He sighed: Germans could be so unpleasantly overbearing. Usually, he could turn aside the questions with accommodating answers: "we had more cement than we could use that month . . . it was only wine and a flat, tasteless cracker – harmless foods . . . we would not *really* have begun issuing the transit visas again (though he was not at all sure that was true) . . .'' But he had to admit this pressure was wearing him down. Something would have to be done, something he could point to and say, "See that? We too are working on the Jewish problem." Exactly what "that" should be, he wasn't sure. But he'd had some ideas – he would talk them over with his colleagues after this afternoon's meeting.

Inuzuka looked critically at the careful array of rocks and shrubs that created an entire landscape out of a corner of ground. Tubercular or not, his wife was a clever gardener. He thought, briefly, of his younger and considerably more vivacious mistress back in Shanghai. Though he'd never thought to ask, he suspected that gardening was not one of her talents. With a private smile, Inuzuka went inside to get ready for the meeting.

A few days later, early in May, Kobe Jewcom received a politely worded order: two leading representatives of the refugee community were to appear in three days time, in Tokyo, for a military interrogation. The order was signed by the chief secretary of the Imperial Japanese Navy.

# 11

THE FULL JEWCOM EXECUTIVE BOARD of directors met that night in Ponve's home. The living room was comfortably arranged, with Chinese carpets on the polished floor and exotically carved teak furniture softened with embroidered Chinese silk cushions. But the room was filled with anxiety and apprehension. The very word "interrogation" was over-burdened with fear. For generation upon generation of European Jews – from the Jews in Rome of the third century through the Rhineland Jews in the Middle Ages, the Spanish communities in the fourteenth and fifteenth centuries, right up to the present day in Germany and Russia – the word "interrogation" had been nothing more than a formal prelude to a whirlwind of chaos and destruction which the majority culture then felt free to inflict upon its Jews. An interrogation always resolved itself into a trial – a trial without jury, a trial in which the verdict was a foregone conclusion, to be reached through loaded questions.

"Why do you Jews drink the blood of Christian children at your Passover celebrations?"

"Why do you Jews write vicious slander against the son of God, and then have the audacity to say we are misinterpreting your words?"

"What exactly is the excuse you Jews have for denying the divinity of the Savior?"

The announcement of an interrogation was the opening move, the formal statement-of-intent that inevitably preceded the destruction or exile of a community.

"But they don't *do* things in this way in Japan," one of Jewcom's directors pointed out. "It *must* be the Germans putting them up to it."

"Not necessarily. The Germans have made enough converts by now. The Japanese could very well have figured this out all by themselves. They know how things like this have always been done."

168

"No! It's not them alone. If the order had come from the super-nationalists in the *Gaimusho*, I'd agree with you. But from the navy? What does the navy have to do with us anyway?"

"Inuzuka is in the navy."

"So Inuzuka knows he's welcome here any time – *any* time – and we will answer any questions on any subject. No, I don't think Inuzuka had any part in this. He knows us too well to use a word like 'interrogation.' And he wouldn't send a *formal* command. He's a friend. . . ."

Ponve rapped on a Chinese cedar chest and order was restored. There could be no question of refusing the order; the point to be decided, therefore, was which two leaders should represent the refugees who, in fact, recognized no single leader because they were by no means a single community. Overall, they consisted of many tightly knit groups, each too fervent in its own beliefs to join even briefly with the others. Only two things did the refugees have in common: they were all, in one form or another, Jews; and the overwhelming majority came from Poland. Beyond that, they shared no political viewpoint; they looked up to no one religious leader. They did not even share a culture hero who might at least speak for the hearts of the people if not for their minds. The executive board pondered the problem, finding no solution. Finally, Alex Triguboff spoke up:

"So, we approach it from another angle. *We* know there aren't any leaders, but who would the Japanese consider leaders? After all, what does 'Jew' mean to them? A religion. And who, in Japan, is the religious leader? The priest. And who is a Jewish 'priest?' A rabbi – these days, that's as close as we can come. So, we simply ask two rabbis to go to Tokyo!"

There was general agreement at Triguboff's premise and his conclusion. The question now was which two rabbis to send. One candidate was apparent: the Amshenover rebbe.

The rebbe was decidedly not the most cosmopolitan of the rabbinic refugees; and as a Hassid, he was certainly not, philosophically, the most representative rabbi. But he was a *mensch* – a fine man, deeply involved with his fellow men, warm, helpful, tolerant – articulate.

The Amshenover rebbe was a talker. He could captivate an audience, of one or a thousand, even if his hearers intellectually didn't believe a word he was saying. Definitely, the rebbe should be asked. And to accompany him? There were several suggestions, but the final choice was Rabbi Moses Shatzkes. Rabbi Shatzkes was not a great orator; but from his youth he had been recognized as one of the most brilliant Talmudic scholars in all of Europe. Besides, of all the rabbis in the Kobe refugee community, Shatzkes had held the highest position. At an unusually early age, he had been chosen to be the chief rabbi of Lomz, a focal point of European Jewish learning.

Anatole Ponve was due to depart for the United States within days, so Leo Hanin was delighted to accompany the two rabbis. It would be the job of Alex Triguboff to drop in at the Kobe office of Naval Intelligence, and, as Ponve suggested, "see if you can find out anything more about the circumstances of this 'interrogation.' Maybe – who knows? – maybe they just pulled the wrong synonym out of the dictionary."

The next morning, however, Naval Intelligence was not answering questions, it was asking them.

"Who will be coming to represent the Jewish refugees?" the officer in charge wanted to know.

"It hasn't been finally decided, but probably two rabbis, two religious leaders."

"Religious leaders, I see. What are their titles?"

"Rabbi Shimon K-a-l-i-s-c-h and Rabbi Moses Shatzkes, S-h-a-t-z-k-e-s.

"Those are titles?"

"Those are their names."

"Ah, yes. But what are their titles?"

Triguboff paused, uncertain. "Rabbi Kalisch is known as the Amshenover rebbe. Rabbi Shatzkes is sometimes referred to as the Lomzer rabbi."

"Is a 'rebbe' higher than a 'rabbi'?"

"Higher?"

"Yes, higher, more powerful, more respected."

"No, not higher. Just a little different. A little more personal."

The intelligence officer appeared genuinely puzzled.

Triguboff tried again: "The difference between 'rabbi' and 'rebbe' is very slight," he said. "Both men can properly be addressed as rabbi. And both are very well respected by all the refugees and all of us. And by Jews all over the world," he added. (There was considerable doubt that anyone outside of his immediate circle of followers and a few acquaintances had ever heard of the Amshenover rebbe; but certainly the Japanese didn't have to know that.)

The officer nodded; but Triguboff's answer wasn't exactly what he had wanted to hear. He too tried again.

"How high are they?"

Triguboff didn't know how to answer that. He knew the officer would never understand an accurate answer that rabbis don't come in grades. There are some who are particularly scholarly. Others, the "rebbes," develop extremely close personal relationships with their followers. There are full-time rabbis, and rabbis who spend their entire lives as shoemakers or furriers and never turn their ordination degree into a profession. But no type is higher or lower than any other.

"They are both very high," he said, finally.

"But *how* very high?" the officer insisted.

"They are as high as possible! They are . . . are next to God!" Triguboff exclaimed.

From a Jewish point of view, this was such a totally meaningless concept that Triguboff wondered later how the words had entered his mind in the first place. But the intelligence officer was not a Jew.

"Ahhh! They are next to *God*. Now I know. Yes, yes, 'Next to God.' That is very, very high. Thank you, Triguboff-san. Thank you for coming."

The intelligence officer rose and directed his visitor out the door. Triguboff hung back, trying to learn more details; but the officer would not hear him. It seemed that the interrogation was not to be discussed beforehand. The two "next-to-God" rabbis would have to cope with it as best they could with no advance information.

Walking unhappily back to his business office, Alex could almost sense what might be coming: the interrogation; some sort of charges, probably espionage; a deportation order. . . . And then what? Would the United States finally let down the barrier? Would Australia open up? Where would nearly two thousand people go? And if Japan expelled the Jewish refugees, how would she feel about the twenty-five resident Jewish families who had been responsible for them?

The Sunday evening overnight train to Tokyo left Kobe exactly on schedule. On board, along with the normal passenger contingent of some two hundred and fifty Japanese was the small entourage of Jews. The Amshenover rebbe and Rabbi Shatzkes had both agreed instantly to represent the refugee community at the interrogation. Rabbi Shlomo Shapiro, a tall young linguist, had offered to help with the translating; and Hanin was ready, as always, not only to translate but to do whatever else he could to bridge the cultural gap between Japanese and Jew.

Because sleeping-car reservations had not been obtainable on such short notice, the rabbis and Hanin rode in a coach – which gave them no privacy whatever. The Japanese were much amused by the long, black formal satin coats and broad-brimmed hats of the two bearded old men. They laughed and pointed and talked, and every so often a particularly brave child would quietly come over for a closer look and maybe a gentle touch of the satin cloth. But the Japanese could not have been more gracious in their actual dealings with the "strange foreigners": extra room was made for the Jews; tangerines, balls of rice wrapped in seaweed, even *sake* was offered to them. The rabbis – accustomed to being the center of attention and knowing full well how similar the response would be if a Japanese in full kimono turned up in Poland – smiled at the children, politely refused the offerings of food and drink, and made themselves as comfortable as possible.

The mood changed abruptly, however, when a group of Nazi soldiers passed through the car. The Germans, taken completely by surprise at finding *Jews* in an otherwise unremarkable Japanese conveyance, reacted brutally. "Parasites! Pigs!" they screamed in German as they kicked at the rabbis legs, grabbed at their beards, spat into their faces. "You think you are safe here? Hah! You are safe *nowhere*. We will annihilate you. We will eradicate your whole stinking, sub-human race from the face of the earth! You are doomed, Jews. Soon you will all be dead."

Hanin could feel his stomach churning. There were few committed Nazis in Kobe, and those few directed their anti-Semitism into non-violent propaganda displays. Bare-faced hatred, physical abuse of defenseless old men was something he had only heard of in the vivid tales of refugees and in the railroad car. Hanin had no idea how to respond. He himself was not a violent person, not a fighter. But how could he simply sit there? Yet the rabbis were doing exactly that – sitting there, eyes averted, turning away from the spittle, avoiding those blows and kicks that they could avoid, accepting those they couldn't. Unlike Hanin, they *had* seen it before and much worse than this. Hitler's army, and Himmler's paramilitary *Einsatzgruppen* police had not come gently into Poland in 1939. The rebbe and Shatzkes and Shapiro knew that here they could make no response. Sometimes a Jew simply has to put up with what comes.

Fortunately, the encounter was not protracted. After one verse of the "Horst Wessel" song ("When Jewish blood flows from the knife, things will go much better . . ."), the soldiers, moved on, bored by the lack of response. In the unnatural silence that followed – the Japanese passengers were aghast at the attack but did nothing to interfere – the rabbis cleaned themselves as best they could. Then, they took out the thermos bottles of hot tea that they had brought along, stirred in a few spoonfuls of jam, and began talking quietly, as if nothing had happened at all. Hanin excused himself and went to the lavatory where he was sick. As an omen, the acts of the Nazis did not bode well for the upcoming interrogation.

Toward midnight, the train passed along a stretch of track that lay right by the Pacific. The night was clear and the moonlight reflected off the quiet waves. The three rabbis talked and talked, about everything but the upcoming confrontation. Hanin, finally, could no longer resist asking a question that had been worrying him: "What will you say if the generals ask you why the Germans hate the Jews?"

The rebbe didn't even look up, only laughed softly. "*Zorg zich nicht:* don't worry about it."

"But I really do not anticipate a pleasant discussion with them, rebbe," Hanin continued.

Because of Hanin's concern, the rebbe gave fuller attention to the subject. "I think such exchanges never begin as 'pleasant.' But the beginning is less important than the end. If we are correct in our suspicions and fears, they will walk into the meeting room despising us. *That* we can do nothing about. By the way, do you know if there will be Germans at the meeting? That is, since you think the Germans put them up to this. . . ."

Rabbi Shatzkes also looked to Hanin for his response. Shatzkes' entire family – parents, brothers and sister and a vast network of cousins and in-laws – was still in Poland. Only his wife and a son had been able to get out with him. Every news report of German atrocities tore at his soul. The Germans were Edom and Amalek,

Sodom and Gomorrah, Baal, Moloch and Haman all together, united and distilled into an essence of unmitigated evil. Violence was not a part of Shatzkes's personality. But he was certain that he could not sit across the table from a German and exchange words on any subject.

Hanin could offer no guidance. "No one would give any details. Naval Intelligence wouldn't even listen to Triguboff's questions. We have never before been in such a situation with the Japanese. Whoever has arranged this must purposely be keeping us in the dark."

"That in itself is, no doubt, part of the threat," Rabbi Shatzkes said. "You have said – everyone has said – that there was never any problem before from the Japanese. So, why now? Is there anything someone might have done wrong? Any incident, any argument, even anything that might appear to be a personal slight or insult?"

"That was *my* first reaction: what have we done wrong?" Hanin said. "But I have wracked my brain and come up with nothing." He considered briefly whether or not to mention Warhaftig's aborted transit-visas-for-tickets scheme to them – in Japanese eyes, the Jews had lost considerable face over that. But he decided it was too complicated, and probably not important after all.

"We have very clean hands, I think," was all he said.

"There was a problem with the steamship company a few weeks ago, wasn't there?" the rebbe asked. A Jew promised something and the World Jewish Congress refused to back him up? But was that 'loss of face', as they call it, serious enough to warrant something like this?"

Hanin just stared at him. The old man said nothing, only sat there, pleased with himself and with the grapevine that kept him informed about virtually everything that happened among the Jews.

Shatzkes had been gazing out the window, watching the shadowy outlines of a small town as it passed by.

"If the Japanese were agreeable before, and if we have done nothing, then why do you think they have had this change of heart? You know the Japanese better than we do."

Hanin could only shake his head. "I think it can only be the Germans. They are very successful right now, and the Japanese are very, very fond of success. Perhaps, up to now, they felt they could, and should, hold out against, the advice of the Germans.

But no one seems to be able to stand up to the Germans – not England, not France. Maybe now the Japanese think: 'We've chosen the winner; why not go all the way with him?'"

They were silent for a moment, the only sounds in the car were the snores of their fellow passengers. "What will you say if they ask you why Jews are persecuted by the Nazis?" Hanin asked again.

The response was no more satisfying this time than last. Rabbi Shatzkes again said nothing. The Amshenover rebbe said only: "We will see. We will simply have to do our best, *im yirzeh ha-Shem*. Now, as I am an old man, I need some sleep." Wrapping his coat more tightly around him, he retreated into his brief night prayers. Shortly thereafter, he was asleep. A few minutes later, after staring quietly out at the passing rice paddies for several miles, Shatzkes too, said his prayers and closed his eyes.

Hanin could not sleep. Tomorrow could destroy the whole refugee effort – and possibly the refugees as well. And tomorrow had been entrusted to two old men who didn't seem to be sufficiently concerned about the danger. They slept – and Hanin worried – till the sun came up not far out of Kamakura.

At 8:17, as promptly as it had departed Kobe thirteen hours before, the train pulled into Tokyo station. Hanin had been informed that they would be met at the station; but he was not prepared for the person who appeared.

"Dr. Kotsuji! Is this a coincidence or are you here officially?"

"Good morning! I am here 'officially,' as you put it. This is Captain Fukamachi," he introduced the young man in civilian clothes standing next to him, "and we have come to escort you to the naval officers' headquarters."

Delighted at this first positive note in the proceedings, Hanin introduced the rabbis. Both Kotsuji and Fukamachi bowed low with respect and the entourage made its way out of the crowded station.

"Dr. Kotsuji," Hanin said quietly as they waited for a driver to bring the official car, "we are a little in the dark as to the purpose of this discussion. Do you know what it is about, why we have been asked to come here, what they want to know from us? It is always better to be prepared beforehand for these things. If you could perhaps enlighten us. . . ."

"Oh, no!" Kotsuji said airily. "Don't worry. I know nothing about it at all. They merely asked me to meet you here and bring you to the correct address. No problem. Weren't the cherry blossoms beautiful this year, Hanin-san?"

Hanin was not reassured. He was even less so when he learned that they would proceed directly to the interrogation, leaving the two old men no time to rest, eat or recover from the rigors of the trip. The Japanese could be inadvertently inconsiderate, but they were usually solicitous for the elderly. The rabbis themselves, however, seemed unperturbed. They chatted with Kotsuji in elementary Hebrew about the state of the yeshivas in Kobe, and expressed their appreciation to him when Hanin told them of Kotsuji's part in finding rooms for the students. However, once again it seemed to Hanin that the two rabbis were not fully aware of the gravity of the situation.

The naval officers' headquarters was four stories of yellow brick gleaming in the sun and set luxuriously back behind a clean sweep of lawn. At the door, waiting to greet them, was a translator introduced by Kotsuji only as Mr. Fujisawa, and an assistant whose name Hanin failed to catch. Much to his dismay, Fujisawa immediately divided the group in two: Hanin, Rabbi Shapiro and Kotsuji were ushered into a small sitting room, while the Amshenover rebbe and Rabbi Shatzkes, with Fukamachi and the translator, were led off down a long paneled corridor. Rabbi Shapiro hung back, protesting with great concern that his place was with the two older men, no matter where they were going. Hanin himself requested, with more decorum, that he also would like to accompany the two rabbis, but to no avail. Dr. Kotsuji politely insisted that both men join him in a small sitting room.

"They will be fine," he said blandly. "Don't concern yourselves. It is not necessary for you to be with them. Mr. Fujisawa is one of the best translators in Japan. Please, sit here. Would you like some tea?"

Kotsuji gestured to a comfortable armchair covered in white linen with antimacassars on the back and arms. Hanin had no choice but to accept the unwanted tea and attempt small talk. Shapiro perched on the edge of another chair and gnawed at his nails.

They waited there only a few minutes before Fujisawa, the translator, appeared. "Hanin-san, would you be so kind as to come with me. We are having small problems."

Hanin rose with a bound, relieved to be included but anxious at the "small problems." Shapiro was instantly at his side. The translator started to say his services were not needed, but noting the determination on the man's face, he was persuaded that perhaps *all* of them should come.

Hanin and Rabbi Shapiro found Rabbi Shatzkes and the Amshenover rebbe seated in the windowless antechamber of a conference room. On the far side of a low table – abundantly spread with non-kosher foods – were four admirals in dress uniforms. Heads shaven, arms folded stiffly across their chests, they sat motionless. The two rabbis were calmly drinking green tea, waiting till their hosts could solve the problem of carrying out the interrogation. Unfortunately Yiddish had stumped Mr. Fujisawa, the "best translator in Japan."

It was Captain Fukamachi's suggestion that Hanin would translate from Yiddish to English and Fujisawa would take it from English to Japanese. This would be tedious but possible. The admiral furthest to the left – the first among equals – grunted a monosyllable of approval. Hanin seated himself beside the rabbis and awaited the customary opening pleasantries.

They were brief. In fact, Hanin thought with dismay, considering the usual time-consuming graciousness that customarily began such formal encounters, they were just short of insulting. "We appreciate your coming today; we appreciate your cooperating with us. . . ." Then, suddenly, the opening shot.

"What is the inherent evil of your people that our friends the Germans hate you so much?"

None of the admirals, not even the one who had spoken, deigned to look at the objects of the question. The query was translated across the double barrier.

Rabbi Shatzkes was the more eminent scholar, and the rebbe deferred to him. But Rabbi Shatzkes had no answer. What could one say to such a question? How does one confront such arrogance, such a void of knowledge. Where does one begin? "Why do they hate us?" Shatzkes had often asked himself exactly that in the face of a lifetime of senseless atrocities that he had witnessed in Europe before his escape. Why? Why? Why was an old Jewish grandmother shot in the eyes for not being able to move as quickly as her grandchild? Why were the beards ripped from the faces of harmless old men leaving white dots of bone visible through the broken, bleeding skin? Why?

"The Nazis hate the Jews because the Nazis know that we Jews are Asians."

It was the Amshenover rebbe who had spoken. Scarcely three seconds had passed between the posing of the question and this calm response. It surprised the admiral, not because the rebbe rather then Shatzkes had answered – in Japan older people are expected to speak first – but because of its totally unforeseen nature. The admiral involuntarily shifted his eyes to look directly at the rebbe.

"What does this mean – you are Asians. We are Asians!"

"Yes," the rebbe agreed. "And you are also on the list."

"What list?"

The Amshenover rebbe smiled a smile so supremely calm, so warm, so totally out of keeping with the threatening atmosphere which the officers had tried to create that, in spite of themselves, all four of them leaned forward, waiting for him to speak further.

"My dear friends, I have just come from Europe. I have lived with the great hate that the Nazis have for others. I think that perhaps no one who has not lived in the midst of it can understand it. But to get even an inkling of the scope of their hate, don't read their writings in the censored translations they give you. Read what Nazis write in the original German. There, you will learn that you also are on their list of 'inferior people.' So are the gypsies, the blacks, the Slavs . . . and the Japanese.

"Let me tell you a story," the rebbe continued, sitting back slightly in the hard chair. "In Berlin, not many years ago, perhaps three or four, a young German girl fell in love with a fine young man, a Japanese man, who was working at the Japanese Embassy. Naturally enough, the two young people wanted to marry, but such a thing could not be in Germany. Such a marriage was for-bidden by law, by the laws of 'racial purity,' which prohibit a fine German girl from marrying a . . . Japanese."

All four admirals were now staring at the rebbe, not even trying to conceal their interest. They had heard such stories about America which had changed its immigration laws to keep out the "Japs" or about the British who called Asians "Yellow Monkeys." And now, what was this man saying? That Japan's most successful ally – those who would rule the world with her – that the Germans too thought in such terms?

"You are lying," the first admiral said.

"No," the rebbe said, calmly. "Consider for yourself: What is the image of Hitler's master race? How does he describe it? In films, documentaries, newspapers, who is shown bringing victory home to the German fatherland? Always, *always*, the so-called Aryans. Tall, broad-shouldered, blond hair, blue eyes. . . . I am not six feet tall. I do not have blue eyes. I don't have blond hair – even before it turned white my hair was not blond. The reason they hate me, the reason they hate all of us, is because we don't fit the image of the Aryan master race."

He said no more. There was no need to point out the scarcity of tall, broad-shouldered, blond, blue-eyed Japanese.

The admirals sat staring straight ahead for a long time after the old man had finished. Hanin, who had been merely a mouthpiece, neither adding nor subtracting an iota of the rebbe's words, seemed to have absorbed, in passing, some of his tranquility. Now he and the others were content to sit in silence. Quiet voices, not associated with this meeting, could be heard occasionally from the corridor outside. Finally, the first-among-equals let out a long nasal sigh and began speaking to his three associates. Barely imposing on the surrounding quiet, the four men spoke in gutteral undertones which even Fujisawa, the translator, could not make out. Eventually, one of the lesser admirals spoke directly to him.

"Tell our Jewish guests there will now be a brief recess. Tell them we have been inexcusably inconsiderate in not allowing them time to rest from their long trip and in not offering proper refreshments. Tell them we will meet in two hours time in a more comfortable place." He paused, then added, "And be polite, Fujisawa-san."

After the translation, the four officers stood as the Jews were shown out of the interrogation room. Fukamachi led the way to a suite of clean, Western-style rooms overlooking the garden behind the building and left them.

Drained, Hanin slumped into a chair and offered quiet congratulations to the two rabbis. Shatzkes said little; the Amshenover rebbe was only a little more communicative.

"The truth is difficult to avoid when it is set before you at your own request," he said. "Now, if you don't mind, I will claim the privilege of age and lie down right here to take a nap." He stretched out on one of the beds. Shapiro laid a blanket over him. Within seconds, he was asleep. Rabbi Shatzkes went into the bathroom to wash.

Hanin stared unseeing at the formal garden, his muscles slowly turning to jelly. He was no more than vaguely concerned about the plans for the afternoon. He had stood on the brink of a catastrophe – the destruction of the entire refugee community as predicated so brutishly by those Nazi soldiers on the train the night before. Then he had witnessed an old man dissolve the danger with a handful of words. Almost too exhausted to feel even relief, he let his eyes close, and he too slept.

When several hours later, the Jews were shown into a large conference room lined with windows, the atmosphere was entirely different. Again the four admirals were lined up proudly on one side of a table – their shaven heads glistening in the sunlight that streamed in past the open drapes. But now, seated beside them, were two newcomers, resplendent in long white robes and tall stiff black hats tied decorously under their chins. They were high-ranking *Shinto* priests Hanin realized, definitely "next to God." The heavy table had been set out with the inevitable tea, but also with bowls of apples and bananas and tangerines, plates of seaweed-wrapped rice balls and small mounds of chilled spinach in a sauce of sesame seeds and soy. Gone were the lobsters and other non-kosher dishes, and gone was the heavy hand of the military. The admirals were merely for show. Throughout the next four hours, they said not a word. From the opening greeting through the final farewells, the two priests were entirely in control.

The discussion centered almost exclusively on religion: comparisons and contrasts between *Shinto* and Judaism, extended explanations of the theory of common origin (that the Japanese were descended, in part, from one of the "ten lost tribes" which had come to Japan) and the so-called "reverse theory of common origin" (that Moses had actually come to Japan to learn the wisdom of ancient *Shinto* during the forty days that the Bible had him on Mount Sinai, receiving the Torah from God). For over an hour, Rabbi Shatzkes described the basic principles, ideas and ceremonies of the Jews. The younger of the two priests responded with explanations of the customs and beliefs of *Shinto*. Of particular interest to Hanin who continued to do half the translating, was the entwined relationship between *Shinto* and Japan as religious and political state.

It was late afternoon before the meeting drew to a close. As a final note, the Amshenover rebbe repeated the gratitude of the refugees to the Japanese for taking them in and treating them so well.

An Admiral spoke briefly to the priests, and then the first admiral, in turn, reassured the rabbis. "Go back to your people. Tell them they have nothing to fear: we Japanese will do our utmost to provide for your safety and peace; you have nothing to fear while in Japanese territory."

As he waited for the rabbis' response to these final sentences, it seemed to Hanin that the other three admirals shifted, just slightly, uncomfortably in their chairs. But it was a momentary thing. When he blinked to look more closely, they were again sitting straight and still. To Hanin, and the others discussing it on the uneventful train ride back to Kobe, it seemed that their trip had been an unqualified success.

# 12

WHILE A TYPHOON of anti-Semitism was creating havoc over much of the globe, the refugees in Kobe enjoyed the tranquility of the eye of the storm. In the late spring of 1941, although these fifteen hundred Jews were totally in the hands of the ally of their most deadly enemy, they had little anxiety as to their immediate safety. For whatever reason, and none of the refugees had the vaguest idea of what that reason might be, they had landed in Japan, a haven for Jews. From Japan, they feared nothing.

By May, it was quite warm in Kobe. With little to do, the refugees relaxed in the rooms of Jewcom or milled quietly around the front-gate bulletin board where notices of accepted visa applications and other important items of news were posted. When Jewcom palled, they walked, and walked, and walked. They walked to the parks and through the parks. They walked along the broad main street of Motomachi, Kobe's colorful, crowded, brightly lit shopping area. Dodging bicycles, skirting the tiny makeshift cooking stoves that turned areas of sidewalk into instant restaurants, they traipsed from store to store, taking in at least with their eyes the abundance of products displayed.

On an allowance of one and a half yen a day, there was little beyond food that the average refugee could afford. But simply looking was a pleasure in itself. Tiring of Motomachi, the refugees might stroll along the busy docks, unwittingly alerting Japanese harbor patrolmen who saw in every foreigner a potential spy or smuggler. Alternatively they might meander through the quiet streets of any of a score of similar neighborhoods, accepting without surprise the curious glances of the Japanese residents and the vigilant observation of the omnipresent police. Until their own visa notifications appeared on the Jewcom bulletin board, the refugees had very little else to do that spring. For them, it was a time of waiting, but a time of peace.

For the refugees still in Lithuania, the spring of 1941 was neither passive nor peaceful. From southern France to central Poland, from the north of Finland to the north of Africa, the Axis was in control. Though the extent of Hitler's plan for the entire Jewish people was not yet unmistakable, the commonplace atrocities – the degradation, imprisonment, starvation and murder that had highlighted his rule from the start – were clearly not abating with time. The exodus from Vilna, which had begun as an anxious but organized journey, became a rout. Those who already had – or had forged – a Japanese transit visa and a Curaçao stamp could no longer afford to hang back, hoping the situation would still allow them to remain safely in Europe. Nor could they now afford the time needed to insure the safety of each step along the way. Cajoling non-Jews into purchasing innocent short-distance tickets for them, many set out on their own once in Russia, avoiding Intourist altogether. Beyond the knowing eyes of the NKVD, refugees with rubles could safely purchase cheap tickets for themselves from one station to the next, and not arouse suspicion. When their money ran out, they hid, trembling with fear, under seats or slipped from one to the next, always looking back, always just a jump ahead of the conductor. Some didn't make it. Dragged from trains, they never were heard of again. But Russia was huge; only so much manpower could be delegated to tracking down fleeing Jews. For many, Vladivostok became a reality.

For the accommodations available in Vladivostok, it was *too* many. The city was soon jammed with refugees, many of whom had to be put up on straw mattresses in a requisitioned high school gymnasium, often for several weeks, until they could find a space on one of the few ships still plying the Vladivostok-Tsuruga route. The system that had been such a boon to a few thousand was breaking down. In all of April, only two hundred and eighty-five refugees managed to reach Tsuruga; in May; only a hundred and fourteen; in June, fewer than sixty-five. But June was another story altogether.

In the spring of 1941, for the refugee relief agencies in Japan, and particularly for Jewcom which dealt most intimately with the Japanese government, the system also was foundering. The Japanese policy of leniency toward the refugees had been based on the premise that those who came in would soon go out again. This was clearly not being realized. The Japanese government was well aware – through its official links to Jewcom and through the confidential reports submitted regularly by Dr. Kotsuji – that the

Jewish community was doing its utmost to find new homes for the refugees. The Hebrew Immigrant Aid Society and its European counterpart both had representatives in Kobe. Working closely with Jewcom's Emigration Committee, a handful of professionals spent days and nights interviewing refugees, cabling requests back to the United States, putting together piece by piece the money or character references or support guarantees needed for the hundreds of people who were so desperately striving to become reconnected to the normal structure of life.

HIAS was the principal channel of hope, but there were others. The Polish government in exile's representative in Japan, Count Theodore de Romer, was more than sympathetic to the plight of the refugees, using his considerable influence with the British to permit additional families to settle in Australia. He also endorsed the applications of some male Jews into Poland's government-in-exile army which was then being formed in Canada. And there was still Wahrhaftig's Palestine Committee. By means of half-truths and the occasional leniency of the British, this organization continued to send a tiny stream of Zionists on the long journey around India to Haifa. But the would-be emigrants were numbered by hundreds, and the responses could be counted by tens.

By the end of April, the Japanese were obviously becoming less sanguine about the situation in Kobe. Little was said, but transit visa extensions began to be issued for shorter periods of time. Surely, *surely* everyone agreed, the United States will soon realize the gravity of the situation. But the American assistant secretary of state, Breckinridge Long, continued to insist that "in view of reports indicating that Nazi and other totalitarian agents are endeavoring to enter the United States in the guise of refugees, it (is) considered essential in the national interest to scrutinize all applications carefully." By late spring, some of the administrators in Kobe were no longer so sure the situation would work itself out.

"Ah, Mr. Warhaftig! Please do come in!"

In his Shanghai office, at the appointed time, Captain Inuzuka looked up to greet his scheduled guest Zorach Wahrhaftig, recently arrived from a brief trip to Yokohama, returned the greeting and shook the outstretched hand. He was not overly fond of Inuzuka and had not been looking forward to his morning's meeting. But the situation had gone beyond choice.

The two men exchanged courtesies over small cups of the inevitable green tea. The wet heat of the Chinese coast hung around them like a third presence, circulated, but not dissipated by the gently turning blades of the ceiling fan.

"I understand you made a very moving address to the Shanghai municipal council," Inuzuka remarked. "We Japanese have great sympathy for those Jews who have been caught by international circumstances in a place they do not wish to be."

As bland an assessment of the situation as has yet been spoken, Warhaftig thought to himself. "We understand you do, Captain Inuzuka," he said. "We are most grateful for all the assistance you have given us."

"And I do hope your cohorts in America are aware of Japan's feelings on this matter," Inuzuka continued as he took a silver case from his pocket and offered a cigarette to his guest. "I trust you are assuring them that we are doing all that we can."

Warhaftig nodded warily. He had heard from more than one source that telling Americans how well Japan was treating Jews was actually counter productive for Japan. Even Dr. Kaufman in Harbin was being considered either a fool for letting himself be duped, or worse, a collaborator, a traitor. The World Jewish Congress and Rabbi Stephen Wise's American Jewish Congress were even now, according to rumor, thinking of curtailing relations with Dr. Kaufman. But Warhaftig had enough to worry about without getting into that.

He reached for his host's silver cigarette case on the table. Boris Topas, the president of the Shanghai Ashkenazic community, had alerted him to Inuzuka's pride in the thing. "May I read the inscription?" he asked.

"Of course!" Inuzuka reacted as expected, then proceeded to recite the words himself to his guest: "'To Captain Inuzuka – in gratitude and appreciation for your service to the Jewish people. From the Union of Orthodox Rabbis – USA Purim 5701 Frank Newman.' Are you acquainted with this Rabbi Newman, Mr. Warhaftig? A fine young man."

Inuzuka had good reason to think positively of Frank Newman. The man *was* very young. Nonetheless, he carried a letter of introduction from the Union of Orthodox Rabbis of America. So at last, Inuzuka thought, even so many months after Tamura's setback in New York with Rabbi Stephen Wise, an American Jewish organization had sent someone over to investigate. It was a very small beginning and, in fact, young Rabbi Newman hadn't done very much since his arrival a few months before. But at least it was a beginning.

Warhaftig knew better. In the first place, though it wasn't of overwhelming importance, Frank Newman was not a rabbi and – he had never pretended to be. Inuzuka had simply presumed that anyone carrying a letter from the Union of Orthodox Rabbis would be a rabbi. But that was Inuzuka's problem. More important, to Warhaftig, was the fact that although pleasant, Newman was by no means an effective force in dealing with the refugee problem. Having completed his studies, the young man had simply come to the Orient to see an interesting part of the world. His letter of introduction from the Union of Orthodox Rabbis was a courtesy, not any form of authorization.

"Newman is definitely a fine young man," Warhaftig said decisively snapping closed the cigarette case and returning it to the table. He had spent enough time on civilities.

"I have a favor to ask of you, Captain," he said. "I want to bring it up now because now I am here in Shanghai. But I hope it is a favor which will never have to be carried out."

"Such a favor is usually the best kind." Inuzuka said smoothly, slipping happily into his favorite role of "benefactor to the Jews." Warhaftig smiled politely, despising the man for his pleasure.

"As you know, in Kobe now there are still about fifteen hundred refugees. Due to the international conditions, we have very few new arrivals. But it is taking some time for us to arrange for the emigration of those already there."

Inuzuka nodded. He still received the weekly reports from Kobe.

"I am not a prophet," Warhaftig went on. "But I would not think it impossible that the time might come when Kobe would no longer be the best place for those refugees to live while arrangements are being finalized for their emigration."

Inuzuka nodded again. There was not the slightest doubt in his mind as to what was coming. But he said nothing: first the Jew asks, then the Japanese responds. To Warhaftig, sixteen hundred lives were at stake; he had no qualms of false pride.

"If such a time should come that the refugees would have to leave Kobe, would you give your permission for them to come to Shanghai?"

186

"Ahhhh," Inuzuka nodded slowly as if only now comprehending.

Naturally, transferring the Jews to Shanghai was the only sensible thing to do with them – he had realized that long ago. As a navy man, he had, from the beginning, been wary of having so many foreigners living so close to the Kobe docks, well-guarded as the facilities were. And as director of refugee affairs in Shanghai, his importance would not be diminished by the arrival of sixteen hundred additional charges. But nothing should ever come easy for the Jews.

Inuzuka rose and went over to the window as if to contemplate. From this vantage point, three stories above the street, he could see trolleys, cars and trucks – many more than in Tokyo – bicycles, rickshaws and pedestrians jostling for space in the mid-morning sunshine. And down every narrow wooden wharf an endless belt of Chinese coolies moved goods from waterside warehouses to open lighters which would ultimately transport their cargo to the large freighters moored in deeper water. Straight ahead of him, out in the middle depths, Inuzuka could clearly see the Japanese battleship *Izumo*, scene of so many meetings between himself, Yasue and Ishiguro about these Jews.

"I already have about seventeen thousand of your refugees here now," Inuzuka began, in a tone meant to convey the hardship of such a situation. "You know, I am sure, the hardship being suffered by those already here. More arrivals will mean less for everyone."

Warhaftig had heard variations on that argument in every refugee context around the world. More refugees would "create anti-Semitism in America . . . disrupt the traditional British way-of-life . . . create chaos in Australia. . . ." Wasn't anyone considering the alternative?

"Of course," he said reassuringly, "we are sure that the Joint Distribution Committee will continue to support the Polish Jews once they are in Shanghai, as it is doing now in Kobe."

"But are you so sure, Mr. Warhaftig, that the refugees will not be permitted into the United States?"

"On the contrary, Captain Inuzuka, I believe they *will* be. It is merely a question of time. It could be that tomorrow the Americans will change their minds. As I said at the outset, this is a favor that may never have to be asked. But if the situation were to arise. . . ."

The two men looked steadily at each other. The Polish lawyer had presented his case. The Japanese militarist knew there could be only one decision. But for effect and for the pleasure it gave him, he dragged the situation out as long as he could.

"I do understand the problem, Mr. Warhaftig," he said at last. "If we Japanese do not provide a refuge for these unfortunate people, there may be nowhere for them to go. Therefore, of course, if the time comes when they must leave Kobe and no other country is open to them, they will be welcome in Shanghai."

Wahrhaftig said nothing for a moment, then he smiled and rose to leave. "I am very grateful to you, Captain Inuzuka. Very grateful indeed."

He continued to smile as they shook hands and exchanged closing pleasantries. But as he closed the door behind him, he swore in his heart that he would *never* rest till the day came that no Jew would ever again have to seek refuge in someone else's land. They would have their own.

A few days after his meeting with Inuzuka, Warhaftig returned to Japan. A few days later the United States did, at last, change its immigration regulations for the worse. One simple question was added to the American visa application form: "Do you have any relatives in enemy-overrun territory?" The refugees were understandably suspicious of its intent. Who did *not* have relatives who had believed that, as so many times before, this too would pass, and that they would be better off staying in their homes? What kind of a question was this for a visa application; and what was the right answer?

"It's just a question," the American consul in Kobe replied blandly. He had been briefed on how to handle these refugees. "Just answer the truth."

So, with that advice, and being afraid not to answer the truth, the overwhelming majority of the refugees admitted that they did leave relatives back home. And that, for them, was the end of America. The State Department had decided that people with relatives in enemy-held lands were vulnerable to blackmail. Such security risks certainly could not be accepted into the United States. From mid-June on, a future in the United States ceased even to be a dream for all but a few of the thirteen hundred refugees who, by then remained in Kobe. By the end of that month, they were just as completely cut off from their lands of their past.

At 4:00 on Sunday afternoon, it was announced that Germany, carrying her treaty allies with her, had declared war on the U.S.S.R.

Now, no more ships at all would come from Vladivostok to Tsuruga. Those parents, brothers, cousins and friends who had not made it out by now, never would. Since the end had begun in 1933, seven hundred and eighty-five thousand Jews had fled from Europe. Of these, approximately four thousand six hundred had escaped through Japan, many of them with no other backing than the strange benevolence of the Japanese Foreign Ministry and War Department. Now all had come who would ever come. A curtain of war was now closed across Europe. When it opened again in 1945, three quarters of the European Jewish population would be dead.

Like the rest of the world, the Jewish refugees in Kobe did not know that. They knew only that there was no America for them to turn toward and no Europe for them to dream of returning to. There was only Kobe, where the Japanese no longer wanted them. And there was Shanghai.

# Part Three

# SHANGHAI
# 1941–45

## The
## Challenge
## to
## Survival

# 13

FOR MOST OF THE REFUGEES, Shanghai was not entirely *terra incognita*. While they were still in Europe they had heard that a few people had emigrated to the International Settlement – though the great majority of those who had done so had come from Germany and Austria and therefore had very little connection with Polish Jews. And it was also known that there was some sort of Jewish communal life in the city. But even after the refugees reached Kobe and heard for themselves the reports sent back by the handful of refugees who had met the immigration restrictions and relocated there, Shanghai continued to have a very poor reputation. The climate was miserable twelve months of the year. The employment situation was impossible: thousands of refugees already there had exactly the same skills you possessed whatever they might be; and the Chinese glutted the manual-labor market, accepting wages one tenth of European standards for comparable work.

Rents were astronomical for even the tiniest room carved out of someone else's already-too-small apartment. And the most destitute refugees were forced by necessity to live in a *heim*, a dormitory housing, not seven or eight people to a room, as in Kobe, but up to two hundred. Moreover the Polish refugees felt that most of the Sephardic or German Jews running the major relief organization, the Committee For Assistance of European Refugees in Shanghai (the CFA for short) had no hearts or feelings and looked down on them as disruptive, undisciplined, obstreperous *schnorrers*. While they were secure in the ministrations of Kobe Jewcom and held the hope that they would soon be departing for America, most of the Polish refugees were not greatly concerned about conditions in Shanghai. In June of 1941, they suddenly became concerned.

The reaction to the prospective relocation to the Chinese port was universally negative. Hoping against hope for a miracle – the United States would change its mind, Hitler would be assassinated, God would visit a plague on the entire German army – each of the refugees plotted to be the last to go. In the yeshivas, Talmudic contests were held – the losers went first. If the healthy were due to be shipped out, illness became epidemic. When the sick were to go, health bloomed. But there was no avoiding it: Kobe Jewcom was closing down.

The Kobe experience had been involuntary and not exactly luxurious; but it had been guaranteed to be temporary. Shanghai would be equally involuntary and surely even less comfortable. Furthermore, in spite of a continuing, though totally unfounded, belief that America might eventually relax its immigration restrictions, there was an unavoidable possibility that the Shanghai experience might be more than temporary.

There was, however, one mitigating factor: Shanghai was less of a closed system than Kobe. Japanese law as well as circumstances demanded passivity. In Shanghai, on the other hand, you would possess an identity card. To some extent, you would become a "citizen." In fact, in the unlikely event that you could find a job – or in the even less likely event that you could start a business – you were welcome to it. At least, the refugees, who had had to be content accepting a dole from Kobe Jewcom, would have a chance to forgo charity and fend for themselves. People began to dredge their minds for the names of contacts – names they might merely have overheard in a conversation. Every conceivable opening was followed up. A shoemaker might have heard of a leather factory – a letter was sent. A tailor might know of a silk firm – a cable went off. Of course, no one turned his back on other destination possibilities, and indeed by August, the number of refugees remaining in Japan was down to eleven hundred. But Shanghai became increasingly the most realistic alternative. And no one, *no one*, wanted to be a dependent on the dole handed out by the CFA.

By the spring of 1941, efforts were already underway in Shanghai to help these new refugees through a new organization. In large part the work of Warhaftig, Eastjewcom, or more formally, the Committee for Assistance of Jewish Refugees was predominantly made up from Eastern Europe of Russian Jews from the masses that had emigrated to Shanghai from Harbin in the thirties or from Russia itself earlier. At least this new organization shared a kindred spirit with the Polish Jews. What the Germans of the CFA saw as "undisciplined," the Russian considered "imaginative." What the Germans called "obstreperous," the Russians called "independent."

# Shanghai

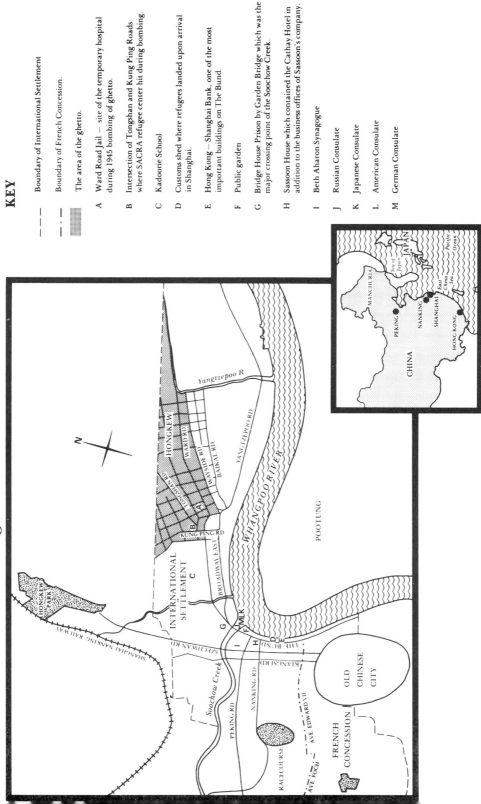

## KEY

---    Boundary of International Settlement

—·—    Boundary of French Concession.

▨    The area of the ghetto.

A    Ward Road Jail — site of the temporary hospital during 1945 bombing of ghetto.

B    Intersection of Tongshan and Kung Ping Roads where SACRA refugee center hit during bombing.

C    Kadoorie School

D    Customs shed where refugees landed upon arrival in Shanghai.

E    Hong Kong — Shanghai Bank, one of the most important buildings on The Bund.

F    Public garden

G    Bridge House Prison by Garden Bridge which was the major crossing point of the Soochow Creek.

H    Sassoon House which contained the Cathay Hotel in addition to the business offices of Sassoon's company.

I    Beth Aharon Synagogue

J    Russian Consulate

K    Japanese Consulate

L    American Consulate

M    German Consulate

A radiogram sent on September 18, 1941 from Kobe Jewcom to Shanghai.

Shanghai – the *Bund* and the docks – the refugees' first view of the city. *Photo. courtesy of Sasson Jacoby, Jerusalem Post.*

Refugees are taken from the docks in Shanghai to the processing center.

The Resident Certificate issued to all refugees in Shanghai—the symbol in the circle is the first letter of the Japanese word *yudayajin* (Jew).

Mir Yeshiva students at work in the Beth Aharon Synagogue. *Photo. courtesy of David Kranzler.*

A geisha party in Shanghai – Captain Inuzuka *far right* entertains Sir Victor Sassoon *second from right*.

Captain Inuzuka *second officer from right* and D. E. J. Abraham *far left* leave a meeting to dedicate a clinic in Hongkew.

Captain Inuzuka in a Shanghai synagogue.

Refugees selling their clothes in the ghetto. *Photo. courtesy of David Kranzler.*

A yeshiva celebration shortly before the bombing of Pearl Harbor.

Nazi colonel Josef Meisinger, the Butcher of Warsaw,
after his capture by Allied forces in Japan, 1945.

This dormitory in the Pingliang Road *heim* slept 200 men. A separate
section of this *heim* was used as the processing center for the refugees
on arrival in Shanghai.

A lane off the Tongshan Road in the center of the ghetto. *Photo. courtesy of David Kranzler.*

The reading room of the Kadoorie School.

Refugees moving to the Hongkew ghetto in spring 1943.

Mitsugi Shibata, the former vice-Consul in Shanghai, in 1976.

And in the eyes of the Russian Jews, a fellow who had his back to the wall but was too proud to beg was no *schnorrer*. Centuries-old antagonism between Jew and Jew would not be erased, even in the midst of war, deprivation and mortal peril. But with the founding of Eastjewcom, the newcomers would not be without representation in this totally new, unfamiliar surrounding.

Moishe Katznelson pressed his foot firmly against his sister's so he could be sure she wouldn't wander off, and leaned over the ship's rail for a better look at the city. After thirty-six hours of moving briskly through the East China Sea, the Japanese ship had steamed up the Yangtze Delta and turned into the mud-yellow waters of the Whangpoo River. With the taller buildings of Shanghai in view on the absolutely flat right-hand bank, the captain had cut the ship's engines. Among the three hundred-odd refugee passengers already on deck there was astonishment at the weather. They had never felt air so hot and wet! Without the breeze of the ship, you could almost pick it up by the handful. By unspoken common consent, the crowd along the rail opened up – skin to skin contact was too unpleasant.

"Where are you going?" Moishe called out when Sophie's shoe moved away from his.

"Just to see Dovid. He's right over there, Moishe, see? It's all right."

He watched her curly black head bob in and out among the adults and finally come to rest by the Syrkins. The father was not there – which didn't surprise him but Mrs Syrkin was standing next to Dovid and would, now he knew be keeping an eye on his sister.

Moishe was depressed as the crowded two-story outskirts of Shanghai slid by. Japan had been clean and fresh, even in the summer heat. By comparison, this place was a pigpen. And even from a distance he could see that the Chinese people didn't move calmly and carefully like the Japanese.

Facing this strange environment, Moishe was apprehensive, but he wasn't really frightened. Somehow, he and Sophie would be taken care of, just as they had been in Vilna and Moscow and Vladivostok and Kobe. By now, they were part of a group. He and Sophie would not be allowed to get lost. But even if he wasn't afraid, he was still lonely. It was a foregone conclusion that he wouldn't see his parents or his two sisters after all until the war was finished and he could go back and find them. Refugee committees in Vilna and again in Kobe had sent inquiries almost everywhere trying to see if somehow the rest of the family had already escaped to some other point. Moishe had to resign himself to the realization that he and his sister were cut off – perhaps forever from the other Katznelsons.

Sophie still hoped, and he was glad she did. And Sophie had found a friend in little Dovid Syrkin. But Moishe had no friends. All the boys even near his age, it seemed, were scholars; they spent all day, every day in the yeshivas. He himself had neither the background nor the interest for that. But he wasn't really old enough to feel comfortable with the men, and not big enough to pass among them anyway. Even the peculiarly unstructured refugee community in Kobe held no place for him. And Shanghai, no doubt, would be just a continuation of that. Or maybe worse. Many people, he knew, had made some sort of contact in Shanghai. Many had somebody who would be meeting the ship, somebody who would at least know who they were and what they were. But outside the group, he and Sophie had no one. Just the strange-sounding name, Eastjewcom.

The ship came to a complete halt in the middle of the river and was instantly surrounded by a dozen motor launches that would ferry the passengers ashore. As the refugees scattered to collect their baggage, Sophie came running back, excited in spite of the heat.

"Moishe, do you see all the Chinamen! Look how crowded it is – much more than Kobe. And it's all so big. Dovid says it's the biggest city in the world!"

"Yes? Well, maybe. Come on, let's get our suitcases. We'll probably have to spend the whole of the rest of the day filling out forms. Oy, is it *hot* here!"

But this was Shanghai: there were no forms. A quick clearance through a stifling customs shed, and the refugees were in. In the blazing hot midday sun, they milled around in a large and noisy group, many looking for faces that seemed to fit the names of the strangers they hoped would meet them. A few simply did what seemed the most expeditious thing: standing in one place and calling out "I am Katzenback; who is Mr. Wilensky?" or something of the sort.

Moishe watched, as the Amshenover rebbe and his wife and son were welcomed by a short middle-aged rabbi, and he saw them all climb into a small car and drive away. Ever since that hopeless, helpless day in Vilna, Moishe had felt a kind of bond between himself and the rebbe. And the old man gradually got to know him a little – at least he remembered Moishe's name and sometimes he even gave him an apple or at least a pat on the head when they happened to meet in Kobe. But the rebbe had his own life and his own son who followed him everywhere, quiet and obedient, like a miniature reproduction.

Moishe sighed and looked for the Syrkins. He knew they also had no contacts in Shanghai. In fact, Mr. Syrkin seemed unable to make real contact with anyone. You could talk to him, but only about the immediate present: "Nice weather, isn't it Mr. Syrkin. . . . Did you see the cherry blossoms, Mr. Syrkin?" But the minute you referred to anything in the past, anything before Kobe, or if you began speaking of the future, he stopped responding entirely. His face took a confused expression and he looked as if he didn't recognize you anymore. Moishe and Sophie had stayed close to the Syrkins in Kobe. While Sophie played with Dovid, Mrs. Syrkin looked after them, and she would do motherly things like sewing up tears and remembering that Sophie needed new shoes even if she didn't complain about the old ones. But Moishe wasn't so sure the relationship would continue in this new place.

In locating the Syrkins on the pier, Moishe also found the Eastjewcom representative, a Mr. Spechman, and another man also wearing a label on his jacket. CFA it read. Gradually, the other refugees who also had no one to meet them collected around the two committee men. Mr. Spechman spoke first, briefly welcoming them to Shanghai, explaining that before anything else they would have to be "processed" for the purpose of record keeping and that afterward, they would be helped to find housing and jobs. He would be going with them now to the Pingliang Road *heim*, which was the processing center, Spechman said, but the CFA was in charge of procedures, so please listen to its representative.

Feeling like a package being passed from hand to hand, Moishe shifted from foot to foot while the CFA man explained that the three open-sided trucks awaiting the refugees with no other place to go were insufficient to carry the entire group of eighty. "You can't all go at once, so some will have to wait."

The refugees groaned quietly at the prospect of waiting in the heat, to say nothing of being driven in what appeared to be open cattle trucks through the streets of Shanghai. But the CFA man paid no attention, merely separated off a chunk of about half the refugees and began hurrying them away. Moishe, the Syrkins, and the rest of the second half away retreated into whatever patches of shade they could find and sat down on their baggage to return the stares of the Chinese stevedores and take stock of their arrival in Shanghai.

If Shanghai was not, as Dovid believed, the biggest city in the world, the particular section of it facing the customs shed was impressive enough. Massive stone-faced buildings, the highest in Shanghai, rose up in a solid wall of five or six stories, with towers and cupolas reaching above that. Parallel stripes of tall arched windows and bas-relief pillars ran far off to both left and right, and blinding sunlight reflected off the broad dome of the Hongkong and Shanghai Bank. The street in between, the *Bund*, was filled with a constant flow of traffic, as busy as Moscow but more varied. Trolleys, cars and trucks veered from lane to lane, maneuvering for dockside space. And rickshaws – dozens and dozens of the little two-wheeled carts being jerked along by Chinese dripping with sweat. Everybody was in a hurry. Only the wealthiest, white-suited European gentlemen, apparently, could afford to walk leisurely. The slowest Chinese gait was a trot.

The slat-sided trucks finally returned. Moishe and the Syrkins made their way gingerly up the ramp to the back of one and hung onto its sides as the trucks jerked to a start and swung out into the chaos of the *Bund*. It was breezy in the truck, but it was a short trip. After a few blocks, they passed beyond the magnificent edifices of the *Bund*, crossed the Garden Bridge over the narrow, filthy Soochow Creek and came into the northern sector of the International Settlement, a district called Hongkew. Beginning with a crescent of consulates – the Russian, the German, the American and the all-important Japanese – then curving off to the right, the road, now called Broadway, passed through the area rebuilt by the German and Austrian Jews in 1938 and 1939. This was a pleasant enough section, so European that it was referred to as "Little Vienna." But right after it, the real Hongkew began. In 1937, the Chinese, retreating before the Japanese, had torched everything that would burn. In the intervening years, a good deal of rebuilding had been accomplished; but the construction was of the most basic nature. Now blocks of houses, some looking like little more than firm piles of broken brick and timbers, stood forlornly overlooking the remaining, as yet uncleared, lots of charred rubble.

The truck pulled into the yard of the Pingliang Road *heim*, originally built to house one large family. Now in the rooms not occupied by the processing center, lived nearly sixty, mostly German, refugees. Climbing down, the newcomers joined a line of forty or so others waiting in the hot sun. It threaded inside slowly; it was going to be a painfully long day.

The members of the Shanghai Jewish communities who had volunteered to help with the processing kept order and organization as best they could. Shouting to hold the attention of the despondent refugees, they directed people this way and that – come here, go there, and always have all papers ready. The procedure was particularly hard on Getzel Syrkin. He jumped uncertainly at each crack of command, and by the time he reached the interviewers inside, he was incapable of doing more than standing very still and shaking his head back and forth, back and forth. Cheya did her best to answer all the questions and cover up for him: she was terrified they would take him away.

One by one, the refugees passed through the doors into the *heim* to respond to a barrage of questions: What is your name? Where were you born? How much money do you have? In what currencies? Who do you know in Shanghai? What is your occupation? And throughout it all, the heat enveloped questioner and respondent alike, shortening tempers, turning requests into orders.

By 4:30, only a few refugees still waited to be assigned housing. Two representatives of the CFA Housing and Disbursement Committee sat at battered desks near the side door of the *heim*. With the assistance of the Eastjewcom representative, the Syrkins, who had preceded Moishe and Sophie throughout the bureaucratic maze, had just received one medium-sized room of an apartment in the back of the fourth floor of a rebuilt house some blocks east of Pingliang Road.

Moishe and Sophie – unfed since breakfast, exhausted by being ordered "now here, now there" for six hours – collapsed into two rickety wooden chairs by the second committee desk.

"You have no family," the committee woman said aloud, looking over an impressive sheaf of forms on the Katznelsons. Moishe shook his head in answer – he had been asked the same question fifty times today. But the lady wasn't looking.

"And you are fifteen and you are . . . nine? Yes, you are nine years old." Sophie, beyond response, stared at the floor.

"Well," the lady went on, looking at the papers rather than the children, "I think the best place for you to be is right here in the dormitories – you with the men, of course, and you with the women. I'll make sure you are introduced to someone. . . ."

As the meaning of her words dawned on Sophie, she looked up, distraught. "I don't want to be with women," she said in a voice rising with emotion. "I want to be with Moishe. He is my *brother*."

The CFA woman looked at Sophie and Moishe. What were they doing here, such innocents as these? What kind of a world was it that sent children like these off on their own to a place like Shanghai? And what was she supposed to do with them? Sophie, in the face of the heat, the exhaustion, the hunger, having heard no retraction of her banishment to the dormitories, fell sobbing onto her brother's lap. "Moishie, where is Mommy? Where is Daddy? Moishie, I want Mommy to *come*. Why doesn't she come and take care of us? I don't want to be with women, Moishie; don't *let* them. . . ."

God, what was he supposed to do! Mommy and Daddy weren't going to come. He was all Sophie had and he didn't know how to help her. With half a mind, he wanted to jump up, run away from all this – from this lady, this horrid hot place. He couldn't do that, and he wouldn't, but he didn't know what he could do. Lowering his head and shoulders over Sophie like a shelter, he put his arms around her shoulders and just held her. She was all he had too.

"They will stay with us." This was Cheya Syrkin's statement, and for once it was not a request – nor was it prefaced with "my husband says." Cheya had heard enough. She had been on her way out, grateful for a place to go, no matter how miserable it sounded, grateful that they had not taken her husband away, grateful to be finished with this "processing" at last, still she had turned back at the sound of Sophie crying. As she had kept half an eye on the girl ever since they had met in Kobe, she also kept half an ear out for how she and her brother were doing during the past few hours. The Katznelsons were not her problem. But a person's heart is not a stone.

"They will stay with us," she said again to the surprised CFA woman.

"That is impossible," the committee woman said, shaking her head. "It is very kind of you; but really, I have seen the room you will be living in. It is simply not large enough. . . ."

Moishe didn't look up. Sophie continued to sob as if her heart were breaking.

"The children will be fine here," the CFA woman began explaining to her.

If Cheya had not taken the opportunity, while seeking out the bathroom, to look around the Pingliang Road *heim* and been horrified by its immense dormitories she would probably have allowed herself to be overruled. If the committee representative had been a man, she certainly would never have let herself speak out so boldly. As it was, she put her suitcase down firmly on the floor and moved closer to the desk.

"I have seen 'here,'" she said directly to the woman. "'Here' is no place for children. 'Here' is nothing but a bed, not a table to put a book on, not a nail to hang up a jacket. 'Here' is no place for children. These have no parents – at least, no parents with them," she added, mindful of Sophie's presence. "They *need* a home and they will stay with us."

The CFA woman stared at this homely, underfed *Ostjuden* villager with her patched, sweaty dress and her dirty hair in disarray. *Five* people in a space already much too small for three was unthinkable for any who considered themselves human beings!

It was Spechman the Eastjewcom representative, who, hearing the dispute, came over to break the impasse: "It's after all the Syrkins' apartment and therefore their choice, I would say. In a day or so, perhaps, we can find another solution to the problem."

The committee representative threw up her hands in resignation. With these people, what could you expect? Marking the appropriate information on Moishe's papers she pushed them back into his hands and managed a small smile. "Good luck to all of you," she said evenly. "Next!"

Dovid, hot and tired but pleased that his friend was moving in, went over to Sophie and put his hand on her shoulder in brotherly fashion. "Stop crying, Sophie. Stop it now."

As best she could, she did. Half-lifted by the two boys, Sophie managed to stand up. Then, with Cheya in the lead and Getzel, who had watched the entire proceding like a man at a play, bringing up the rear, the five newcomers trudged out into the hot sun and headed for the tiny apartment at 14B Tongshan Road.

# 14

BY THE CONCLUSION of the High Holy Days in September of 1941, all eleven hundred of the Kobe refugees who had been unsuccessful in obtaining destination visas had relocated to Shanghai. Kobe Jewcom reverted to being simply the Kobe Jewish community, and its activities as Leo Hanin described them once again became "ninety percent gin-rummy and ten percent social gathering." But as Japan approached Pearl Harbor it increasingly restricted the kind of international trade from which the Jews of Kobe made their living. From one week to the next, the size of the community decreased, as whoever could manage it left permanently for the security of America or Canada or Australia. For them, Kobe became only a memory – as it did for the eleven hundred refugees now in Shanghai. But for the latter, in retrospect, their months in Kobe would seem like a dream-memory, an idyll when compared to the unending harshness of the reality of their new home.

Nothing was the same about the two cities, and everything about Shanghai was worse. Where Kobe had been temperate, Shanghai was miserably tropical. Where Kobe as a city had been well built and maintained, other than the few blocks of handsome European edifices, Shanghai still suffered visibly from the bombing and burning of the battle of 1937. And even in the neighborhoods that had come through unscathed, the cityscape was nothing but a flat jumble of dark, overcrowded, closely built two- and three-story brick boxes. The mass of Japanese in which the refugees had found themselves had been alien, but well-mannered and generous. The Shanghai mass was made up of four million people whose tradition did not so strenuously dictate politeness and whose total being was consumed in a relentless struggle simply to stay alive. Existing hand-to-mouth in a heartless, unforgiving world, most Shanghai Chinese had neither the energy nor the money for luxuries like cleanliness or generosity. Moreover, the refugees had been a rarity in Kobe and their plight a cause for sympathy, while in Shanghai, Caucasians were commonplace, and for valid historical reasons, not well liked. With all the chaos that had been sweeping across their land for the past hundred years, the Chinese themselves had been refugees often enough – and how often had the whitemen ever felt sorry for them? Shanghai had consistently attracted refugees. There was nothing so special about these. Why shouldn't they, too, have to make it on their own? Anyway, the Jews had their own kinsmen to look after them, didn't they?

They did. By the fall of 1941, there was a major relief undertaking going on in Shanghai. But for the incoming refugees, the organization of relief efforts represented one more point of comparison – again negative – with their experience in Kobe. The comparison was not fair. Kobe Jewcom had, at the most, two thousand refugees to care for at any one time; the average refugee contingent in Japan over the twelve-month period was less than eight hundred (many of whom were "just passing through"). Shanghai, on the other hand, had a constant refugee population of seventeen thousand. And for many thousands this was the end of the line.

The situation among the relief workers – as distinct from the refugees themselves – was also quite different. In Kobe, those involved with relief work, totalled less than fifty. Except for a handful of professionals, they were all newcomers to the problems of organizing and maintaining destitute strangers; but they were virtually all Russian Jews, and as such shared a common background and point of view with their Eastern European charges. In Shanghai, due to the multi-cultural make-up of the Jewish community – and due to the size of the refugee problem – not one but six major organizations (with many more committees and subcommittees), each with its own viewpoint, served the refugees. Until 1940 and the arrival of a few relief workers from various worldwide Jewish self-help organizations, the Shanghai relief scene was well-intentioned chaos. The professionals who reorganized things *their* way, created yet another dimension of friction, and the chaos subsided into simple bureaucracy. Hardly anything was possible, but everything was difficult. In the memory of one exasperated diarist: "In those days, a most ordinary thing could only be effectuated by utmost persistence . . . the energy spent was in no proportion to the success attained."

By the time the Polish refugees arrived from Kobe, in the late summer of 1941, the professional relief workers at least had shifted the work onto a reasonable level of efficiency. Thus, it should have been a simple matter for HICEM, the European refugee – aid organization, and the Joint Distribution Committee to redirect funds from Kobe to their representatives in Shanghai (just as Wahrhaftig had promised Inuzuka the previous spring). The additional money would be added to the already existing funds, the additional refugees would be added to the already existing population. . . .

Life should only be so easy. When confronted with the living arrangements established by the Shanghai relief workers, the Polish refugees were by no means as tractable as their German predecessors. Under no circumstances would they accept what they considered the "degradation" of living as many as two hundred to a room in a Shanghai *heim*! To the envy of the Germans – and the exasperation of Laura Margolies, the JDC representative from America – the Polish Jews made their refusal stick. Backed-up by the vociferous arguments of Eastjewcom, the Polish refugees convinced HICEM and the JDC that they should receive their share of the funds directly through that organization. With the HICEM–JDC stipend as a base, and small additional allotments from *Va'ad Hatzalah* and other Orthodox groups in the United States, even those Polish Jews who could not find so much as occasional employment could maintain a basic level of independence. Of the eleven hundred who arrived in the late summer of 1941, no more than a handful actually had to spend any time in a Shanghai *heim*.

Not that where they did live was so much better. Within a few weeks, the Mir Yeshiva was set up for living and learning in and around the beautiful Beth Aharon Synagogue in Hongkew. But for the rest, aside from a few dozen, like the Amshenover rebbe, who had been welcomed into the pleasant French Concession, housing meant half a floor or less in one of the twelve-by-thirty-foot houses that lined the close, dank lanes of Hongkew. But they didn't care. If they weren't housed luxuriously, they could at least maintain a pretense of privacy. And if the food allowance, particularly for those who had no other income, was never enough, at least they could decide for themselves how and when and what they wouldn't have enough of – and they didn't have to stand in line for two hours for the privilege of doing it. (*Heim* food was worse than plain. A popular cartoon showed two residents in conversation: "Well, Max, what day of the week is it? Red beans or white beans?")

The eleven hundred Polish refugees worked themselves into the Shanghai economy as best they could as waiters, secondhand dealers, tailors, and so on. One man, the proud possessor of an alarm clock, organized a "wake-up service" for his less fortunate fellows. And, considering their number, they made a remarkably strong impression on the entire Jewish community of Shanghai, but particularly on those culturally closest to them – the Russians.

The Poles were much more "Jewish" than their German cousins. They were less secular, less interested in assimilating themselves into the mainstream culture. They were more observant of the *halakah*, the law that governs the lives of religious Jews. And they were energetic in their encouragement to others to observe as well. The Polish refugees set up two schools – one for boys, one for girls – where a strong secular education was combined with in-depth religious learning. Several of the yeshiva boys even undertook crash courses in English simply for the purpose of teaching Judaism to Sephardic children who spoke no other language. The most pervasive influence of the newly arrived Poles, however, was not religious but linguistic: they spoke Yiddish.

Among the Russian Jews of Shanghai, Yiddish – that magnificently expressive language made up of German, Hebrew, Russian and miscellaneous bits of half a dozen other East European tongues – had been spoken only at home. Suddenly the words came out in public. Yiddish newspapers and magazines appeared – *Unser Leben, Unser Welt, Dos Wort, Der Yiddisher Almanach.* . . . Yiddish theater which in the late nineteenth century had exploded with creative enthusiasm in Europe and America, was suddenly right there in their midst. Even on the radio, for a brief period every day, one could hear Yiddish newscasts, music commentary, even lectures in *mama-lashon*. With the arrival of the Poles, "to be a Jew in Shanghai" took on new meaning.

Avram Chesno rolled over in his bed and tried to bury his head in his arms against the intrusion of the morning light. Last night had been *impossible*. No sooner had the Russians below finished their screaming match – uniting thereafter in conjugal bliss, the sounds of which seeped through the floorboards with uncanny clarity – than the Chinese across the lane began a battle with cooking pots and tin buckets. Avram groaned into his elbow. But the sunlight was relentless – which was just as well. He rolled over again onto his back and opened his eyes. After eight weeks, his twelve-by-sixteen foot cubicle with a seven foot ceiling was only too familiar. But it was reasonably clean. It gave him enough space for a bed, table, a straight-backed chair and some hooks for his clothes. And small as it was, it was his alone. At least that he thought was as it should be. Because Avram Chesno had earned the money to pay for it.

Five months ago, in Kobe he had again been refused an American visa. What the hell was he doing here? Why could he not seem to break out of this dead-end entanglement of dependence? Where could he go to get back into the world of *real* people – a place where people did things for themselves, where people were liberated from begging favors? Why did America not accept him? The visa officer in Kobe gave him no reason but said Chesno could apply again in six months if he liked. Avram stared at the man uncomprehending. Didn't he know what a length of time six months was? It was almost July then. Was he supposed to wait out the entire year doing *nothing*? Avram had felt like grabbing the bland, blond American and hurling him headfirst through the third floor window. Instead he turned on his heel and stamped out. Who needed America?

After two days, he had calmed down sufficiently to be more constructive. Jewcom maintained a list of all the foreign schools in Shanghai, and he had written to each of them. Only one had been interested, but one was enough. A Miss Lucie Hartwich, headmistress of the Shanghai Jewish Youth Association School, 100 Kinchow Road, Hongkew district, Shanghai, offered part-time employment teaching science. Standing in the doorway of Kobe Jewcom headquarters, reading her brief, formal letter, Avram remembered the day he had been accepted in the university, the day Ruthie had agreed to become his wife, the day he had been hired by one of the most prestigious high schools in Warsaw. A part-time post in a little Jewish school in a burned-out section of a city on the edge of Asia? For a teacher of his attainments, this was nothing! But for Chesno now, this was everything. A job. A job doing something he was trained for, something he liked. Never mind that the salary she offered was only barely enough to live on. With a job, he would be back in the world of men. Immediately, savoring every stroke of the pen, Avram had accepted the offer.

Now, from the other side of a plywood partition, he could hear Mrs. Tookansky setting out cups for breakfast tea. A frugal woman with a husband and a father to look out for, she had been quite happy to make "an arrangement." Every week Avram contributed some of his precious Shanghai dollars to her budget; every breakfast and every dinner, he partook equally of whatever she was serving. Mrs. Tookansky was not an award-winning cook; and she was further limited by the strict laws of *kashruth*. But somehow, despite escalating prices in Hongkew – where everything nonetheless was at least thirty percent cheaper than in Shanghai's International Settlement or the fashionable residential Frenchtown – she managed to serve at least part of a chicken every Sabbath. Avram was well satisfied with the arrangement.

When the bell rang at the end of that morning, Avram's students streamed out of the classroom, their imaginations full of the strange properties of sodium, "the metal you can cut with a butter knife!" Avram was pleased, as he had been pleased with every class since he had begun teaching here. The enthusiasm of these children inspired him. They devoured knowledge. After a tortuous trek across half the world, their minds were burdened with tragedy and emotional upheaval. Their home lives, where everything was "make do," were punctuated by short-tempered, jobless fathers and anxious mothers. Despite, or maybe because of, these appalling drawbacks, the students wanted to learn, were avid to learn, about everything and anything. And not only science. The French- and Chinese-language teachers said the same, as did the music teacher, the English teacher, the Bible and Hebrew teachers, even the gym teacher.

Someone had recently written in the visitors' book: "Happy laughter resounds again in a world that had forgotten how to smile." A little sentimental, Chesno thought, but true nonetheless. In the beginning, the enthusiasm and proficiency of his students had put him to shame at first. English was the school's language of instruction. And from the start of the first day, it had been clear that Avram's English was not up to the students' standards, though it was as much a second language for them as for him. Cursing himself for having "wasted his time" studying Hebrew in Vilna, Chesno spent hour after hour in the school's wicker-furnished library devouring grammar books and English-language science texts. Within a couple of weeks, he had lost his disadvantage and even gained a certain amount of added respect from his students.

"Mr. Chesno?"

Avram looked up to see a small boy in the doorway.

"Syrkin, isn't it? Yes, what is it?"

Dovid was too young to be in one of his science classes, but Avram had not been surprised to meet the boy in the hallways of this particular school. He had gathered from seeing the family intermittently after that first time in the Vilna library that it had no money. And the Kadoorie School – as it was commonly called after its Sephardi founder and benefactor – was the only school in Shanghai that never turned a child away if his family could not pay the tuition.

"Mr. Chesno, if you twist your ankle so hard you can't walk on it, will it just get better by itself after a while?"

Dovid did not appear to be limping. "Your ankle?" Avram asked.

"No. A friend of mine."

"Well, I should say your friend should go to the school clinic and have the doctor look at it."

When Kadoorie had founded the school, he had not confined himself to books and teachers. There were vocational programs, after-school clubs, sports teams, religious services and a well-run clinic that kept detailed records on every child.

Dovid let pass the reference to the clinic. "But will it get better by itself?" he repeated.

"It's impossible to say, you know. I'm not a doctor. Maybe yes, maybe no. You really need a doctor."

Dovid looked at him with soft brown eyes, too large for such a small face. "All right," he said, wanting, Avram thought, to say more but instead saying only, "Thank you very much," and turning back toward the door.

For God's sake, what is this? Avram thought.

"*Dovid'l, kum aher. Vos is mit dir?*" For some things, only Yiddish will do.

At the familiar sounds, Dovid gave in. Perching himself on the edge of one of the desks, he gave a deep sigh and began on the problem.

"We have a boy living with us, you see. Moishe is the older brother of my friend Sophie. You know Sophie? No? Well, Moishe is too old for school because he is over fourteen, so he found a job."

Very enterprising of him, Avram thought, what with so many of the few employment ads now specifying "Refugees Need Not Apply."

"He works for this Chinaman who has a peanut-crushing factory," Dovid went on. "Moishe crushes the peanuts. He works a machine that is kind of like a bicycle. At least, it has pedals and a chain like a bicycle. But yesterday when he came home, he almost couldn't walk because his foot had slipped on the pedal. And today he can't walk at all. And he's afraid if he can't go to work tomorrow, too, the Chinaman will fire him."

"I see," Avram said. "Well, since he has a job, I would think he might have enough money to pay for a visit to the Jewish Hospital in Frenchtown. It doesn't cost much, you know. Anyway," he added, "maybe Moishe has insurance?"

Two years before, the Association of Central European Physicians (refugees all) had been formed in the knowledge that far too few refugees could afford even the low fees that the doctors charged. Now, for a dollar a month, one could be insured for fifty percent of any medical bill, and even twenty-five percent of a dental bill.

Dovid shook his head sadly. "There's no insurance. The Chinaman hasn't paid him yet. Just to get the job Moishe has to work free for the first two weeks."

Avram had decidedly mixed feeling about the mass of Chinese among whom he was living. By no means could they be faulted for being too poor to be clean. There had been enough Jews in Europe who had been in the same predicament. And manners and customs varied so much from one place to another that he couldn't simply dismiss them as savages for not behaving like Europeans. But exploiting fifteen-year-old boys was too much.

"Where is this Moishe now?" he asked.

14B Tongshan Road, where we live," Dovid said hopefully.

"Stop by at 1:00 after your last class. I'll go home with you."

Dovid looked as if the weight of the world had been lifted off his shoulders. "*Danke shein, danke shein,*" he said, then hurried off down the corridor.

Chesno heard the scope of the problem before he saw it.

"Moishe, it's just a cloth with warm water." A young girl's voice drifted down the dark stairway as Avram carefully made his way up the rickety steps. The October weather had cooled off a little, but the higher he went, the stickier and more odorous the air became.

"Don't put *anything* on it, I told you. Just leave it alone." Moishe's voice was brimming over with anger and agony.

Dovid opened the door. The room was about twice the size of Avram's own, but quite obviously it was living, eating and sleeping space for five people. The boy lay on a mattress on the floor, his foot raised on a kind of cushion formed from a twisted dirty sheet. He was white with pain.

"Dovid, I told you, no doctor!" Moishe said harshly.

"I'm no doctor," Avram said, vaguely recollecting having seen the boy before. "I'm a friend of Dovid's. Can you stand on it at all?"

"No," Moishe sighed, angry not at Dovid or Sophie but at himself. He'd managed to get a job so at least he could contribute to the household a little. After all the hassle of bargaining with the Chinaman, after working like a coolie for nearly two weeks, after all *that*, what had he done but stupidly, stupidly put his foot down wrong on the pedal on the very last day before he actually started earning money.

Avram bent over the ankle. It was swollen and red, possibly broken, certainly in need of treatment.

"I'm afraid you're going to have to see a doctor."

Moishe only shook his head. "No, no."

Avram looked first at Sophie, then at Dovid. Both were looking down at the rough bare floor. Even so young, they were embarrassed by the poverty.

"If you ever want to walk again," Avram added as an afterthought.

Moishe's head stopped shaking.

"I'm not a doctor, but I know something about bones. If you don't get that ankle looked at, it will turn gangrenous and you know what that can lead to."

Moishe turned even paler. Nothing was said for what seemed like a long time. Finally the boy shifted his eyes to look at Avram who for his part was now looking studiously out of a window.

"You know, there's a difference between accepting charity and taking out a loan," he said as if it wasn't of any particular interest to him one way or the other. "For instance, if I were to advance you the money to cover the cost of the doctor – and the cost of getting there in a rickshaw because you obviously can't walk two kilometers – if I did that, I would consider it only a loan which I would expect to be paid back once you were on your feet again."

The silence returned. Avram continued studying the dismal view out the window.

"Paid back how?" the voice finally responded from the mattress.

"That would depend on what I needed done when the ankle was healed," he said, having absolutely no idea what a fifteen-year-old boy could do for him at any time.

Moishe tried to shift his leg and a jab of pain shot up from his foot. *Oi!* What choice did he have?

"All right, it'a deal," he said, forcing himself, in spite of the pain, into a half-sitting position.

Sophie turned away quickly, burying her face in her hands and weeping with relief. As Dovid went over to comfort her, Avram reached down and pulled Moishe up by the arms.

"The deal was the easy part," he said. "Now comes the hard part: getting you down those three flights of stairs isn't going to be a picnic."

"Right," Moishe said quietly. "Unlike everything else over the past two years, this is not going to be a picnic. Give me that shirt, will you Dovid?"

Avram steadied him as he stood on one leg and finished getting dressed. They then started the agonizing maneuver of descending to the street.


By December, where the refugees had cursed the heat, now they cursed the cold, the rain, and the flooding that the rain created. It wasn't a European winter. The temperature rarely dropped below forty degrees and there was no snow. But a damp chill pervaded every place, and fuel was too expensive to use except for cooking. Even the wealthy European traders were uncomfortable, in their mahogany and marble mansions set graciously out in the outskirts of the International Settlement. They were forced to go more often to the posh Shanghai Club to savor the warmth of whisky served up along what was believed to be the longest bar in the world. The Japanese soldiers had their thick winter uniforms but huddled closely in their barracks.

But on the night of December 4, there was no cold in the world that could chill the spirits of a mass of yeshiva students who had gathered for a party. Six days a week, for twelve, fourteen, sixteen hours a day, the yeshiva studied in the magnificent, high-ceilinged white sanctuary of the Beth Aharon Synagogue that never closed. The synagogue had been turned over to them by its founder, Silas Hardoon, an extremely charitable Sephardic millionaire with a

Chinese wife and a dozen adopted children of several races. Hardoon had built the synagogue during the 1920s in response to a dream in which his father praised him for having done so much for the Chinese but chided him for doing so little for his fellow Jews. In spite of its beauty, the synagogue had never been put to much use. To the students and faculty of the Mir Yeshiva, it seemed that the building had been destined all along for their use. There were exactly the same number of seats in the sanctuary as there were students in the yeshiva. There was no doubt in anyone's mind that Beth Aharon had been simply waiting for their arrival.

On this night, most of the school, and visitors from other yeshivas, were giving an enthusiastic send-off to one of their number who, miracle of miracles, would be sailing within the week for America and a waiting fiancée. The singing and dancing had already been in progress for hours, song after song, the young men dancing back and forth, swinging each other around with beards and jackets flying. After weeks of unrelenting dedication to studies, it was good just to feel one's body move again.

Yankel Gilbewitz and Gershon Cohen, who these days saw each other only on special occasions, had just finished a whirling rendition of the *mitzvah tantz* – eighteen boys circling round and round the groom-to-be, clapping in time to the increasingly rousing verses of *Od Yishama* till the room itself seemed to throb with the beat. The two boys collapsed, breathless, on a couple of chairs near one of the cloth-covered tables at the side of the room.

After the scare put into him by the combined forces of a Kobe police sergeant and God's own retribution, Yankel had retreated entirely from the world of commerce. Though he had continued to pick up the bread ration for his section till the yeshiva departed for Shanghai in late August, to the disappointment of the shopkeeper, he no longer stopped by the fruit store. Anyway, he had discovered that socks could be had for the asking from the Ladies Committee.

In Shanghai, at least, Yankel had less need of secular success. For one thing, the quality of life in the yeshiva was clearly much better than on the outside. The Orthodox congregations in America might not have had much clout with the Jewish community that Inuzuka was interested in: but they were totally and selflessly devoted to rescuing their religious brethren from the harsher rigors of refugee existence. With contributions coming in steadily from abroad, the students, teachers and families of the Mir Yeshiva were far more secure and comfortable than all but a few of the most well-connected of their fellow refugees. Just as Yankel's interest in feathering his own nest had propelled him away from the yeshiva in Kobe, it encouraged him to retreat even further into it in Shanghai. He was quite content to be eating after-dinner cake and nuts here now while others in Hongkew scrambled for bread.

Yankel helped himself to a cup of the always-available tea. From the first day it had been crammed into their heads: don't drink unboiled water. It was important not to eat raw vegetables. It was important to slice the bread very thin to check for worms. But it was most important *never* to drink unboiled water. Luckily, tea was cheap.

Gershon, having caught his breath, was ready to fill Yankel in on what had happened to him in the months since they had last been together.

"Well, I have come to the definite conclusion that the Japanese are, without doubt, *avodah zorah-niks*."

"Ehhh?" Yankel had never concerned himself with the religion of the Japanese. But "polytheists?"

"Exactly. Just like the ancients. By them, different gods hold sway in different places. Just like the Canaanites or the Assyrians – I'm sure of it. 'Here, our god is powerful, so *here* we must act in such and such a way. But over there? Our god doesn't exist over there. So, over there the rules of our god don't apply! We can act any way we please.'"

"I thought the Japanese were rather nice," Yankel began, remembering the old lady with the shining gold teeth.

"*Absolutely*, in Japan they were *very* nice. That's the point! The gods of Japan tell them: be nice, be polite, be gentle. But here in Shanghai – no gods of Japan. So, no more 'nice,' no more 'polite,' no more 'gentle.' Listen, I'll tell you what happened to me, how I know." Gershon stuffed an entire piece of cake into his mouth and began his story.

"We are staying at the Jewish Club, right? Us from Ramailes, a few from Tels, Lubavitch, the other yeshivas? Well, you know that. But there are a couple of married boys, right? Naturally, they don't live in our dormitory but they have little apartments, rooms really, alone to themselves near the club. So, one night I am visiting one of them and there's an air raid drill. Well, we all have been told what to do. We put up dark curtains over the windows and shut all the lights and sit there, maybe talking a little, very quietly in the dark. Suddenly," Gershon paused for effect, "suddenly there comes a terrific pounding on the door and a lot of yelling. None of us understood Japanese of course, but we can tell it's the police. But what have we done? I open the door a crack. They burst into the room, push me back against the wall and start waving their red flashlights all over. They're slamming the furniture all around, over-turning everything, scaring the wife half to death and my friend and me too, I must admit. Suddenly one comes back to me, probably thinking it's my room since I opened the door, and starts slapping me back and forth and pointing to his flashlight, and finally we figure it out, that they are looking for a light. One of us says the word in English, and the policemen at least understand that. But there is no light on. We had shut everything. Suddenly the other one starts jabbering and pointing out the window, first up at the moon, and then down the street. So the one holding me stops slapping, and finally we all see what happened; from down in the street, they've seen the reflection from the moon on our window, and they thought we were violating the blackout. So, of course, we're all waiting for some kind of explanation, apology, or some-thing. Did we get one? No, all that happened was that the guy holding onto me throws up his hands like he is very impatient with the whole thing, grabs me by the shoulders, throws me out of his way and stalks out of the door. Then they're both gone, pounding down the stairs and out the door. No apologies, no bowing, no helping us pick up the furniture. *Avodah zorah!*"

His point proved, Gershon stopped talking and reached for the tea. Yankel could scarcely believe the story. The same Japanese who had been so nice to all of them – letting them come to their country in the first place, giving them gifts of apples or eggs, per-sonally leading them home when they'd gotten lost. . . . Even that *farshtunken* police sergeant, Okuda, hadn't done anything really violent. Yet, he thought, on the rare occasions that he'd been out walking in Shanghai, hadn't he sensed a different feeling on the part of the Japanese here? Had any of them gone out of their way to help him here like they did in Kobe? And when he happened to be walking toward a Japanese on the sidewalk wasn't it always he who had to step aside and let the other go straight on? Such little things. But maybe Gershon was right.

"*Avoda zorah-niks,* I tell you, Yankel," Gershon said, absolutely sure of his interpretation. He stood up. "Come on, they're giving Binyomin the send-off present. Oh, how I envy him, going to America in less than a week!"

Yankel agreed, with his whole heart and more. He didn't want to stay here. He didn't like the city or the weather. And now that Gershon had made him think about it, he didn't care so much either for the Japanese in Shanghai. He also stood up and followed his friend over toward the head table. But, if Binyomin can get to America, he thought, maybe, somehow, some way, others of us can too. And if others, why not me? It will just take time. Just be patient and give it time.

It would take a great deal of patience and more time than Yankel had ever imagined. In fact, even Binyomin himself would never leave for America; never join his fiancée . . . and never fully recuperate from the trauma of the disappointment.

On December 8, at 1:58 in the morning Shanghai time, the Japanese attacked Pearl Harbor.

When Yankel heard the news, all he could think about were the words of a letter the Mir Yeshiva had recently received from Europe: "There remains but one thing you can do for us now: Say *kaddish* for us, and mourn." Trapped here, under the rule of Germany's ally and America's enemy, weren't they, too, as good as dead? Who was there left to say *kaddish* for the Shanghai refugees?

# 15

As the first bombs dropped on Pearl Harbor, Japanese troops and artillery in Shanghai were taking up positions along the *Bund* and beginning to fire on the Royal Naval gunboat *"Petrel"* moored offshore. The attack was quickly over. The *Petrel* expired in flames, her crew swept rapidly downstream on the outgoing tide. The only other Allied ship on the river, an American gunboat at anchor nearby, surrendered without resistance. At last all of Shanghai, even the International Settlement and French Concession belonged to the Japanese.

The midnight rattle of distant artillery seeped into Avram Chesno's sleep, creating a semiconscious nightmare: his wife, his lovely, lithe, brown-haired beauty slowly disintegrating, exploding in a long, silent, macabre death before his eyes. But the bombing was brief, and when Avram awoke shortly after dawn, his deep inner unhappiness had been supplemented by a surface annoyance at the mechanical sputtering which had disturbed his sleep. Unaccustomedly claustrophobic in his small room, Avram rose and began dressing. The noisy sputtering that had drifted off returned. Now fully awake, he recognized it as the sound of a small plane flying very low overhead. He went downstairs and outside.

Groups of excited Chinese crowded the narrow streets of the neighborhood, jabbering, gesturing, some weeping, a few laughing nervously. Recognizing one fellow, a tall thin pharmacist named Chin with whom he occasionally had exchanged some simple sentences in English, Avram hurried over to him.

"It is war!" Mr. Chin called out as he recognized Avram. "From last night; Japan has struck America. Now, Japan is at war with America, England, Australia, Holland. . . ." Folding his long fingers over his palm one by one, Mr. Chin ticked off the names of the Allies. "You look worried, Mr. Chesno. I am also. Now it is war for everyone. The world. . . ."

The remainder of Chin's thought was drowned out in the racket of the returning biplane. Passing directly over their heads, the machine suddenly dropped a batch of leaflets which fluttered down like giant snowflakes onto the rooftops and into the streets. The leaflets' message, translated meticulously into Chinese, French and English as well as Japanese, was brief. "Due to errors and failings on the part of the Allies – and in small part to errors and failings of Japan, an unfortunate state of war has come about between Japan and the Allies." As a result of the unfortunate state, the Japanese authorities were now responsible for administering all of Shanghai. There should be no panic, the pamphlet concluded – all necessary information will be given out in good time.

As Avram stood studying the minimal information offered by the pamphlet, he wondered what difference this would make. Two years ago, he had fled from one war, *his* war, to a haven half a world away. The fact that Japan was even then at war with China had had little meaning for him: it was someone else's war. Now, as Chin said, it was the whole world. Now there was nowhere left to run to. But what an idiotic thought that was. Really, there never had been any secure refuge from the beginning! This expanded war, this world war, only made the inaccessible unattainable.

More Europeans were out on the street now, jabbering and gesticulating, in their own way very much like the Chinese. How the war might affect their already meager chances of moving on to the United States was one thing. How it would affect their immediate lives and their strange incomprehensible relationship with the Japanese was another. Avram glanced briefly at the sky. The light had not brightened appreciably since sunrise. It promised to be a very gray day – cloudy, damp and chill.

Several blocks away, from his office, Captain Inuzuka also briefly studied the day. It was indeed inauspiciously dark and cloudy. But from his higher vantage point, he could see that it was graced by not one but two rainbows. Pleased with the omens, he began to dress.

Although he had not been briefed in advance on it, the attack on Pearl Harbor had scarcely come as a surprise to Inuzuka or to any of the other Japanese officers. Preparations had long since been made, wall posters and the aerial-drop leaflets had been printed up; soldiers and tanks were already being organized for a prearranged parade of strength. Within hours, to the extreme gratification of the

Japanese, the previously inviolate International Settlement and French Concession would be brought officially under their direct rule. Inuzuka, as director of refugee affairs, would of course take part in all the historic activities. But first, he had a personal score to settle.

The office of Sir Victor Sassoon was, appropriately, in Sassoon House. Covering nearly an acre of the most expensive real estate in Shanghai and housing the grand Cathay Hotel, this building was one of the largest and easily the most luxurious on the *Bund*. Inuzuka could hardly wait until the start of the business day. Then he marched into the sparkling glass lobby and took an ornate elevator up to the third floor, headquarters for the entire multi-million-pound-sterling Asian financial empire of E.D. Sassoon and Company. At Sir Victor's very British office, he paused only momentarily before stomping across the carpeted floor, seating himself proprietarily in the leather desk chair and swinging his feet up onto the desk to survey the scene.

"This is now *my* office," he announced loudly to the employees who stood nervously at hand. "This is now *my* building. Henceforth you will, *all* of you, follow Japanese policy!"

So much for you, Sir Victor, with your arrogant and never-concealed disdain for the Japanese. The times have changed, Sir Victor; we Japanese have *made* them change. No more are your kind the ones in charge; no more will you lord your ways over us. From now on, Asia, free and united in the Greater East Asia Co-Prosperity Sphere, will go her own way under her own banner!

The British employees stared with horror at this crude defiance of their established world. The man was a barbarian, a monkey! But they had all seen the posters in the streets and heard the newscasts over the radio. Whatever was right or wrong, there was an unassailable reality to the situation. No one said a word to oppose him.

Sassoon's Chinese employees found Inuzuka's performance equally tasteless. After four and a half years of war against the Japanese, the Chinese despised and detested them. But of all the Asian peoples, only the Japanese had been able to stand up against the *ta-piza* (big noses). What Inuzuka had just done individually, his countrymen were doing on a grand scale. Hadn't they already liberated the southern provinces, which the French had called "Indochina?" And weren't they at this very moment shelling the British Crown Colony of Hong Kong? At least the crude Japanese were freeing China from its one hundred years of slavery to Western economic interests, Asia would again be, in the words of the Americans, "of and by and for" Asians.

But what a pity, they and Inuzuka himself, thought, what a gross injustice against the order of the world that Sir Victor himself is not here to witness his own demise! Pearl Harbor had caught the chief Sassoon on a business trip in Bombay. Unlike lesser known "enemy nationals" in Shanghai, Sir Victor would not have to wear a red armband or personally oversee the Japanese usurpation of his holdings. He would spend the next five years in Bombay, another stronghold of his financial empire.

Inuzuka savored his moment of glory in Sassoon's office all the more because he knew his days in Shanghai were about over. With the declaration of war, his Jewish contacts and Jewish expertise had become meaningless. All his work, his patient, exhausting manipulatory deals had come to naught. The Jews were supposed to have persuaded Roosevelt to yield gracefully to Japanese domination of the East. Japan should not have been forced to war with the United States. Hadn't that been the purpose of the *fugu* plan? But the Jews had failed the *fugu* plan totally; and in their failure, they had kept Inuzuka from achieving his life-long goal of entrée to the high-level policy-making circles of Tokyo. Even forty-eight years of training in the fine Japanese art of concealing emotions could not completely overcome the fury of his disappointment. The first time thereafter that he met with representatives of the Shanghai Jewish community who were courteously requesting permission to undertake a major fund-raising project – Inuzuka practically threw them out of his office. The *yudayajin* would get nothing more from him! A few days later, however, after he calmed down, when Laura Margolies, the Joint Distribution Committee's representative, came for the same purpose, he responded politely, not only giving her permission for the fund-raising but also turning over to her five thousand sacks of cracked wheat from the International Red Cross.

But Inuzuka had been correct about the events that would flow from Pearl Harbor. In a matter of weeks, communiqués began coming down from Tokyo. From Shigenori Togo, the new foreign minister: "Since the outbreak of the great East Asian war, it has been necessary for us to reconsider the problem of the Jewish population; the resolution of the Five Ministers' Conference must be set aside. . . ." Henceforth, the Jews of Shanghai would have no special place in the scheme of things. From the headquarters of the Bureau of Military Affairs: "Jews are to be treated according to their nationality, but considering their unique character, it will be necessary to keep them under strict surveillance. . . . Those antagonistic are to be suppressed and dealt with." Thus, all "enemy nationals" – including most of the wealthy Sephardim who held British citizenship – were to be transferred to special internment camps on the outskirts of the city. The others – virtually all the seventeen thousand refugees and the four thousand Russian Jews – would be protected according to the "principles of universal harmony" (the same principles that had "protected" three-hundred thousand Chinese who had been killed in Nanking four years before).

But Inuzuka himself, as he had foreseen, was to play no further role in Shanghai: in February 1942, he was relieved of his post to return to sea duty. The photo of Theodor Herzl was taken down from his office.

As the Year of the Serpent gave way to the Year of the Horse, it seemed less and less likely that Japan needed help from anyone, Jewish or otherwise. Even before Pearl Harbor, she had been in control of Korea, Manchuria, Taiwan, huge sections of China and all of French Indochina. Hong Kong had fallen by the year's end. And now, in a matter of a few spring months, Japan conquered the key remaining strongholds of her enemies: in February, Malaya and Singapore; in March, the Dutch East Indies; in April and May, the Philippines. All over, victories for the Axis. On the other side of the world, Germany and Italy were having equal success with their chosen enemies. The entire European continent (excepting the four neutrals: Switzerland, Sweden, Spain and Portugal) from the west coast of France to the gates of Moscow and the vast expanses of North Africa, from Casablanca to within sixty miles of Alexandria, were securely under their control. Russia, already deeply invaded by the Germans, would surely fall – Hitler guaranteed it. Much to Japanese relief, no more would the Land of the Rising Sun have to fear the Bear of the North. As for Great Britain, it could only be a matter of time before she was brought to her knees. And then, of course, the United States would be forced to come to terms. Jews? Who needed them!

Since those unnecessary Jews had never known about the Five

Ministers' Conference or the *fugu* plan or their responsibility to bring it about, they did not recognize their "failure" or even that they had fallen from some strange "state-of-grace" vis-à-vis the Japanese. But the refugees in Shanghai knew very well that the attack on Pearl Harbor and the subsequent declarations of war put an absolute and final end to any hope any of them might have kept about going to America; practically, it was also a shattering blow to what little economic security they had been able to create. With the cessation of trans-Pacific shipping, a major chunk of Shanghai's import-export business was ruined. Some firms ceased entirely, carrying down with them many of their suppliers. Even those companies that remained had to accept Japanese "advisers" who invariably redirected supply contracts into Japanese-owned shops. Every aspect of life became more difficult. Tight rationing was imposed on gasoline (putting an end to a well-organized training program for would-be auto drivers and mechanics which had attracted many of the Polish refugees). Inflation ran rampant; bank accounts were frozen except for small withdrawals for day-to-day expenses; and the wealthy Sephardim who, heretofore, could be counted on for help, had less and less control over their businesses or their profits. And at this point, exactly when it was most needed, relief money from the United States was drastically curtailed.

From the late thirties, the Joint Distribution Committee had been the major source of those overseas funds which covered the everyday expenses – food, housing, medical care – of the refugees. (The other overseas source, HIAS/HICEM, dealt both before and during the war with emigration costs, legal problems, reconnecting scattered families, and so forth.) With the declaration of war, however, the JDC faced a crisis of conscience. The Anglo-American Trading With the Enemy Act clearly prohibited all communication, direct or indirect, between Americans and people in enemy-occupied lands. In the months after Pearl Harbor, there was a great deal of discussion and soul-searching at the JDC headquarters in New York. Finally a decision was reached. In order not to give ammunition to the anti-Semitic elements in America, in order to be "super-patriots," beyond even the shadow of reproach, in order not to contribute so much as a penny that might help the cause of the Axis, the JDC felt compelled to break off all relations with Shanghai. No more transfers of money, no more repayment guarantees which had proved so helpful in eliciting loans from the Shanghai community itself. After May 21, 1942, no more communication of any sort between any branch of the JDC and its office in Shanghai.

The Japanese were dumbfounded: where was the historic "family spirit" of the Jews? For Laura Margolies, the JDC's representative, it was disaster. This American source had been contributing thirty thousand dollars a month to the relief effort. How could they possibly get by without it? But New York headquarters was adamant. She had no choice but to appeal on all levels to the remaining local financial sources (particularly the Russian Ashkenazim) and to try to squeeze every last drop of efficiency from the relief distribution system. The free-meal program was cut in half; the rolls of those eligible for relief of any sort were gone over name by name to catch those who did not fully qualify; and the refugee hospital which had handled over fifty-four thousand cases and handed out twelve thousand vaccinations was closed down. The closing of the hospital was all the more poignant because it coincided with a serious outbreak of typhus and a heatwave so severe it caused the deaths of sixteen refugees. But there was no other solution; the money, one thousand dollars a day, just wasn't there.

The irony of the situation was that even the U.S. Treasury Department was less stringent than the JDC in the enforcement of the trading act. Treasury officials hinted broadly that although cables could not be authorized, not every cable would necessarily *need* to be authorized. Perhaps, they suggested, the JDC could make arrangements with a neutral third-party country through which the funds could be sent. But the JDC chose to stand firm: "We, as an American organization, cannot be involved in anything that has the remotest color of trading with the enemy." And that was the end of it.

Fortunately, however, not all the funds for the refugees were cut off. Outside the JDC effort, money still trickled in from the United States, and a little from England.

Rabbi Abraham Kalmanowitz of the *Va'ad Hatzalah*, for example, still managed to find ways to raise – and send – money. Occasionally this required both persistence and extraordinary ingenuity. One afternoon, after he had been kept waiting several hours in the outer office of Secretary of State Cordell Hull, the Rabbi was informed that Mr. Hull would not be able to see him after all. Kalmanowitz rose graciously from his chair . . . and collapsed on the floor. Aghast at seeing this venerable, white-bearded gentleman in a heap on the floor, Hull's receptionist called out to the secretary for help. Together, with great concern and care, they lifted the old man onto a couch in the inner office. But no sooner had Hull turned to call a doctor than Kalmanowitz regained consciousness. He was *most* apologetic. He had been working too hard . . . he was too old for this . . . and the devastating plight of those poor unfortunates in Shanghai. . . . But as long as he was here, he said more briskly, could the secretary of state spare just a moment to discuss this particular problem while he regained his strength?

With the cooperation of the Japanese, funds from organizations such as *Va'ad Hatzalah, Agudath Israel*, and the Polish government-in-exile were transferred through Switzerland or Portugal directly to the various groups in Shanghai or indirectly to them through Eastjewcom. Since the Poles, in Shanghai only a few months, were among the hardest hit by unemployment, this additional relief money did not provide luxury for anyone. But it did allow for necessities – and in the case of the Mir Yeshiva, there was even enough to begin printing, book by much-needed book, almost an entire edition of the Talmud and several other basic Jewish texts.

The loss of income had been devastating but, remarkably, by the start of summer 1942, no Jew in Shanghai, was starving; none was without a home; none was in danger for his life. Then, in July, a middle-aged, balding, cigar-smoking German colonel arrived from Tokyo. The "final solution" had at last come to Shanghai.

# 16

SOME MONTHS before Pearl Harbor, in the late summer of 1941, Heinrich Himmler's plan for the outright and total annihilation of the entire Jewish people had been openly adopted as Nazi policy. In every country where Jews were found, they were to be systematically sifted out of the general population and exterminated. Once this decision had been announced, there remained only a question of means. In Europe, under the direct administration of the German ss, work was speeded up on various technological experiments. One of these, involving the use of cyanide gas, designated Zyklon B, which could be released into airtight chambers, was finally put into widespread use.

Asia was a different question. There were, of course, far fewer Jews to be concerned with there, but the Germans encountered unexpected resistance in persuading their Japanese allies to deal with "their Jews" in an appropriate manner. It was a resistance that rankled ss Reichsführer Himmler. In mid-1942 the chief of Gestapo for Japan, China and Manchukuo was directed to leave his Tokyo headquarters temporarily and go to Shanghai where most of Asia's Jews were concentrated. There, working with the local Japanese authorities, he was to arrive at a final solution to the Jewish problem.

The Gestapo chief, a colonel named Josef Meisinger, was no neophyte when it came to dealing with Jews. As chief of the secret police in Warsaw in 1939, he had been responsible for the murder of so many (estimated at one hundred thousand) that he had been labeled "the Butcher of Warsaw." Warsaw, however, had been the zenith of his career. Even for the Gestapo, Meisinger had been too enthusiastic. In 1941, he was exiled to the relative obscurity of East Asia where he would be assigned principally to ascertain the loyalties of resident non-Jewish Germans to the fatherland. There was, in fact, little for him to do. Thus, when the order came down that he was to help the Japanese solve their "Jewish problem" once and for all, the "Butcher of Warsaw" responded with enthusiasm.

In July of 1942, proposals in hand, Meisinger boarded a submarine in Tokyo Bay for the trip to Shanghai.

Mitsugi Shibata sat on a bench in the small garden near the Japanese Consulate, outwardly serene, as befitted a vice-consul, inwardly exploding with emotion. It was Friday afternoon and he had just left a two-hour meeting of the newly created Jewish Affairs Bureau, which was composed of representatives of the Japanese Consulate, the *kempeitai*, the military and Mr. Tsutomu Kubota, a former naval officer now serving as the director of refugee affairs, and three Germans: Adolph Puttkamer, the chief of the German Information Bureau; Hans Neumann, lately of the Bergen-Belsen concentration camp, and Colonel Josef Meisinger.

After the customary formalities, Meisinger had come right to the point.

"There are now in Shanghai, over seventeen thousand Jews who have chosen to leave the fatherland. In January of this year, the German government very wisely deprived these traitors of their citizenship. They are enemies of the German state and potential, if not already actual, saboteurs against you, our ally. For the good of our alliance, we strongly feel that the entire Jewish plague must be eradicated from Shanghai. You need not worry about the mechanics, we will handle all the details. You will merely reap the rewards of our labors: you, of course, will inherit everything the Jews presently own or control."

There was a brief pause. Simple greed, Meisinger was sure, would take care of any lingering doubts the Japanese might have about the action.

"With your permission," he began again, nodding deferentially to Kubota, "I will now outline our proposed plans for dealing with the Jewish problem."

Kubota, the director of refugee affairs, sat passively, smiling slightly. This type of undertaking, he knew, would not need special permission from Tokyo. Dealing with problems like the Jews certainly came under his purview. So he who had heretofore only written about the Jewish menace would now actually be able to act. Kubota nodded. Meisinger began.

The first step would be to round up the potential saboteurs, preferably all at once so none would have a chance to escape. It is never easy to catch all dogs in one net, of course; but on the Jewish New

Year holiday of *Rosh Hashanah*, which begins the evening of September 1, almost all of them will be at one or another of their synagogues. It will be a simple matter to surround the buildings at that time.

As to what was then to be done with the Jews, Meisinger went on, there was a choice. First, like garbage, they could simply be thrown away. There were several old, unseaworthy ships docked across the Whangpoo River at Pootung. The Jews would be stripped even of the clothes on their backs and loaded onto the boats. These would then be towed out to sea, their rudder cables cut; and the Jews would be left to drift helplessly till they all died of thirst and hunger. At some later point, a naval detail could go out and sink the ships thus disposing of the worthless corpses.

A second possibility: upriver, there were several abandoned salt mines. The Jews could be put to some honest work for a change, they could dig salt for Japan. Most of the Jews would not last long at this, Meisinger admitted, but the Nazis knew from their experience in Europe the maximum amount of labor that could be gotten from a Jew for a minimum of nourishment. The equation was profitable enough to justify the trouble.

Another recommendation, one which Meisinger himself put forward, would be to build a concentration camp on the island of Tsungming in the mouth of the Yangtze River. There the Jews would be permitted to volunteer for medical experiments . . . on the human nervous system's tolerance for pain, for example.

Shibata couldn't take his eyes off Meisinger. The German kept rolling his fat black cigar between his wet lips, his balding head was sweating with excitement, his hands trembling as they lay on the edge of the table. Shibata found particularly revolting the saliva around Meisinger's mouth as the German described several of the "experiments" that Neumann had supervised at Bergen-Belsen.

Kubota cut off Meisinger's revolting descriptions by asking several questions. The Germans consulted their maps and charts and replied in concise detail. The meeting ended without a formal decision; but clearly the representatives of the army, navy, *kempeitai* and Refugee Affairs Bureau had been receptive to the suggestions.

"How can we be doing this?" Shibata demanded of himself as he watched a stream of emaciated rickshawmen trundle a party of military officers toward the *Bund*. "What is happening to the

Japanese that they should even be thinking these things?"

Shibata was a bright fellow – vice consul while still in his thirties.

In the three years he had been in Shanghai, one of his principal duties had been to keep the *Gaimusho* informed of what Inuzuka, whom they never did trust, had been up to. Shibata had many friends among the Europeans in Shanghai (he also kept a Chinese mistress, a risky venture for a representative of the Japanese government). He was familiar with the position of the refugees, and how that position had deteriorated. But this? Where was the justification for anything like this?

Undecided what to do, he began walking toward the residential area of the former French Concession. On the way, he met one of the men he most admired in Shanghai, Reuben Abraham. Shibata tried to chat with him casually as he would have done ordinarily. It was impossible.

"Mr. Abraham," he finally blurted out, "we *have* to talk. I can't give you any details, but the Jews in Shanghai are in the greatest danger. Please, we must have a meeting soon, tonight, tomorrow at the latest."

Shibata was aghast at himself: he, an official of the imperial government, privy to top secret information, was about to commit treason. His own ears could not believe they were hearing his words.

Abraham was unperturbed. "Tonight and tomorrow are the Sabbath, you know. The Sabbath is a day of holiness, a day of rest. We can't possibly descrete it."

"Mr. Abraham, this is not a social gathering. It is a matter of life and death for all the Jews here."

Abraham only shook his head. "It's more than the Jew protecting the Sabbath, Mr. Shibata; the Sabbath protects the Jew."

As the tall, proud man sauntered off, Shibata shook his head in disbelief. But his amazement was quickly washed away by relief: after all, he had not yet blurted out the secret. His position, his life as a Japanese, was still secure. Shibata began walking again, but even as he walked away, he knew what he had to do. Turning into a broad driveway, he knocked at the door of Elias Hayim. Hayim was less strict in his observance of the Sabbath.

Early the following day seven men, representing the Sephardi (Hayim and Michael Speelman), the Russian (Boris Topas and Joseph Bitker) and the German Jews (Dr. Kardegg, Fritz Kaufmann and Robert Peritz), met in Speelman's luxurious living room.

As Shibata described the details of the Meisinger meeting, the atmosphere in the room grew heavier.

"Pogroms happen, of course," one of the Russians said, "but of such a magnitude? Whoever heard of annihilating *every* Jew in such a big city?"

But the German Jews had fled from exactly that. It didn't matter, rich engineer or poor peasant, one said. The Nazis are out to destroy every Jew, every single Jew in the world. "Are you really surprised at twenty thousand?" he asked. "In Europe they murder in *batches* of twenty thousand – one batch today, another tomorrow." In Speelman's living room, the Jews were, for once, united . . . in terror.

But there was no time for terror. The date that Meisinger had spoken of, *Rosh Hashanah*, was only a few weeks away. What could they do in such a short time to avert a pogrom they were not even supposed to know about?

There was only one ray of hope in all the words Shibata had spoken: the extermination plan was a local undertaking. The Shanghai *kempeitai*, military and Foreign Ministry representatives were working on their own; they were not carrying out a directive from Tokyo. Possibly, if the higher ups were told about the plan, they would order it stopped, cold. As far as the seven men at that meeting could see, it was their only chance. In order to bypass the telegraph censors, they would send a Chinese messenger to Dr. Kaufman in Harbin – and through him, try to inform Yasue in Dairen and Matsuoka who was no longer foreign minister in Tokyo, but was still influential in the government. General Matsui, the commander of all Japanese forces in Central China would also be approached. But the chief of the *kempeitai* was another matter. None of the Jews knew him; none of them even knew his name. And the *kempeitai* was by far the most dangerous, most ruthless branch of the whole Japanese occupation structure.

"Nevertheless, there may be a way to reach him," Shibata said to the men seated anxiously around him. "There is a Japanese woman here in Shanghai who is a member of the nobility, not far removed, it is said, from the imperial family. She knows the head of the *kempeitai*. But what is most important about this woman is, she is very, very close friends with a Jewish man, Fritz Brahn. If you could inform this Fritz Brahn, of the extermination plan, perhaps he could try, through that woman, to reach the *kempeitai* chief."

It was a dangerous course to follow. No one knew Brahn very well, and he would be one more potential leak, and the leaders were trying to avoid a general panic. But it was a chance they would have to take.

Feeling he had done all he could and fearing the Speelman house might be under surveillance, Shibata left before the others, but not until each of the Jews there had thanked him emotionally for his warning and had promised him that its source would never be revealed.

After Shibata left, the seven continued to sit in Michael Speelman's living room. The difficult world outside now threatened to become devastating.

"There is one other person who might be able to help us," Boris Topas said, "Dr. Abraham Cohn."

His suggestion was met with approval but not enthusiasm. All seven men knew of Cohn, but each of them mistrusted him.

When Topas spoke with Cohn the next day, he discovered to his amazement that the doctor knew about the extermination plans.

Even in cosmopolitan Shanghai, Abraham Cohn was unusual. The fellow was unquestionably Caucasian: a tall, broad-shouldered Rumanian with fair skin, black wavy hair and handsome features. Also unquestionably, he was a Jew. But he was more. Cohn had been raised, from the age of six, in Nagasaki, long after the foreign community had moved from that city to Yokohama. Necessarily, he had had to study for his *bar mitzvah* under a Jesuit Hebrew scholar, but other than that his education had been entirely Japanese – kindergarten through medical school. Thus in many ways, the thirty-four-year-old Cohn was totally fluent in every aspect of Japanese culture. He was an award-winning master of the *haiku* poetic form and a triple-black-belt karate expert.

Cohn's karate skills had been put to an ironic use during the last of his Nagasaki days. The violently anti-Semitic White Russian General Gregorii Semonov had moved to that city after his defeat by the Communists in 1922. Late one night in the narrow dark streets of the city, Semonov was attacked by two Russians who blamed him personally for the Communist victory. Cohn, walking home down a nearby street, heard the commotion and rushed to prevent what was clearly about to be a violent murder. After both the assailants were on the ground, unconscious, Cohn took the victim to the hospital – and only there learned who he had saved.

Semonov's views of Jews remained unchanged by the incident, but he considered himself to be a man of honor. "You have without doubt, saved my life tonight," he said. "If ever I or any of my family can help you, we will consider it an honor to repay the debt." At the time, Cohn shrugged off the proffered thanks, but the incident would have repercussions years later.

Cohn was entirely too Japanese to be trusted by Topas or any of the other Jews: all too often they couldn't understand him, verbally or philosophically. And yet, they were greatly in need of, under these circumstances, those traits of his that they mistrusted. Topas was not happy to be meeting with him but he was very curious as to how the doctor had learned of the extermination plans.

Abraham Cohn had been practicing as a physician in Shanghai since his arrival from Hankow in 1939. He was popular among all the refugees and well liked also by many of the port's bar girls whose unique problems he treated with discretion for low fees. One evening, as he told Topas, he had been having a drink at the La Conga bar when a White Russian waitress named Vera approached him.

"There are some German soldiers at my table," she had whispered. "They are talking about the most horrible plans for the Jews here!"

Cohn had asked her a few questions, realized how serious this might be and asked her to keep the soldiers drunk and occupied for a while. Audaciously, he then went next door to the hotel where the Germans were staying, talked the Japanese desk clerk into giving him their key and went upstairs to search their room. Neither the Germans nor the waitress had been exaggerating: Laid out on the bed were plans, charts and maps for "dealing with" the entire Jewish population of Shanghai. Cohn touched nothing. He walked out, went downstairs, signalled Vera that he had finished and went home.

This much of the story Cohn related to Topas. The rest, he did not.

The following morning, Cohn went to visit one of his former classmates from Nagasaki, a Mr. Akiyama, who was now in the Police Department in Shanghai. Traditionally, such early friendships remain for life: without hesitation, Akiyama agreed to arrange for Dr. Cohn to meet with the director of refugee affairs, Tsutomu Kubota.

The two men met a few days later in Kubota's office. The director, as was his custom, had called in an interpreter before his foreign visitor arrived. When his secretary knocked on the door and ushered in the foreigner, Kubota bowed perfunctorily and waited for an incomprehensible stream of words to begin.

To his amazement the foreigner began speaking Japanese. Not only the right words but the right forms, with the right gestures. Politely hiding his surprise, Kubota asked his visitor to be seated. After a few minutes, he dismissed the interpreter. After half an hour, he rang for his secretary and cancelled the meetings he had called for the rest of the afternoon. This foreigner was a godsend! He knew Japan as well as any well-educated Japanese; and more important, he knew what had always been a total mystery to Kubota, the whys and wherefores of Western culture.

Satisfied with the impression he had obviously made, Cohn spoke calmly and casually about matters of no particular importance. All he wanted from this first meeting was to establish a relationship but Kubota was willing to waive the normal courtesies when he saw an opportunity.

"Would you be willing to act as our agent among the foreign community?" the Japanese asked Cohn. "To help keep us informed of what is going on, particularly among the Jews?"

There was a moment of silence.

"No," Cohn said clearly, "I will not do that."

"But why?" Kubota asked, surprised. "Japan is your home, you have said as much – and Japan is in control here now."

"Japan is my home," Cohn agreed. "But the Jews are my people. I will help both. But I will not help either side against the other."

Another silence.

"You are a Jew?"

Kubota was dumbfounded. He was one of the leading experts on Jews in Japan. He had studied Jews for years. He had read scores of books, written dozens of articles, given many, many lectures on Jews . . . but he had never met a Jew before.

Seizing the opportunity of Kubota's silence, Cohn embarked on the strategy he already had outlined in his mind.

"It should not surprise you too much, Kubota-san. No doubt, you are familiar with the theory that the Japanese and the Jews were at one time closely related?" Cohn happened to believe in the theory of the common origin of the Japanese and the Jews.

Kubota needed no briefing on the theory that the ten lost tribes of Israel had wandered across Asia as far as Japan, intermarried with the Japanese and mixed in their culture as well as their blood. Certainly, this was a most logical way of accounting for the wealth of little details that the traditional *Shinto* religion shared with ancient Judaism.

The theory was also, for the purposes of both Cohn and Kubota a mutually acceptable point of interest. Before he left the Japanese official's office, the physician promised to stop by the next morning at eight with a book on the subject. Not a word had been said about the pogrom – an entirely proper Japanese way of beginning a serious discussion of it.

Cohn's relationship with Kubota developed slowly. It was not till the third or fourth meeting (always at eight in the morning) that Cohn mentioned, in passing only, that he had been distressed at the recent flurry of strongly anti-Semitic newspaper articles appearing in Shanghai. Despising any group of people was not part of the Japanese way of thinking he said, so he believed there must be a foreign influence working on the Japanese.

Kubota did not immediately reply. Instead, he leaned back in his chair, folded his arms across his chest and looked steadily at Cohn. "Do you know who I am?" he asked.

"You are the director of refugee affairs for Shanghai."

"Yes. And that is no accident, Cohn-san. For nearly twenty years I have been engaged in studying the Jewish conspiracy in the world. I have written for journals devoted entirely to the Jew race. I have given lectures at the War College on Jews and Jewishness. I have shared in panel discussions and seminars about Jews so often I have lost count. But still, I was not the government's first choice for this position. First choice was General Shioden, now a member of the Diet. But, as we know, 'the frog that opens his mouth reveals his whole body.'"

Cohn smiled at the well-known Zen proverb.

"Shioden was such a *blatant* anti-Jew and his views were *so* well known, he was thought to be too obvious for the job. So, here I am."

"You are an 'expert,' Kubota-san, and yet you didn't recognize that my name is the oldest and most 'Jewish' Jewish name in the world?" Cohn said mildly.

"You have been a problem to me from the start, Cohn-san. To be

230

candid, I like you; I find you interesting. But I don't know that I can trust you."

"I am very trustworthy," Cohn said, accepting a cigarette from the proffered pack.

Kubota nodded noncommittally.

"Even my 'sworn enemies' will tell you so. Isn't Semonov one of the strongest anti-Semites in Shanghai? Semonov? Ask Semonov about me. Even he will tell you. . . ."

Kubota snorted with disbelief. The Semonov now in Shanghai was the son of the famous general. Kubota himself had served under General Semonov in the Siberian campaign, and he knew how he felt about Jews. "Semonov is like his father: he has no use for any of you! He'd see you all dead very happily."

"Nevertheless, Kubota-san, ask him," Cohn said. "See what he says."

At their next meeting, Kubota made no reference to Semonov; but he looked at Cohn through new eyes. Semonov had kept the promise his father had made so many years before.

In the same period that he was meeting with Kubota, Cohn was also meeting regularly with Topas. Their mutual distrust did not diminish over time, however Cohn's aloofness – and his disdain for the Jews' lack of understanding of the Japanese position and national personality – only grew. At Cohn's request, Topas had promised to include him at all meetings of the other leaders. In fact, Topas did not. And for his part, Cohn never spoke openly of his discussions with Kubota. By nature, he was a loner. In this crucial situation, the last thing he needed was to have to carry a bunch of clumsy foreigners on his coattails.

Weeks passed. The Hebrew month slipped from *Av* into *Elul*. *Rosh Hashanah* was only twenty-nine days away. Nothing had been heard from General Matsui in Nanking. From Dr. Kaufman in Harbin came a promise that he would try to exert his influence in Tokyo. Even more promising, though, was the news that Fritz Brahn, the Jew with the aristocratic girl friend, had been granted an appointment to meet with the chief of the *kempeitai*.

Brahn was carefully coached on what to say. He should not try to do too much. He should merely sound out the *kempeitai* chief. He should express the concern of the Jewish community at the sudden barrage of anti-Semitic articles – untrue, defamatory, totally out of keeping with the Japanese ideals of brotherhood – which had been appearing in the Chinese press for the past few weeks. He should impress upon the chief that the Jews in Shanghai were loyal members of the community and that they were not opposed to the Japanese. Definitely he should not say anything about extermination plans. Brahn understood and agreed. But his meeting with the *kempeitai* officer was very unpleasant from the beginning. The chief did not want to see him, couldn't understand why he was making such a fuss over "a few" newspaper articles, was very unsympathetic and antagonistic from the start. In the heat of what became a kind of confrontation, Brahn inadvertently let slip that he had heard a great harm would be done to the Jewish people in Shanghai. The *kempeitai* chief reacted with fury. Brahn was propagating false rumors! Who had said such a thing? Where had Brahn gotten this information? Terrified, Brahn implicated the Jewish leaders. Within forty-eight hours, Topas, Hayim, Speelman, Bitker, Kardegg, Kaufmann, Peritz and vice-consul Shibata had been arrested.

Without hearing or trial, all were sent to the infamous Bridge House Prison which was already jammed with "saboteurs," "foreign agents," and others who had somehow aroused Japanese suspicions. The eight men had no chance to correlate their stories. Seized individually, they were held in separate cells: Interrogators played heavily on their lack of knowledge of what the others might have confessed to.

Conditions in the prison were grotesque. Prisoners were forced to sit cross-legged for twelve or fifteen hours at a time, allowed less than fifteen minutes of exercise a day, and fed nothing but a weak gruel of boiled rice in water. Lice were the constant companions of all the Bridge House inmates: and the typhus that spread from man to man was responsible for as many deaths as the punishments of the Japanese guards. Neither advanced age nor social position had any bearing on one's treatment in the Bridge House. Even Shibata's position as vice-consul did not protect him from the *kempeitai*. They were a law unto themselves. After weeks of beatings, Shibata was deported in shame back to Tokyo, under threat of immediate execution if he so much as set foot in China in the next fifty years.

But the worst treatment was received by Boris Topas. Topas was beaten without mercy. Under interrogation, he was burned on the back and chest. His fingernails were pulled out. And worse was to come. One of the Japanese officers in the prison had been involved, nine years before, in the Manchurian kidnapping and murder of Simon Kaspé. Topas had written and signed a widely circulated statement protesting this brutality, and now fate placed him in the hands of this same Japanese officer. Topas was led to the old stone-built section of the prison, to the top of a long flight of sharp-edged steps leading down to a cellar. Suddenly, with no warning, he was thrown headfirst down the stairs. The guards came right down after him. Seizing him by the wrists, they pulled him up, across the sharp edges of the treads, to the top . . . then hurled him down again, over and over till his broken body lost all consciousness. It was treatment Topas never would recover from.

The seven community leaders were punished severely, but they were neither executed nor allowed to die. Except for Topas, who was held for six months, in a matter of days or weeks, the other Jews were released. Before being freed, however, each was subjected to a stern lecture by the prison sergeant. "How could you believe such nonsense, that we Japanese would harm you? We are your friends! We are your protectors! We have always treated you well. We will always treat you well. The only reason you were brought here was that you didn't have faith in us. Now go – do not spread any more false rumors. And tell your co-religionists that no harm will come to them from the Japanese."

And none did. Kubota had been unwise in his initial reaction to Meisinger's proposals. Slaughtering the Jews of Shanghai did not bear scrutinizing by Tokyo. Once Dr. Kaufman in Harbin got word of the extermination plan to Matsuoka with his contacts in the Foreign Ministry and to Yasue with his friends in the upper ranks of the army, Meisinger's dream was doomed. The beginning of the Great East Asian War might have forced Japan to re-appraise her relationship with world Jewry, but neither the *Gaimusho* nor the military saw any reason to alienate that community unnecessarily. Registration of Jews, internment of Jewish, as well as non-Jewish "enemy nationals," strict and continuing surveillance of all Jews – these measures were in order and had been officially sanctioned in Foreign Ministry memos as early as January, 1942. But very prominently paragraphed in Foreign Minister Togo's overriding "Emergency Measures for Jewish People" was this directive: Nothing shall be done to or with the Jews that might inspire "enemy counterpropaganda." Even to accommodate her ally, the Japanese government was unwilling to engage in a "final solution."

*Rosh Hashanah,* the first days of the year 5703, came and went in peace. Nothing more was heard of the Butcher of Warsaw, his rudderless ships, his salt mines and medical experiments. In Europe, six million Jews – an entire people – would die. In Shanghai, a tiny remnant of European Jewry would live.

How they lived was another matter. "I was originally sent to take your head," Kubota once said to Cohn. "I must at least take an arm."

In November, 1942, a top-secret dispatch was sent from the Japanese consul general in Shanghai, Seiki Yano to Kazuo Aoki, minister of Greater East Asia: "Relative to measures pertaining to the Jewish people in the Shanghai area, the plan established by the Japanese navy of that area, having been approved by the central government, will shortly be carried into force. . . . It is as follows: A Jewish district will be set up in the Hongkew area. The Jewish people scattered within the city will be collected together in order to live in this district. Surveillance, control and guidance will be a military function."

The Japanese did not carry out a pogrom – instead, they created the first Jewish ghetto in Asia.

# 17

A RAW FEBRUARY WIND blew in gusts past the tattered, nondescript buildings lining Tongshan Road. Getzel Syrkin, hunched up against the cold, stared without expression at a notice pasted to a brick wall. Stiff, black letters, stood out arrogantly against the unbleached-white paper:

PROCLAMATION CONCERNING RESTRICTIONS OF RESIDENCE AND BUSINESS OF STATELESS REFUGEES:

I Due to military necessity, places of residence and business of the stateless refugees in the Shanghai area shall hereafter be restricted to the undermentioned area in the International Settlement: east of the line connecting Chaoufoong Road, Muirhead Road and Dent Road; west of the Yangtzepoo Creek; north of the line connecting East Seward Road and Wayside Road; and south of the boundary of the International Settlement.

II The stateless refugees at present residing and/or carrying on business in the district other than the above area shall remove their place of residence and/or business into the area designated above by May 18, 1943.

III Persons other than the stateless refugees shall not remove into the area mentioned in Article I without the permisson of the Japanese authorities.

IV Persons who will have violated this proclamation or obstructed its reenforcement shall be liable to severe punishment.

Commander-in-Chief of the Imperial Japanese Army in the Shanghai Area.

Commander-in-Chief of the Imperial Japanese Navy in the Shanghai Area.

February 18, 1943.

As people stood motionless near the wall, other people hurried by – Jews, Chinese, Japanese, even some Gentile Europeans, lived in this slum section of Shanghai or came to it to take advantage of its cheaper prices. Few even glanced at the poster: it wasn't news any more. Yesterday, Thursday, February 18, it had been news – horrifying, totally unexpected, suddenly leaping out at them from official broadsides like this one, or radio broadcasts, or four-column headlines on the front page of every newspaper in Shanghai (and in smaller type in papers in Tokyo, Peking, Manila and Harbin). But already by Friday, the nineteenth, the "stateless refugees" had begun coping, in their minds if not yet their lives, with the prospect of a ghetto. Only Getzel, it seemed, could not get beyond the paper on the wall.

He spread open his hands in his trouser pockets, trying to warm them against his thighs. Protected only by thin cotton pants, his legs had little heat to give. Nothing about Getzel had very much more to give. He had tried – God, he really *had* tried. After they had moved into the fourth-floor room and Dovid started school, his life seemed to be returning to some slight degree of normality. He seemed almost about to shake off the *dybbuk* of fear that had been in his heart since that afternoon in Moscow. He went out every morning, rain or shine, to beg from one tailoring shop to the next – not for a handout, but for the opportunity to do a little work for a little pay. Some days he was lucky: he'd work a few hours, maybe even the full day, often for a Chinese who made him take a place near the window so every passerby could see that in *this* shop the whiteman was the worker. On those days, even with the Chinaman, he'd feel almost human again. The pay was only a few hundred dollars . . . a few hundred! In Alexandrov, a few hundred of any denomination made a man wealthy! But here, two hundred dollars now barely bought a loaf of wormy bread. But with even this paltry sum in his pocket, he was a *mensch*. He'd head for home, maybe buy something nice for his family – a little ersatz coffee, a couple of rolls, maybe even a packet of sugar. He'd felt such a part of things on those days. Now there would be no more of those days. Oh, of course, if he had a regular job, he might be allowed to leave the "designated area" during working hours. At least that's what the papers said. And he'd heard that some of the leaders were protesting that the Polish Jews weren't "stateless" at all, because there was a recognized Polish government in exile that stood one hundred percent behind their citizenship. But a ghetto for Jews was a ghetto for Jews no matter how often the Japanese referred to it as a "designated area for stateless refugees." It was another step toward extermination.

Getzel tried to remember his life – Alexandrov, its familiar dusty streets, his own tiny house, the *shul* full of old men and their endless discussions. All dead now. His own survival still puzzled him. Alexandrov to Vilna; Vilna to Moscow, to Vladivostok, to Kobe; and Kobe to Shanghai. For four years, he had managed to stay half a step ahead of utter catastrophe. And here, in this totally alien corner of the world, in China, he had tried, with the utmost of his shattered abilities, to start life again. But even in the whale's belly, the worthy prophet Jonah couldn't escape the wrath of God, so how could a poor *schlemiel* like himself hope to escape just by fleeing to an unheard-of land? The catastrophe had leap-frogged seven thousand miles and caught up with him. Getzel wouldn't even have to move to be shut up in the ghetto: he was already living in the very center of the slum that was to be the "designated area."

Why did they bother to avoid the word ghetto, Getzel wondered idly, watching an emaciated cat disappear down an alley. Why "stateless refugees" instead of "Jews"? The Nazis used the words freely enough each time they proudly announced shutting people up in the Warsaw Jewish ghetto, the Vilna Jewish ghetto, the Riga, Shavli, Berdischev, Bialystok, Minsk Jewish ghettos. . . . Moishe, that gawky adolescent, brought home news of all of it. "From where?" he'd once asked. The boy wouldn't say. Just from "someone" who had a radio, who had hidden it before the Japanese confiscated all the long-range receivers. Through Moishe, when the little ones were out of hearing, he and Cheya received a periodic supply of grisly stories about the formation of ghettos, firing of ghettos, calculated starvation in ghettos. Recently, just a few weeks ago, from Warsaw, there was even word of a rare, brief uprising within a ghetto. But uprisings inevitably failed and inexorably brought down still greater terrors upon the heads of those trapped helplessly inside. That was the thing about a ghetto, Getzel thought: it was just a prison with a little extra distance between the walls.

Getzel was shivering compulsively now – but too despondent to care. He knew he'd feel even worse later, after they'd built their gates and strung up their barbed wire. Colder, hungrier, sicker. And more hopeless. There was nothing more he could do – nothing any of them could do – to escape the destruction that God seemed to have chosen for His chosen people. "I will die in this strange, unheard-of land," he thought, more sure of it now than ever before, "and be buried far away from the graves of my father and my grandfather."

There arose before his eyes the gentle faces of those two old men. Getzel stood motionless on a street in Shanghai, filling his heart with the warm smiling faces of his father and grandfather.

Moishe trudged up the three flights of rickety stairs, glad to be home in plenty of time to prepare for the Sabbath. Friday was only a four-hour day at the Organization for Rehabilitation and Training School on Jansen Road. In the spring of 1941, an ORT professional had arrived in Shanghai to help some of the uprooted refugees make the change from *shtetl* life to the careers demanded by the twentieth century: electrical work, locksmithing, automobile driving, engine repair. . . . For teenagers, like Moishe, who were too old for the Kadoorie School, a full-time program was set up in a former Chinese knitting factory – practical technical training in the morning, book-learning in the afternoon. By the end of even the short Friday schedule, Moishe was glad for the exercise of walking home. But it was a long trip, particularly on a cold day. Passing through the built-up area of Hongkew, he could smell Sabbath meals being prepared on the tiny flower-pot shaped devices that served as stoves for the poorer refugees. Coal was expensive, wood unattainable. But the little stoves burned a homemade concoction of coal dust, sand, cinders, ashes and straw, pressed into cakes and dried. Along with billows of smoke, enough heat was produced for cooking; and starting shortly after breakfast on Friday, Jewish women begin the preparation of the Sabbath meal for their families.

Moishe paused briefly to rest on the middle landing. Mrs. Syrkin and Sophie, and probably Dovid, would be all involved with that now, no doubt, not in the room – the smoke there made cooking impossible – but down in the courtyard. Moishe was of half a mind to join them – it would be warmer there than in the unheated room. But he was already halfway upstairs; he went on up and opened the door.

His hand never left the metal latch. He stood absolutely still, willing himself not to scream out loud.

"My God! Oh, my God!" he whispered. The body of Getzel Syrkin, a leather belt around its neck, hung lifeless from a hook in the wall.

Moishe released Getzel's old body from its unnatural pose, laid it out on the floor under a sheet and stumbled down the stairs to break the news to Cheya. As always on a Friday noon the courtyard was full. No sooner had Moishe spoken the words – God knows which words, he could never remember afterward – than other women were crowding round, holding Cheya, crying for her loss, consoling her with words and prayers. Clutching Dovid, who was too stunned to cry, Cheya made her way back up the stairs to the miserable room. Sophie, sensibly went to fetch people from the burial society.

After their arrival, within minutes of Sophie's summons, Moishe, himself, was sent out to call the Amshenover rebbe at his apartment in the former French Concession.

The rebbe had been spending his early Friday afternoon as usual, organizing his mind and his wardrobe for the Sabbath that would begin at sunset. His long black satin jacket, with frayed cuffs and dangerously thin at the elbows, was already waiting, hanging softly around the back of a wooden chair. One brightly brushed black shoe sat on the floor beside it. Humming a rhythmic, wordless little *niggun*, the rebbe was buffing the other to a matching shine. As he would have dressed to greet a queen, so he dressed to greet the Sabbath. A day of rest, a day of holiness, but more than that, *shabbos* was a day-long intimation of the world to come – a weekly preview of the peace, the satisfying wholeness of the life that would open for a Jew after God had brought this life to a close.

His wife knocked gently at the door and came in. There had been a phone call, she told him, not good news: in Hongkew, Getzel Syrkin had died.

The Sabbath-eve pleasure faded from the rebbe's eyes.

But it was still worse, his wife went on. Getzel Syrkin had not waited for God to bring his life to a close. The representatives of the burial society were with the body now, she said; but they did not know what to do.

The rebbe put down the shoe and reached for his small, well-worn Hebrew psalm book.

"Tell them to do nothing until I get there," he said. "And if anyone else is looking for me, tell him I will see him in *shul* at 5:43."

With that, he hurried out to the street. If humanly possible, the burial question would have to be settled and the body laid in the ground by sundown. Otherwise, it would have to wait until Sunday morning – an unnecessary hardship on everyone concerned. The Amshenover rebbe did not like riding in rickshaws, as a principle, he objected to causing some poor man to act as a draught animal solely for his benefit. That, and his desire for speed, persuaded him, in spite of the cost, to flag down a passing taxi.

Getzel Syrkin's body lay, still untouched, on the floor of the room. Cheya sat in one corner with Dovid and Sophie, both of them sobbing softly. The four men from the burial society stood, unsure and ill-at-ease on the opposite side of the room near the window. The neighbors, as custom required, waited outside. Panting from the effort of climbing four flights of stairs, the Amshenover rebbe paused at the open door. Cheya looked up at him, beseechingly, but said nothing. One of the four men from the society hurried out into the hall. Anxiously but quietly, so that Cheya would not hear, one of the four began speaking.

"It was not a natural death, rebbe! It was a suicide. We cannot bury a man who takes his own. . . ."

"I am well acquainted with Talmud, Mr. Lewin," the rebbe cut him off as gently as possible. "The person who takes his own life denies the partnership of God in that life. By denying God His role, the person implies that God does not exist. And in denying the existence of God, a Jew denies his fellowship in the Covenant with God."

"Well, can we bury such a man in a Jewish cemetery?" Mr. Lewin demanded, speaking more loudly than he had intended.

In her corner of the room, Cheya heard the question. He was not "such a man," her heart silently cried out. He was a good man. He was a good Jew; a good husband. Getzel never was a strong man, but he did all he could. How can they now refuse him the honor and peace of a proper burial? How can they refuse it, even in the face of his son?

Almost unnoticed, Moishe joined the group of men in the hallway. The prompt arrival of the rebbe had taken a burden from his shoulders.

In response to Lewin's outburst, the rebbe put his finger to his lips to remind them all of the importance, the simple decency, of not troubling the widow with this discussion.

"It is not a matter of law only. It is also a matter of interpretation. A man who takes his own life surely is committing a crime," the rebbe said in almost a whisper. "But to be held responsible for a crime – any crime – the person committing it must be conscious of the reality of what he is doing. Is that not so? If he is too ill, or too upset, or too despondent to realize what he is doing, how could we hold such a man guilty? Now, I have seen Getzel only occasionally in the past several months. But would you say he was fully conscious of the reality of the world around him?"

"I would say he was not, rebbe," one of the other men replied after a short pause. "He tried, but . . . he was not entirely here."

The rebbe gestured with his hands. "So?"

Mr. Lewin, however, was not entirely convinced. "Won't it set a poor example, if we allow a proper burial in this case?" he whispered. "Life is hard for all of us here. Getzel was not the only one to be discouraged. If people begin to feel that there is no shame, no dishonor to committing suicide. . . ."

The rebbe looked at him in wonder. Does the man really believe people cling to their lives out of fear of shame? he thought. Then softly he said, "You are right, Mr. Lewin. It would be best not to make a great to-do over the suicide aspects of this. A man died. That alone is unfortunate enough. Getzel Syrkin was a Jew: he will be buried as a Jew with all respect in our cemetery."

Persuaded by the rebbe's authority if not his argument, Lewin gave in. The men of the burial society began preparing the body. Cheya had not heard the final exchange of words, but she understood the meaning of the activity.

"Thank you, rebbe," she said to the man who approached her. "He was a good man, *such* a good one."

He looked down at her with gentle pity. "His suffering is over now, Mrs. Syrkin. God is with him. There is time yet to bury the body today. Is someone making the shroud?"

"I took a sheet to Mrs. Ershowsky downstairs," Moishe said. In accordance with the law. Getzel's body would be dressed simply in a loose fitting cotton shroud, and a *yarmulka*. His prayer shawl, one of four fringes cut off, would be wrapped around the body before it was placed in a plain wood coffin.

"Rebbe, though he was not my father, I would like to say *kaddish* for Mr. Syrkin." Moishe's tone of voice questioned the propriety of this as much as it stated his desire.

The rebbe looked approvingly at him. "Dovid is not yet *bar mitzvah*, is he?" he asked.

"He is only ten," Cheya answered, shaking her head.

But I *know* the *kaddish*, rebbe," Dovid spoke up. "I know it, and I will say it for the rest of my life," he vowed miserably.

"Every day for eleven months, will be sufficient to honor your father," the rebbe said gently. "He was a fine man, Dovid. You must do his memory honor by also being a fine man."

Tears again running down his cheeks, Dovid could not respond. There was so much he had never been able to talk to his father about, so much that he had been putting off until things got a little better, until his father really seemed to be here with them, completely. Now all he could do was put his arms around his mother's shoulders and cry out at the unfairness of it.

The rebbe went to him, putting his hand on the boy's small head, saying nothing, merely being there for a few minutes.

"If you just go with him every morning," he said when he turned back to Moishe, "it would be a *mitzvah*. I'm sure it would be appreciated by everyone."

Moishe nodded, grateful for the rebbe, grateful for the burial society that took care of the coffin, the cemetery plot, all the mechanical details. What this poor family would do later, with no one earning any money at all, he didn't know. Somehow, they would manage; they always had. Except Mr. Syrkin. Poor, unhappy, lost Mr. Syrkin. But in his own way, Moishe supposed, Mr. Syrkin had managed too.

For seven days, Cheya and Dovid sat *shiva* on low stools in the small room, receiving visitors who came to offer condolences and gifts of food. Sophie took care of the daily chores. Moishe went with Dovid to *shul* every morning and otherwise just sat with Cheya, listening to her reminiscences. At the end of the *shiva*, Eastjewcom was informed that the family of Getzel Syrkin had become "widow, three dependents." Beginning the following Sunday Cheya received a weekly cash allowance, meager, but sufficient to feed the four of them. The rebbe, moreover, spoke to several of the Russian Jews, suggesting that it would be a particular *mitzvah* to offer Mrs. Syrkin whatever occasional work they might have. The children kept a sharp lookout for the few part-time, odd jobs available.

Getzel's response to the proclamation of the ghetto was not unique, but it was rare. For the most part the refugees were deeply frustrated that the structures of their lives, which they had struggled so hard to build were to be so summarily demolished. But there was no alternative, and so the German and Austrian Jews, the overwhelming majority of the seventeen thousand affected, resigned themselves with characteristic discipline to make the move. Equally characteristically, the Polish Jews began protesting the injustice.

As Getzel had foreseen, their first reasoned argument had had no effect whatsoever on the Japanese decision. The manifestos that followed were less restrained: "... why do you compel us to be stateless.... We are not and we will not be stateless! The whole world will know that you have compelled us! We informed from this to the Swiss Consulate and to the International Red Cross! Better for you and for us give us a red belt [armbands worn by "enemy nationals"] and take us to the [internment camp] ... The war is not finish and you can not know! We are and remain Polish citizens till our die!"

The Japanese were still unmoved. Their definition of "stateless refugee" included those from Germany, Austria, Czechoslovakia, Hungary, Latvia, Lithuania, Estonia and "former Poland." The Nazis didn't recognize the London-based Polish government in exile; and since the entire designated-area affair had been intended principally to mollify the Nazis, the Poles must necessarily be redeemed as stateless. Ultimately, the Polish Jews like the other "stateless" refugees, prepared to move.

For their part, the Japanese also responded to all those protests by pointing out – correctly, if somewhat ingenuously – that the relocation order made no mention whatsoever of Jews. The refugees, and all other foreigners in the city, they said, were to be treated according to nationality. And, in fact, those Jews – principally Sephardim who held passports of Allied nations had already been interned along with their non-Jewish countrymen in unused factories and schools on the outskirts of Shanghai. Some internees would ultimately be repatriated; some would die, and some would remain in the camps for the duration. Living space was greatly restricted in the internment camps, and both boredom and diseases were endemic. But, with a few horrifying exceptions, the internees were not mistreated.

Other foreigners, Jews and non-Jews alike, managed to obtain the money and connections to produce passports from neutral nations. All this the refugees could accept. But what really rankled the seventeen thousand Jews who were eventually shut up into the ghetto was that the city's four thousand Russian Jews, since they held citizenship in a nation recognized by Japan, should remain exempt from the ghetto – and, in fact, totally free of restrictions.

The refugees resentment was soon further exacerbated. Within two weeks of the proclamation's appearance, Kubota's bureau had announced that the Russians themselves would be put in charge of moving the refugees into the ghetto. This step was one tangible result of the long conversations between Kubota and Dr. Cohn. During the early winter, before the proclamation had been released, the two men had spoken briefly about the ghetto concept.

Cohn's hope was that such a major upheaval would be less traumatic if it were kept within the Jewish family. "If you close up all the stateless Jews in Shanghai in a restricted area," he had said, "it's going to cost you a tremendous amount to relocate them, feed them, house them, etc. Instead why not let us organize ourselves into a group, with representatives from your office on hand at every meeting, of course, and we will take care of the relocation? After all, who knows better than a Jew how to get another Jew to do something?"

A similar thought had also occurred to Kubota, but he was delighted that once again a Jew had made the necessary offer. Within the Japanese government itself, no one department had wanted to take the sole responsibility for forming the designated area – the final decision had been endorsed jointly by the army, the navy and the Ministry of Greater East Asia with the prior approval of the central government. And now here was a chance to broaden the responsibility further by making Jews themselves a party to it. Kubota had a drawerful of reports on the problems Jews had in working together, but this did not seem an opportune time to allude to that. Besides, Cohn was even now improving on his offer. The Russian Jews, the physician was hinting, would be glad to contribute at least part of the cost of this expensive relocation of their fellow Jews.

Of course, the exclusion of the Russian Jews from the designated area had already been discussed at length among the policy makers.

At this point in world affairs, the Japanese were particularly anxious not to upset the Russian government. A mutual neutrality pact which had been signed with Stalin in mid-1941 had given Japan some sense of security on her northern borders that was much too important now to Japan's foreign policy to be threatened by such a small matter as the living arrangements of four thousand Russian Jews. Now Cohn was offering to let the Russian Jews do the work of relocation and supervision. Had word of all this reached the Russian Jewish community? Was Cohn now here as its agent? Kubota was familiar with duplicity in many forms. The physician looked innocent, though it was hard to tell with a foreigner. Still, Kubota had nothing against the Russian Jews. And the idea of using them – and their money – to accomplish Japanese ends appealed to him.

"It is something perhaps to be considered," Kubota said. Then the two moved on to other topics.

Within a week of the ghetto proclamation, Kubota was invited to speak at a general meeting of the Shanghai Russian Jewish Club. In the course of his talk, he mentioned that it was due to his own personal intervention that the Russians had been exempted from the proclamation. It was hoped, he said meaningfully, that in return the Russians would cooperate fully in the job of organizing the relocation of those people who were not exempt. That very evening a committee of eighteen men was elected to oversee the cooperation. Unlike all the other Jewish committees that had been formed over the past eight years, this group had an emblem: a Star of David which was surrounded – as if being protected – by a stylized cherry blossom. The cherry blossom, one of the symbols of imperial Japan, is called in Japanese, *sakura*. The name of the committee of eighteen was SACRA – the Shanghai Ashkenazi Collaborating Relief Association. The name, so close to the Japanese word, was the suggestion of Dr. Cohn. The emblem, with its symbolic overtones, was a design created by Dr. Cohn. And the chairman chosen by SACRA was Dr. Cohn.

As Kubota had foreseen, SACRA was not an internally harmonious committee. The same suspicions and disdain that had colored Cohn's dealings with Topas and the other community leaders immediately surfaced in SACRA. The question of Cohn's loyalty was never answered to the satisfaction of the other men. The fact that Kubota's representative, a Mr. Kano, was always present as secretary, and that Cohn often chatted with him in Japanese added to the strain.

SACRA's external relationship with the "stateless" community ran even less smoothly. The committee was deeply resented; it was believed by most of the refugees that the Russians had sold out to the Japanese to save themselves, at the possibly fatal expense of their fellow Jews.

To all this, SACRA had no answer. Its overriding purpose-refined in dozens of small get-togethers, unattended by either the chairman or the secretary – was to stall. Its other seventeen members knew they had no choice but to go along with the Japanese; but they would go along as slowly as possible. Maybe the Japanese would have another change of heart. Maybe the German retreat from Stalingrad, triumphantly reported by TASS shortwave, did signal a turning point in the war. SACRA was in a position to play for time – but if that position became public knowledge. If Kubota ever suspected that SACRA was, in the words of one of its members "using every form of sabotage that was possible . . . to stall the implementation of the relocation," he would immediately have dismissed the committee and imprisoned its members. Then, as he had threatened at the initial Russian Club meeting, the Japanese would "take matters into their own hands and do it their own way." In spite of their true feelings, SACRA formed its committees, recruited refugees to man the subcommittees, which would do most of the actual work, and set out with an apparent will to meet the May 18 deadline. By this date, the eight thousand or so refugees who did not already live in the "designated area" were to be moved into it.

The area, slightly under one square mile of Hongkew, was already jammed with some nine thousand refugees, several thousand Japanese and nearly a hundred thousand Chinese. In theory, as 'was "requested" in the proclamation order, the Chinese and Japanese would simply trade their Hongkew apartments for "comparable quarters" among the apartments which would have to be vacated by the stateless refugees. In practice, there was very little comparability. Many of the refugees, particularly the earlier arrivals, scrimped for years to be able to afford small apartments in the French Concession or the International Settlement – places with electricity, phone service and Western-style bathrooms. Few such palaces were available in the Hongkew slum; and those that were were often available only upon payment of "key-money," amounting to four or five months' rent. The most an average refugee could hope for was a couple of tiny, sunless rooms, badly in need of fumigation and separated from the next unhappy family by a plywood partition. Flush toilets were rare in Hongkew; electricity was limited; even phone service could not be transferred without a lengthy appeal through the Bureau for Refugee Affairs.

From SACRA's point of view, the May 18 deadline approached with unnatural speed. Not only did reluctant individuals have to be assisted in transplanting their residences (and, in a few hundred cases, also their businesses); but virtually everything had to be done for the refugees in the *heime*. The higgledy piggledy Chinese style housing was not at all suitable for *heim* living. New residences had to be created virtually from scratch, out of unused warehouses or factories – with every stage of construction needing to be supervised and, of course, paid for. And what of the establishments that had served the whole community? Clinics, schools, meeting halls, the semi-charitable Polish Refugee Kitchen Number One Kosher Restaurant – everything had to be relocated. Primarily for those refugees who held jobs outside the ghetto, an incredibly cumbersome pass system had to be established in order to allow those within the designated area to venture out at certain times, along certain routes. Even if SACRA had worked with the best will in the world, it would have been impossible to do so much so quickly. By the end of April, with less than three weeks to go, only about two thousand of the refugees had been relocated. Among the six thousand still free were the students and faculty of the Mir Yeshiva.

SACRA's business headquarters was on an upper floor of an unimpressive building in the International Settlement. It was a small space, scarcely larger than the Kobe Jewcom headquarters. Standing in the middle of it, Yankel Gilbewitz found that it shared very little else in common with Kobe Jewcom. Certainly the two obstinate and totally unreasonable SACRA committeemen attempting to deal with the yeshiva delegation bore no resemblance to Mr. Hanin or Mr. Ponve.

The yeshiva's position was adamant: The rabbis and students had absolutely no intention of living or studying in the Hongkew Salvation Army compound. When Yankel had first heard this SACRA proposal, he'd thought it was a joke. There were still inmates living in the compound – drunkards, crazy people, prostitutes. . . . The Mir Yeshiva was one of the most illustrious centers of Jewish education in Europe! How could this devoted congregation of scholars, with its reputation for dedication, be asked to study in such a place? Yankel had immediately joined the group going to protest at SACRA's downtown headquarters.

"What *are* we?" one of the boys was now declaiming. "Are we beasts? Pigs? Are we *nothings* that we should be pushed off into some toilet of the world of sin?"

The confrontation had been going on nearly an hour, tempers and voices rising, goodwill diminishing.

"If you will let me say . . ." the SACRA committeeman began.

"Those people are still there!" The yeshiva boy was beyond listening. "Drunkards! Convicts!"

". . . something, I will explain to you our predicament and perhaps . . ."

"Women of the street! The dregs of this abysmal pit of a city! Our yeshiva cannot be insulted this way! It is the total denial . . ."

Even Yankel himself joined the battle.

"What kind of a Jew are you?" he shouted. "Do you consign the elite of Jewish scholars to such a place? Have you no respect for Torah? *Apikores!*"

The SACRA man gave up and turned away. It was enough that he had been forced to volunteer for this thankless, unpopular and misunderstood labor, that he was being forced to contribute most of what little money he still had after the war had closed off his markets and the Japanese had all but taken over his office. It was enough that he was quite convinced that the Russian Jews would also be consigned to the ghetto once they had accomplished the unpleasant task of moving all the refugees into it. But it was too much, *too* much, that his loyalty to Judaism should be questioned, that he should be cursed as an *apikores* – a worldly, anti-Jewish, anti-God Epicurean!

The first yeshiva boy paused to catch his breath. Yankel, hearing only his own voice, stopped too. The second SACRA man seized the opportunity of silence.

"You will not be sharing the compound with the 'dregs of society.' The few unfortunate people still living there will be separated from you as far as possible. You *need* a school in the designated area. And you need a place to live, don't you?"

"We *have* a school," Yankel said. "And we absolutely do not need to live together. We *need* to live apart, separately. Don't you see how easy it will be, if we are all in one place, for them to come and round us all up while we are sleeping? The danger is too great!" This fear, of being forced into a situation where they could all be seized at once, was in fact more of a drawback to the compound

248

than the continued presence of its "inmates."

The SACRA speaker laughed deprecatingly. "No one is going to come and 'round you up.' Think how convenient it will be for you to . . ."

The laughter was the final straw. Yankel jerked his head back just in time to get out of the way of a straight-backed chair that flew past him on its way toward a window. In the silence that followed, he could hear the tinkle of glass pieces as they hit the pavement below. Miraculously, none of the passersby was hit.

"You will *not* behave that way in this office," the SACRA man said. "We have not got the time or patience for these childish outbreaks! You will simply have to . . ."

The students never heard what they would simply have to do. Another chair went the way of the first. Tables were kicked over, drawers yanked from their desks and emptied out onto the floor. Two lamps were seized, the shades shredded, the bases hurled out of another window. And then everything was flying through the broken panes. What was too large was first smashed and then thrown out. The SACRA committeemen fled in terror.

The Japanese police were not long in coming. But by the time they arrived to seize every one of the thirty students, the office was a shambles. SACRA did not protest the arrest.

It was several days before Rabbi Ashkenazi, one of the leading figures among the Ashkenazim, and the principal of the yeshiva could persuade the Japanese authorities not to impose long and probably fatal prison terms for these "revolutionary activities." Apologies were made; SACRA headquarters were cleaned up and refurnished; money changed hands; and one afternoon, the boys turned up again at the yeshiva.

Yankel spent much of his time in jail pondering with a few Mir Yeshiva cellmates the suitability of their response. However, they had won their point. The Yeshiva would have nothing to do with the Salvation Army compound; it would, at its own expense, rent private rooms within the designated area, but would be given passes to study daily at their Beth Aharon Synagogue. Yankel sensed a new fullness to his spirit, a new strength in his devotion. This was, at least, a partial compensation for the typhus he contracted there.

In the course of his leisurely discussions with Dr. Cohn, Tsutomu

Kubota had softened his attitude toward the Jews. He had gone so far as to suggest in a letter to Prime Minister Tojo that some of Japan's suspicion of the Jews might be "erroneous." But the ghetto proclamation had come down from the highest authorities – Kubota had no choice but to carry it out. So, in spite of extensions and SACRA's foot-dragging, in spite of *die Arroganz der Polnischen Fluchtlinge* (the arrogance of the Polish refugees) a few of whom, to the admiration of the other Jews, continued to defy the order till they were finally jailed (where six of them died of disease), the relocation proceeded. The May 18 deadline passed with no great fanfare; but by the early autumn of 1943, all but a few hundred stateless refugees were confined behind the guarded gates of the Hongkew designated area.

Now began the darkest days for the Jews of Shanghai. The ghetto – though the Japanese never referred to it as such – had been carved out of the city's most dismal area. Within the square mile, there were no parks, not even a tree; the closest thing to nature, one refugee noted, was a bench painted green. Aside from the Cafe Louis and the Roof Garden Restaurant, which were patronized by successful blackmarketeers, and a few people, like the owner of the local bakery, who made a good profit in supplying absolute essentials, poverty was everywhere in Hongkew.

The pass system was the only way out. Three-month passes and one-month passes were issued to those who had jobs on the outside (and to the Mir Yeshiva) by a Japanese official named Ghoya. Ghoya was infamous. An exceedingly ugly man, and so short he had to stand on his desk to reach eye level with some of the refugees, Ghoya was a psychotic who gloried in his position of power. "I am the King of the Jews!" was one of his favorite announcements; yet simultaneously wanted to be loved by them. Ghoya's moods shifted like quicksilver. When he happened to be in good humor, word of it spread rapidly throughout the ghetto: Hurry, now is the time to get your pass renewed! Outside his office, refugees would line up to apply for another three months' possession of the precious little metal lapel button that said "May Pass" in a Chinese character. But suddenly something would seem to go wrong: Ghoya would seize on some imagined slight, jump up on his desk, and slap some unfortunate refugee across the face . . . and the line of pass applicants would quickly dissipate.

This bully and tyrant could sometimes be manipulated, however.

One refugee invariably wore a tall top hat when applying for his pass renewal. Initially, Ghoya believed the man was making fun of him and threatened to shoot him on the spot. "But Ghoya-san," the refugee said with wounded innocence, "I *always* wear this hat when approaching a great man!" Thereafter, the refugee received his pass with no difficulty.

Ghoya slapped people, screamed at them, threatened them, insulted them; everyone in the ghetto was terrorized by him; yet actually he never seriously hurt anyone. The official in charge of daily and weekly passes, was more dangerous, however. His name was Okura and on most occasions refugees would have to stand for hours in the scorching sun just to see him. He often beat those he didn't like, and with very little provocation would throw a man into the Ward Road Jail which, as conditions there deteriorated, became the equivalent of a sentence of death by disease.

Passes were distributed by Kubota's men; but the ghetto gates were guarded by the Jewish branch of the foreign *Pao Chia* – an international force which the Japanese had organized in 1942 to police the entire city. The Jewish *Pao Chia* ("protect the home" in Chinese) consisted of men aged twenty to forty-five who, on a rotating basis stood at the gate just beyond signs that read "Stateless Refugees Prohibited Without Permission." They checked every pass for the slightest discrepancy, and many of the *Pao Chia* were despised for being entirely too scrupulous in their work – reporting people for being just one minute late, catching children trying to sneak out to a nearby park. . . . But under the direct supervision of the Japanese, the Jewish *Pao Chia* guards, like their counterparts in the ghettos of Europe, were in an untenable position.

The only refugees exempted from the pass system were the children attending the Kadoorie School. For them, a school ID card was sufficient for any time during school hours on school days. With its green open playing fields, its clean classrooms and a teaching staff determined to make even these depressing years as rewarding as possible, the school was a large oasis of pleasure in the otherwise dreary, uncomfortable, anxious lives of its five hundred and fifty pupils.

As winter came on, the Russian Jewish community, though still free outside the designated area, was rapidly exhausting its resources. Voluntary contributions and loans had long since been replaced by a straight system of taxes levied by SACRA over the signatures of Kubota, his secretary and Kano. But inflation continued to diminish the value of the levy and the Allied blockade of shipping was disastrously effective. The Joint Distribution Committee representative, Laura Margolies, had already been interned and was soon to be repatriated. Before she left, Margolies arranged with Joseph Bitker a SACRA member who had also been one of the city's original Jewish leaders, to take over as director of the internationally disconnected Shanghai JDC. Margolies promised that after her repatriation, as soon as she was successful in lifting the JDC embargo on funds to the refugees in Shanghai, she would let him know by sending a telegram wishing his daughter a happy birthday. In the meantime, everyone would just have to subsist on whatever could be raised locally. Dr. Kaufman's Far Eastern Jewish Council in Harbin sent several generous donations. The wealthy industrialist, Lew Zikman who spent the entire war in Japan, sent money over. But demand always outpaced supply.

The winter of 1943-4 was the harshest that Shanghai had seen in a generation. Coal virtually disappeared. Electricity was rationed. Refugees who, in the heat of the summer, had set up tiny stalls along the sidewalks and sold their heavy clothing for extra food, now had nothing but thin cotton to shield them from the cold and rain. Burlap sacks were reborn as topcoats; people walked the street wrapped in threadbare blankets and little else. For the first time, Jews could be seen begging for handouts along the sidewalks. To alleviate the unremitting cold and hunger, the unthinkable grew into the possible. Prostitution increased noticeably. Seven women were even licensed by the Japanese and many more plied the trade unofficially. In a few instances, mothers of newborn babies gave them up entirely – to other Jews or even to Chinese families – rather than try to keep them in conditions of such privation. Among the men, idleness was the most devastating factor. Raised in a strongly patriarchal society, it was nearly as hard on them to have to live on charity – or on the income of a wife able to secure domestic work – as not to live at all. Husbands would sit for hours in the tiny ghetto coffee shops, staving off rage and depression only through their mutual support. But a few gave up entirely.

As the winter progressed, the Japanese further tightened the restrictions on passes. Those of the Mir Yeshiva were withdrawn altogether, forcing that group to relocate first to a very dilapidated building, then to a former hotel on Wayside Road. The former collapsed entirely several days after the Yeshiva moved from it.

These new pass restrictions hit hardest at more than a thousand of the refugees who had secured from some of the Russian Jewish companies certificates that, falsely for the most part, attested to their employment outside the ghetto. Thus they had secured passes that enabled them to pass the gates every working day. Once free in the open city, they could sometimes get the kind of pick-up work that Getzel Syrkin had done. But now, under the scrutiny of the pass officers, even this intermittent source of income would dry up. A cartoon of the times shows a Chinese peasant squatting by a mound of disintegrating vegetables. The caption reads: "Rotten foods: Japanese no buy . . . Coolie no buy . . . White refugee people, they buy!"

By the winter of 1943, an increasing number of refugees could no longer manage to get by at all. Very simply, even with rotten vegetables there was not enough food to keep from starving. For these, the only place to turn was the communal *heime* cafeteria where, once a day, up to five thousand hot meals were served. Portions were carefully weighed, but even the poorest refugee could count on a minimum of one thousand three hundred and fifty calories every day. The sick, elderly, and almost a thousand young children, were also eligible for a second smaller meal in the evening. A ration of one thousand three hundred and fifty calories even under good conditions is only slightly more than enough to prevent outright starvation. Strength and resistance to disease are another matter.

The SACRA medical committee and the clinics worked constantly innoculating refugees against various kinds of avitaminosis and the epidemics that periodically swept through the crowded houses of the ghetto: pellagra, beri-beri, cholera, typhus, and various parasitic worms were the most common diseases. Amoebic dysentery, at first a curse on all the refugees, was finally successfully dealt with by a ghetto physician, Dr. Theodore Friedricks. After months of experimentation, Friedricks discovered a cheap, effective remedy which he derived from a particular kind of nut and called *ku-san-tzu*.

Those refugees who followed most strictly the laws of *kashrut* suffered nutritionally more than those less observant. At one point a form of beri-beri swept through the yeshiva population leaving many of the students with mouths so painfully swollen they could scarcely speak. Once diagnosed, the problem was cured by a local brewer who contributed a daily ration of yeast to relieve its cause, a vitamin B deficiency. But in spite of the innoculations and the free meal service, disease and malnutrition, combined with psychological depression, took their toll. Before 1943 was over, more than three hundred ghetto inhabitants had succumbed, twice the earlier death rate of the refugee population.

The world outside was not unaware of what was happening to the Jews of Shanghai. In June of 1943, a Red Cross delegate had reported on the conditions of "the German-Jewish immigrants [sic] of whom at least six thousand are on the point of starvation and about nine thousand more are not far better off." The report detailed the economic and emotional devastation caused by the creation of the ghetto and the lack of resources within the local community to deal with it. American newspapers published articles (*"Japs in Shanghai Rob, Banish Jews"*) based on the Red Cross report and on reports from the few civilians who had managed to be transferred to neutral Portuguese Goa on the ship *Gripsholm*. As winter began, there was a report of a State Department plan to exchange a group of so-called "disloyal" Japanese-Americans for some fifteen thousand North and South American nationals in Shanghai. The World Jewish Congress pleaded with the State Department that at least some of the starving Jewish refugees be included. Their pleas were rejected. Secretary of State Cordell Hull allowed no refugees among the small number of exchanges ultimately made. The same people, it seemed, who had refused to open the country to the refugees from Poland in 1939, from Lithuania in 1940, and from Kobe in 1941, still refused them refuge from the Shanghai ghetto in 1943.

But there was more to the government than the State Department. In December, 1943, thanks to the ceaseless importuning of Rabbi Kalmanowitz, the first-hand reports of Laura Margolies who had finally returned, the vigorous efforts of Henry Morgenthau Jr., the secretary of the Treasury, and John Pehle, the director of the Division of Foreign Funds Control, the interpretation of the Trading with the Enemy Act was finally relaxed. Early on one of Shanghai's coldest, rainiest mornings, Joseph Bitker received a cable from New York that warmed him more than the greatest coal fire in the world: Laura Margolies wished his daughter a very happy birthday.

# 18

IN THE TWENTY-EIGHT MONTHS of the Shanghai exile nothing did more to raise the spirits of the refugees than Laura Margolies's telegram. On a practical and immediate level, however, it did little to improve living conditions. The Shanghai JDC did soon receive a cable from the New York JDC – the first in a very long, arduous nineteen months. But the cable wasn't money; it merely gave permission for Bitker to raise money ("up to twenty-five thousand US dollars per month") against a formal guarantee of repayment. New York continued to be fearful of the response to anything that might be perceived as "aiding the enemy." It might now be legal to send relief funds to aid refugees held by the Japanese enemy, but would it be seen by the public and by the United States government, as a moral and ethical thing to do? Might not the Japanese simply confiscate the money? Better, they decided, to start off slowly. But Shanghai had little need of a guarantee. There was no lack of faith that the JDC would honor its debts. The difficulty was simply that money for any purpose was not easy to raise in Shanghai. Inflation had soared into the realm of the ridiculous: by January of 1944, the Shanghai dollar which had been valued at six to the US dollar before the war, was down to a hundred per US dollar and dropping steadily. (By the end of the war, the ratio would be one hundred thousand to one.) Even fortune-sized bank accounts dwindled to nothing in the face of such inflation. And there was little hope for future improvement. From the opening months of the war, such trade as had been possible within the vast Japanese-occupied areas of Asia began to dwindle in the face of the Allied approach. Few people in Shanghai felt that the first quarter of 1944 was a good time to be lending large sums of money, even for the worthiest of causes.

Yet the need had never been so great. Over seven thousand Jewish refugees were now almost entirely dependent on the relief committees for everything; rare was the refugee family not in need of some help. And to this expanding emergency, the committees responded with maximum inefficiency. In mid-winter, 1943–4, an indigent Jewish refugee had to deal with directions and procedures from the following ten organizations: SACRA (with six subcommittees); the Joint Administrative Committee (an extension of SACRA with five subcommittees of its own); the *Juédische Gemeinde* (a conglomerate, mostly of German Jews, which had subcommittees for every aspect of a refugee's life); the Shanghai Joint Distribution Committee; Eastjewcom (for Eastern Europeans); Centrojewcom (for Central Europeans); the Kitchen Fund (concerned primarily with housing and food); the European Refugee Union (which, among other activities, kept statistics on many things); the Medical Board; and the Arbitration Board which settled at least some of the disputes that arose from the others' overlapping jurisdictions.

Not only was there no one centralized source of aid for the distraught and needy refugees but the different committees went so far as to work against each other. The Kitchen Fund, in one instance, flatly refused to accept food supplies purchased by another organization, in this case the JDC. The rivalries never were settled – worse, they were exacerbated. In the summer of 1944, SACRA set up two more committees to supervise and investigate all the others. By that time though, the financial corner had been turned: in March, New York finally began to cable money again with a remittance of twenty-five thousand dollars worth of Swiss francs.

Pawns for so long in the political and military games of the world, most of the refugees could not summon the energy to look beyond their immediate needs. They had and could take no control over their lives and futures, particularly since they could place little credence in the reports they received from TASS and the Japanese as to what was happening in other places. Their world had shrunk to a forty-square block ghetto area, and their aspirations were limited to getting enough food at any one meal to stave off hunger till the next.

As soon as the immediate food-clothing-shelter problems began to be resolved, however, at least several of the ghetto refugees, along with the Russians still leading normal, if increasingly austere lives began looking toward the end of the war. Already, MacArthur, Halsey and Nimitz were steadily retaking the Japanese outposts of the South Pacific. The Chinese – Chiang Kai-Shek's Nationalists and Mao's Communists – were forcing Japan to begin withdrawing from the interior, and to consolidate forces in the major coastal cities of Canton, Tientsin and Shanghai. And in Europe and North Africa, the other two-thirds of the Axis was also in retreat. This much the refugees could see. What they could not predict was Japan's response to losing. Would she choose to go down in flames, taking everything and everyone, with her when she went? Might she try to use captive Westerners as hostages against better peace terms? (And how concerned would the Allies be over the fate of such hostages?) Or might the Japanese even make a final show of loyalty to Hitler by rounding up and executing all the Jews in the Co-Prosperity Sphere?

These fears were not limited to the Jews of Shanghai, of course, and, in fact, when Hitler toppled, one faction, the *kempeitai* did draw up a list of all Jews under Japanese control with the intention of shooting them all in his memory. But higher level policymakers had other plans for "their Jews," not only in Shanghai and Manchukuo, but also among the captured populaces of Singapore and Hong Kong. And there were a few Jewish families in Japan itself, from Kobe or Yokohama, who had been relocated inland to small resort towns like Karuizawa in the mountains. One of those who lived out the war in Karuizawa was Dr. Karl Kindermann, the professor who had corresponded briefly in 1940 with Rabbi Stephen Wise about possible settlement of refugees in Japan. From the start, Kindermann had been specially protected by Japanese friends who were high in the ranks of the ultra-rightest Black Dragon Society. But even he was to be surprised at how high his influence went.

The war had long since turned against the Japanese when one of Prime Minister Tojo's advisers, Colonel Tsugio Sekiguchi, called Dr. Kindermann in for a discussion. After the opening courtesies, Sekiguchi began to speak of the grave situation of the war and the difficulties of settling it. "We are ready for a compromise," he admitted to Kindermann. "We have tried different ways to contact Washington, but they have refused to speak to us. Now we have a new plan."

Sekiguchi paused, expectantly.

"Of course, if there is anything I could do to help . . ." Kindermann interjected.

"Excellent!" Sekiguchi said. "In that case, you will go immediately to Dairen and meet with Admiral Nakamura."

A few days later Kindermann was in Dairen listening to Admiral Nakamura's presentation of the "new plan." It was in fact, a reincarnation of the *Fugu* plan.

The twenty thousand Jews in Shanghai, Nakamura said, are suffering more and more as the war continues, and the Nazis are putting intense pressure on us to deal with them. However, "we Japanese admire the Jewish intelligence," he said. "We hope to cooperate with the Jews after the war in building a better society. But first, we must end this war."

The key to ending the war would be the Shanghai Jews. The refugees would be moved out of their horrible living situation to a "Jewish state" in Manchukuo. They would be guaranteed everything necessary for a good life there. In turn, the "powerful American Jewish community," realizing the sincerity of the Japanese, would persuade Roosevelt to come to the peace table.

As in 1940, when he'd heard the first mention of a Manchurian settlement scheme, Kindermann agreed to try to help. Once again he wrote to Stephen Wise, still president of the American Jewish Congress and adviser to FDR, explaining the plan and encouraging interest in it. And once again, as in 1940, Wise was totally opposed. "My heart is bleeding when I see what the Japanese have done in other territories," he wrote Kindermann. "The Jewish Congress in America will not enter any negotiations with Japan without the consent of the State Department."

The Kindermann peace feeler had failed – but the Japanese would keep trying in other ways to reach the "powerful" American Jewish community.

Second to Shanghai, the largest concentration of Jews in China was in the coastal city of Tientsin, about fifty miles from Peking. The community there was a very close-knit group of about two hundred and fifty, almost all originally from Russia, and it was led by a broad, solid Siberian named Zelig Belokamen. From the beginning of the war, the Tientsin community had sought to maintain good relations with the Japanese occupiers and keep its life uneventful. On the whole, it was successful. But in the spring of 1944, several unfamiliar Japanese officers walked into the Tientsin Jewish Club, the *Kunst*, and began to question its members. "Have you been treated well here by our government? Do you have all the basic necessities for your religious practices? Is all going well with you?" The officers' tone was pleasant. The mystified Jews replied truthfully that all was fine and the Japanese left. Nothing happened for a few months. Then suddenly the *Kunst* received a cable announcing that a high-ranking Japanese mission from Peking would arrive the following Saturday and was to be met at the railway station by "an officer of the community." A formal visitation of the Japanese military was a frightening event. Belokamen was apprehensive as he met Colonel Tomiaki Hidaka and a full complement of assistants and escorted them from the station to the club.

The dining room where the Japanese were brought had been arranged for maximum effect. On a center table, to welcome the guests, was a Russian-style buffet – chopped egg, smoked salmon, chilled potato salad, liver paté, eggplant salad . . . and bottle after bottle of ice-cold 120-proof Russian vodka. The purpose of the food was to encourage the drinking. The purpose of the drinking was to help Belokamen and the others learn the purpose of the visit.

Hidaka and his assistants did their part by drinking a great many tiny glasses of the vodka as toasts were made to the good health of practically everyone. But then, without warning, Hidaka stood up and blurted out the message.

"This war has been going on for too long. Americans are killed, Jews are killed and Japanese are killed. Japan is not in Washington; the Americans are not in Tokyo. There seems to be no need to continue this senseless war. We know of the great Jewish influence in America and that President Roosevelt is Jewish, as are his top advisers. We believe that you can influence Roosevelt to bring this war to a speedy and proper conclusion. We are asking that you broadcast to your brothers in America, informing them of the truth – that Jews are not mistreated under Japanese rule, that Jews are treated well; and perhaps an arrangement can be made to bring this war to an end."

The colonel sat down. The Jews were totally at a loss as to how to answer. Was it a trap to see if they were loyal to the Japanese? What kind of answer were the Japanese looking for? Stalling for time, they kept the vodka flowing. But after only a few minutes, Hidaka again rose unsteadily to his feet. His face was bright red from his drinking. He was also tired of waiting. Slamming his hand down on the table he shouted, "Enough is enough! It is now time for an answer!"

Slowly, Belokamen also rose and began speaking as if he had been thinking about the proposal for ten days rather than ten minutes.

"We Jews know our American brothers better than you do, Hidaka-san. If we broadcast to them, they will be very surprised. They are sure to ask: Why now? Why not two years ago or two months ago? They may think that the reason for the broadcast is that Japan is now weak. If they do conclude in this manner, they will not react as you hope but will come after you with greater strength and fury. Perhaps, this would not be to your best advantage."

Hidaka listened carefully, then conferred with his assistants. "Your answer is wise," he finally said. "I will report it to Tokyo. *But*, if we request you to make the broadcast, you will do it?"

"Absolutely," Belokamen said, "immediately and just as you say."

On this positive note, the meeting broke up. The Japanese were escorted back to the station in time to catch the next train to Peking. The Jews of Tientsin never heard anything further from Hidaka.

As the war situation grew more hopeless though, the Japanese tried other approaches to come to terms with the United States on some basis other than unconditional surrender. In Manchukuo, Colonel Yasue tried to work through his connections. Ayukawa, the originator of the Manchurian settlement scheme, tried to promote peace negotiations through one of his former Jewish employees. There were also dozens of peace feelers which had nothing whatsoever to do with Jews at all. But nothing worked. Manila fell in January 1945, Iwo Jima in February; by March, the Chinese were within a hundred and fifty miles of Shanghai, and the devastating fire-bombs were falling on Tokyo. Early in April, President Roosevelt died of a stroke. But even on the editorial pages of Japan's major newspapers, it was conceded that this would have little effect on the American war drive: the demand for unconditional surrender would stand firm. In May, Germany collapsed. Japan tottered, both domestically and militarily; but, supported by an unyielding concept of national honor, she fought on. On July 16, the United States test-fired the first atomic bomb at Alamogordo, New Mexico. On the other side of the International Date Line in Shanghai, it was July 17.

Trudging through the wet July heat, Avram felt as if he were pushing himself through a wall. It was a Tuesday, a half day for the Kadoorie School science teacher, and he was on his way home – if the tiny, airless cell he'd been forced to accept when the ghetto was created could be dignified with the name "home." Crossing the dusty street that formed one of the outer boundaries of the ghetto, Avram approached the main checkpoint. Every time he had to pass through this gate – every school day since Kadoorie was outside the designated area – he was filled with loathing for the pass procedure. It really didn't matter that this year it had become a little simpler. At last, SACRA had screwed up its collective courage to request that Ghoya be replaced . . . and at least the new man, Harada, was sane. However, everyone still needed a pass and still had to have it checked as if he were a dangerous felon who could not be let loose to run freely in the city. Avram groaned to himself as he came up to the checkpoint where a particularly alert young member of the *Pao Chia*, under the supervision of a Japanese, appeared to enjoy playing soldier. Since Avram was a teacher at the Kadoorie School, his pass was in order. But approaching the point from the inside were two yeshiva students. Because they were ninety-nine percent of the time totally engrossed in the world of talmudic scholarship, these young men seemed always to have trouble passing the gate. Their papers were never in order, something was always wrong. . . . The diligent young guard, anticipating that most heinous of sins, an irregularity, was examining their papers with meticulous care. Having no alternative, Avram stood and studied the students awaiting the guard's pleasure.

Avram had had virtually no contact with the yeshiva. Many months before, when he'd first heard its members were foregoing one meal a day for money to print the books they needed, he'd made a small anonymous contribution in memory of his "Hebrew days" in Vilna. Many in the ghetto had experienced a religious revival – nearly half the Jewish shops were now closed on the Sabbath – but so far observant Judaism had continued to pass Avram by. Had he not been a teacher, he would have worked on Saturday. And on those rare occasions when he could afford meat, he bought it where it was cheap – not from the kosher stalls set up in the marketplace but from the local Chinese purveyor of pork and, probably, dog.

Yet as he stood waiting for the guard, he realized he'd seen one of the boys before, at least a lifetime ago, carrying an arm load of bread down one of the streets of Kobe. What a change there had been in him! Such a nervous, eye-darting *boychickel* then, so young, with just the beginning of a thin beard. And here he stood like a man, with an early morning dark shadow all over his face, so much calmer and more solid, though just as thin as everyone else. For himself, Avram had gotten used to the ravages of age – his hair was completely gray now, the skin of his face was beginning to droop like an old man's, his eyes were starting to recede beneath his brows. Still, it was a surprise to see that that boy had become this man.

The yeshiva student felt himself being watched and glanced over to Avram. Recognizing him as someone he'd seen, so long ago, probably at Kobe Jewcom, he nodded a polite greeting. But the yeshiva lived according to its own schedule of observance, was supported in large part from its own sources, was enveloped in its own scholarly activities. . . . Though they both were "Hongkew ghetto Jews," the science teacher and the yeshiva student had little else in common.

"Your name?"

The youth glanced back at the guard.

"Yankel Gilbewitz."

"Gilbewitz, Yankel," the guard punctiliously corrected him. "You don't look anything at all like this photo."

"One gets sick, one gets well: one even gets older," Yankel replied mildly. "I am the same person still."

Reluctant to concede the point, the *Pao Chia* studied him for a moment before sharply returning the papers.

"You may pass," he ordered.

"Into the promised land," the second boy muttered in Hebrew.

But the soldierly Jew understood no Hebrew and took no notice. Seeing Avram's pass, he waved him through without hesitation. Avram glanced into the small guard box where a very bored soldier was seeking protection from the sun. The clock on the wall beside him showed twelve-ten.

Moments later, as he was nearing Tongshan Road, Avram heard a rumbling roar; more curious than apprehensive, he looked up toward the apparent source of the sound. The sun glinted silver off the wings of a diamond formation of American bombers approaching steadily from over the North. Avram had seen bombers like these several times before during the past few months – still they thrilled him. They were, after all, bringing the Japs to their knees – Americans from America, that wonderland that none of them had ever stopped dreaming of. Following the curve of the river, steadily,

262

majestically, totally unopposed by the feeble Japanese defense system, each plane in turn released a consignment of destruction on a ship, a dock, a warehouse. Avram stood and watched, hypnotized by the relentlessness of the machines. Other pedestrians also halted. Vehicle traffic slowed and stopped. The ghetto was a safe place to be. The residents knew, from experience and from a downed American pilot they had helped escape – that the bombers had strict orders to avoid civilian areas.

Scarcely audible against the roar of the engines, a cry rose from the clusters of spectators – the planes had turned inland opposite Pootung and were now coming directly over their section of Hongkew. In an instant, excitement turned to terror: the small black biscuits that were now tumbling out of one of the planes would land right in the ghetto.

Avram threw himself to the ground just as he heard the first explosion; then the whole world became one terrible roar. For less than an instant he shut his eyes against the shock. When he looked again, a building directly opposite him was in flames. Groggily shaking his head, he tried to pull himself to his feet.

"Are you all right?" The question came from another man nearby, also picking himself up from the street.

"Yes. No. I think . . . All right. Over there. . . ."

The wall of a building a few doors away had collapsed into rubble, and fire was spurting up through what was left of the roof. They began running toward it when a husky shopkeeper in a dirty apron hurried out into the street as if to shoo them away.

"Forget it – it's empty! Down *there*. . . ." Trying to take off his apron at the same time, the man pointed to a far greater catastrophe.

Less than two blocks down Tongshan Road, where it was crossed by Kung Ping Road, there had been a SACRA refugee center. Now it was a center of hell. The main building had been hit directly and totally destroyed; two adjoining buildings were in flames.

Still shaking from the shock of the explosions, Avram staggered after other men who were racing toward the intersection. By the time he reached it, a bucket-brigade had already formed – not that it could do much to contain the fire. An ever-mounting number of casualties lay on blankets in the center's vegetable garden. Some moaned in pain and shock; some lay silent and too still. From the one remaining building, totally destitute refugees – the only ones who had qualified to live at the center – streamed out, tearing up their one last sheet, their shirts, their towels for bandages. Half a dozen elderly women tottered out from the side door of the building, teapots and cups in hand. Calmly they set up a work area out of the way of the activity and began serving tea, first to the wounded, then to the volunteer firemen for whom the intensity of the heat, a normally scorching July midday augmented by the fire, was almost unbearable.

"Aren't you the science teacher?" Avram was pulled out of the bucket line by a SACRA committeeman who had been organizing the evacuation of injured from the burning buildings.

"A hospital of sorts is being set up at the Ward Road Jail," the man said. "Go there. You'll do more good there than here. Can you manage to take this one with you? She doesn't have much of a chance, anyway; but if she stays here. . . ."

The SACRA man gestured to a teenage girl lying amid the lettuce plants. Her hair had been completely burned away, leaving her scalp, like her face, a deep unnatural red. The flesh was swollen beyond any hope of recognition. Except for her shoes, whatever she had been wearing had been blasted away. Dry and charred, the structure of her rib cage poked through the broken flesh. Avram looked at the man, hopeless.

"We can try," he said, taking off his shirt. The SACRA man helped him lift the girl off the ground and draped the shirt over her to keep away the already swarming flies. The girl moaned but did not regain consciousness.

The jail was five blocks away. Trying to keep the girl's head elevated so as not to put any additional strain on her lungs, Avram trudged through the crowded streets, detouring back and forth around burning buildings. Chinese and Jews together were trying to beat out flames with blankets or their bare hands. A few low-level Japanese officials had come to survey the damage and stayed to do what they could to help. But if there was any fire-fighting equipment in the ghetto, it was no more evident than the emergency first-aid stations that existed, on paper, in Kubota's office. Miraculously, the girl was still breathing when they reached their destination.

The largest building in the area and by far the most solid, the Ward Road Jail surrounded a large open courtyard. At this moment its doors were open and the courtyard looked exactly what it was – a battlefield medical station. Maimed and burned victims were being brought here from all over the area on contrived stretchers or in the arms of their families. The bombs had shown no national favorites: Jews, Chinese, even a few poor Japanese civilians lay together. Purposefully, the refugee and Russian Jewish doctors moved from injury to injury, concentrating first on the most serious, returning later for the superficial. They made no distinction by race. Each victim was treated in turn, as thoroughly as conditions allowed. But conditions were atrocious. There were only those few instruments that the doctors had brought with them; painkillers and drugs were totally lacking.

Avram laid the unconscious girl down as gently as he could, folding one end of the blanket into a makeshift pillow. Immediately a volunteer – a woman who in calmer times, might have allowed herself to faint at the sight of blood – came running with a damp cloth and a bowl of water. Avram joined the doctors, asking how he could help.

"You can change the damned Chinese doctors into human beings! You can march into that clinic where half a dozen of them are sitting around on their hands and pull them out here to act like doctors! You the science teacher?" The question followed the outburst with no change in tone. "Hold this arm while I try to get this piece of metal. . . . Those bastards have got everything in there – instruments, anaesthetics, sterile needles, the works. But they won't do a thing till someone comes in with the money to pay for it. What the hell kind of doctoring is that?"

As the refugee doctor continued to probe for the base of the metal, the patient, an elderly Chinese, groaned and turned his face away from the wound. There were many more Chinese victims in the compound than refugees.

"Will you hold the arm *still*, for God's sake. . . . Ahhh!" Allowing himself a fraction of a moment's satisfaction, the doctor triumphantly held up a vicious ragged piece of metal, then dropped it into the dirt and moved on to the next. The women came up behind him, bandaging the bloody wound; and so it went for the remainder of the afternoon. One by one, the most traumatic cases were moved to the refugee hospital. But the girl from the SACRA compound was not among them. Balanced so tenuously on the edge of life, she lay as Avram had placed her, breathing in shallow little gasps, too injured to move – and there was no suitable place to move her to anyway. No Shanghai hospital had facilities for burns that severe.

By early evening, everyone who could be helped had been. The Chinese, grateful for the care given by the foreigners, brought fruit and cakes. This was a rare moment of amity between the Chinese and the Jews and, perhaps rarer still, between the Russian Jews and the refugees. Avram was exhausted. The Chinese food revived his failing spirit, but he was tired down to his bones. Sitting on a stool, Avram held his head in his hands, peering out toward the courtyard entrance, like a child, through his fingers.

Suddenly a familiar figure came slowly through the gate. A chill of apprehension washed over Avram, settling into all the fatigued places. "Moishe!" Avram got up and went toward the haggard boy.

"I can't find her." Moishe was at the end of his strength. "I've spent hours at the *heime* clinics. I went to the refugee hospital. I've asked everyone."

Moishe, who had given up expecting much from anyone or anything, looked at Avram as if begging for life itself: "Have *you* seen her?"

Avram put his arms around the boy's shoulders. "I haven't seen her. But there is a girl, Moishe, very badly burnt. . . . Come."

Avram led him to the still unconscious form lying in the shadow of the jail. Moishe looked at the face, still swollen into anonymity, then down at the shirt, rising and falling with every shallow breath, then finally down to the bare legs and shoes. He shuddered and, just as four and a half years ago in Vilna, he collapsed sobbing onto the ground.

The sun set and darkness filled in the shadows of the courtyard. By the harsh light of acetylene lamps and soft moonlight a few volunteers remained to watch over the last of the injured victims. Moishe sat on the ground by his sister, not touching her, only occasionally looking at her legs and her shoes.

They had been through so much hell together, since that night at the Polish border – come so far, struggled so hard to stay alive and together. The year following Getzel Syrkin's death had been the hardest. Moishe, by default, had become the man of the family. But not the bread-winner. Never able to find work, he quit trying, spending most of his time at his school, learning as much as possible in preparation for the end of the war. Cheya – who aged twenty years in twelve months – had spent more and more time in a desperate search for part-time jobs to augment the tiny ration that was all the relief agencies could afford then to dole out. This search for work had become a compulsion, and even after relief money for food became available from abroad again, in the spring of 1944, Cheya had kept right on going out day after day, asking if anyone, *anyone*, had work for her to do. So it had fallen to Sophie to cope with the daily running of this household and to take care of Dovid who was still small, not strong and immature even for his eleven years.

She had become so practical, his little Sophie, so sensible; her jumpy little-girl gaiety had been burned away by the harshness of Shanghai refugee life, but what remained was a solid core of capability and resilience. Though only two years older than Dovid, she seemed more mature by decades. "And all for what?" Moishe asked himself, looking at the broken body lying in front of him. "All for nothing, just to die, to be killed in a mistake." His heart cried out as if it would break; but he didn't make a sound.

Avram stayed with Moishe until he realized the boy neither knew nor cared that he was there. Then, too tired to fight sleep any longer, he moved a few yards away, sat down on a blanket and dozed.

Close to midnight, he awoke to find Moishe, plain in the moonlight, tying a knot in each corner of a handkerchief to create an acceptable head covering. This time the young man did not have to ask the rebbe's permission: "*Yisgadal v'yiskadash sh'meih rabbo.*" Avram rose, as did the other men, to the words of the mourner's *kaddish*.

The bombs that fell on Hongkew had been targeted on a Japanese radio transmitter within the ghetto. In silencing the radio station, however, the Americans killed two hundred and fifty people, thirty-one of them Jewish refugees. Three weeks later, two single bombs destroyed over one hundred and fifty thousand people in Hiroshima and Nagasaki. On August 15, a strange stillness fell over all Shanghai. Coming through the loudspeakers which hung above the streets at various points in the city, was the high-pitched voice of the Japanese emperor. Soldiers stood stiffly at attention, young civilians bowed their heads, older ones knelt to the ground, their faces within inches of the dust. His words burned a new reality into their hearts: Japan had surrendered.

For several hours the refugees were not sure exactly that the war was over. There had been false alarms before during the past few days: Chinese Nationalist and Allied flags had been run up amid much cheering – only to be hauled down again on orders of the Japanese. Rumors of peace skittered everywhere. But on August 16, newspapers announced it officially. Then the streets were jammed with people, singing, dancing, celebrating the end of the nightmare. Firecrackers exploded everywhere constantly. Blackout curtains were pulled down and burned. Carefully hoarded bottles of Johnny Walker were brought out and drunk with laughter and tears of joy. The poorest of the refugees joined with the wealthiest of the residents in cheering the Allied victory and congratulating themselves for having come through the war in one piece.

The Japanese forces, stunned that their homeland which had never been invaded was about to be occupied, withdrew completely at first, but, thanks to the prudence of the military leaders, only briefly. Among the most desperate of the Chinese poor, looting broke out with the coming of darkness on the evening of August 16. The *Pao Chia* and the other remaining branches of the Shanghai Volunteer Corps were called upon for help. But only the Japanese were armed and trained, and within hours, Japanese soldiers were more in evidence throughout the city than they had been since 1941. The wave of looting scarcely had a chance to get underway before everything was secure again.

Politically, the surrender created a vacuum in Shanghai. The Japanese there could not lay down their arms until the arrival of someone whom they could surrender *to*. In the face of their mutual victory, the union of the two Chinese forces – Chiang's Nationalists and Mao's Communists – disintegrated. With every passing day, it became more and more a race between them as to who could occupy the greater number of strategic cities. Finally, the theoretical problem was solved by the arrival of a small landing party of American forces. America was backing the Nationalists; the Japanese commander was informed he would make his formal surrender *only* to Chiang's forces. However, until those troops arrived, which wouldn't be until August 26, the Japanese were to continue maintaining order.

With the announcement of the surrender proclamation, the Sephardic Jews immediately left the internment camps and returned with relief to their own comfortable homes. The Russians and the other officially "non-stateless" Jews began planning for a future which, they believed, would be not too different from the prewar past. But for the seventeen thousand refugees, after the singing and dancing were over, life went right back to being what it had been. The Mir Yeshiva went on studying fourteen hours a day. The Kadoorie School opened for a new term. Those few who still had jobs continued to work. And the JDC went right on channeling the support that would keep the refugees alive as long as they needed it. The Jewish refugee area of Hongkew remained intact because no one had the money to move from it, or the knowledge of what the future would hold outside it. Only the pass system was definitely, totally and forever laid to rest.

It was Saturday, September 13. Pleased to have the day for his own business, Avram Chesno sat on a bench in the public garden at the northernmost end of the *Bund*. The typhoon that had battered the city the previous day had washed the air clean of dust and brought the temperature down to a reasonable degree. Waiting for the hour to be chimed by the big clock on the Customs House tower, he watched sampans glide cheerfully out of Soochow Creek into the broad muddy Whangpoo River. Aside from the inflation that had brought the exchange rate to one hundred thousand Shanghai dollars, the city now seemed almost a pleasant place – life here might not be bad at all. In time, Shanghai would no doubt again become an exciting, cosmopolitan highly civilized city. For some people, perhaps, but never for Avram. His own feelings about the city were too strong ever to allow him to feel comfortable here.

From the reports and stories now coming out of Europe, Avram realized he had been extremely fortunate in making it all the way to Shanghai. He wondered how many other Jews besides those skeletal forms that hung half-dead over the barbed wire fences in the pictures from Auschwitz and Treblinka and the rest – had managed to come through alive. They would turn up, of course. Even Hitler couldn't have killed all the Jews in Europe. But there was no question that, in Shanghai, he had been safer than he would have been in Poland. So, he didn't hate the Japanese. And he didn't hate the Chinese. What he hated was what had been done to him: he, Avram Chesno, sound in mind and body, a law abiding, hard-working full-grown adult member of society, had been reduced from a person to a category. He had been controlled, confined, forced to live where, and in ways, he detested, compelled to ask permission – from a madman! – to be allowed to go from here to there. He had been denied his own life, his own individuality because of something he had no control over. Avram didn't want not to be a Jew. If anything, the experiences of the past six years had heightened his sense of identity with his fellow Jews. But he never, never again wanted his Jewishness to be the one factor by which he would be classified.

The smell of newly cut grass drifted across from the adjoining British Consulate. "Big Ching," as the expatriate Londoners had dubbed the tower clock, began ringing 9 o'clock. Avram rose and just as countless times before, in Warsaw, in Vilna, and in Kobe he set his direction toward an American Consulate.

# EPILOGUE

*"The sun rises and the sun sets"*. The Talmud interprets this biblical verse to mean that even before the sun has set in the western sky, it has already begun to rise in the east. Sadly, the sun has already set on most of the major figures whose stories are told in *The Fugu Plan*. But at the same time, a keen interest in the Jewish experience in the Far East has been kindled.

THE AMSHENOVER REBBE, Shimon Kalisch, came to the United States in 1946, after the end of the war. He organized a synagogue in Brooklyn shortly after his arrival; others of his family founded a yeshiva in his name in Jerusalem. The Amshenover rebbe died in 1954.

GISUKE AYUKAWA, the industrialist, was imprisoned briefly after the war. He went on to become an influential member of the Diet and a personal advisor to Prime Minister Nobusuke Kishi, his former junior colleague in Manchuria. Ayukawa died in 1967.

ZELIG BELOKAMEN left Tientsin for Israel after the war. He soon returned to the Orient, served as Israel's honorary consul to the Republic of Korea, and was engaged in international trade in Japan and Korea. He died in Tokyo in 1984 and is buried in the Jewish cemetery in Yokohama.

AVRAM CHESNO, MOISHE KATZNELSON, MRS. SYRKIN and DOVID – like the rest of the eighteen thousand Jewish refugees in Shanghai who came through the war safely, if not comfortably – did not leave Shanghai immediately after Japan formally surrendered to the Chinese in September 1945. It was, in fact, well over a year before the United Nations Relief and Rehabilitation Agency which was in charge of resettling all the refugees of the war could begin to clear the way for their move to the United States, Canada, or to various Latin American countries.

Some Jews in Shanghai, refugees and prewar residents alike, knowing of the former commercial possibilities of the city, were not anxious to leave. But in

1949, Mao's Communist forces took Shanghai and left no doubt as to the future of the capitalist order there. The subsequent mass emigration had been made easier by the creation, in 1948, of the State of Israel and the enactment of a Law of Return. By the mid-1950s, with the cooperation of the People's Republic of China, almost all of the ten thousand Jews remaining in Shanghai had left for Israel and other countries. None remain in Shanghai today.

DR. ABRAHAM COHN owned a pharmaceutical business in Shanghai until the Communists took over. At first the new regime denied him permission to leave, but in 1957, Cohn was allowed to emigrate to Hong Kong where he resumed his medical practice. The British, however, continued to be suspicious of his wartime contacts with the Japanese and refused his application for citizenship. He died, stateless, in 1972 in Hong Kong.

SAM EVANS spent the war years in the small, central Japan mountain town of Karuizawa. Afterwards, he returned to Kobe where he was once again the honorary president of the Jewish Community of Kobe. He died there in 1975.

GHOYA, the official in charge of passes in the Shanghai ghetto, returned to Hongkew shortly after the surrender, "to be friends again with the Jews." Members of the Zionist youth group, Betar, did not consider him a friend. In one of the few violent encounters that marked the end of the war, they set upon him and left him in the middle of the street – alive, but in a bloody heap. But that was not the last that was seen of him. During the Korean War, a former yeshiva student who had known Ghoya in Hongkew and had later joined the US Army, happened to be in a police station in Moji on the southern island of Kyushu when a short, middle-aged policeman walked through the door. "I know you!" the former yeshiva student cried out. "You are Ghoya!" "Yes," Ghoya acknowledged, bewildered that this American soldier should have identified him. "You were in Hongkew!" the soldier continued. "You called yourself 'the King of the Jews'!" Ghoya blushed scarlet, glanced briefly at his superiors, and ran back out the door as fast as his stumpy legs could carry him.

NATHAN GUTWIRTH reached Kobe in early 1941 and left soon after for the Dutch East Indies (later Indonesia) where, with the start of the war, he was interned by the Japanese. After the war, he emigrated, first to the United States and then to Antwerp, Belgium. He died in Belgium in 1999.

LEO HANIN left Kobe and was in Shanghai during the war, after which he emigrated with his family to the United States. He now lives in Los Angeles.

KORESHIGE INUZUKA was arrested in 1945 as a war criminal and was to stand trial in Manila for crimes allegedly committed during 1943-4, while he was serving as a fleet commander in the Northern Philippines. In his own defense, Inuzuka produced the inscribed cigarette case given to him by Frank Newman. It was proof, he said, that far from harming non-Japanese, he had in fact often gone out of his way to assist them. Freed, he returned to Tokyo and was active in forming the Nippon-Israel Friendship League. He also attended the opening ceremonies of the Tokyo Jewish Community Center. By the mid-1950s, Michael Kogan, of the Kogan Papers, had read enough of the secret Foreign Ministry documents to confront Inuzuka publicly with the evidence that he had never been a friend of the Jews, and had, in fact, written virulent anti-Semitic propaganda. Thereafter, Inuzuka dropped out of the Nippon-Israel Friendship League altogether. Inuzuka lived in Omori with his second wife, Kiyoko, the woman who had been with him in Shanghai, until his death in 1965. In 1981, the inscribed cigarette case was donated by Kiyoko to the Yad Vashem Holocaust Museum in Jerusalem.

DR. ABRAHAM KAUFMAN was part of the delegation that joyously greeted the Soviets when, having just declared war on Japan, they seized Harbin in August 1945. The joy of Kaufman's delegation was short-lived. He and other Jews were promptly arrested for having "collaborated with the enemy." Like many others, Kaufman was sent to Siberia. He was not released until 1956. Five years later, he finally managed to leave the U.S.S.R. and emigrate to Israel to join his family. He died there in 1969.

DR. KARL KINDERMANN was imprisoned by the Allies in Tokyo at the close of the war. He was charged with collaborating with both the Nazis and the Japanese, and was deported in shame back to Germany. A journalist, Kindermann spent many years trying to set the record straight as to his activities during the war. His claims to have promoted peace and provided the British with valuable military information were finally verified and his name and reputation cleared. He died in Germany.

MICHAEL KOGAN lived for many years in Tokyo and was a pioneer in developing the video game industry. In 1984, when he was visiting in Los Angeles, he died of a sudden heart attack.

SETSUZO KOTSUJI came under heavy *kempeitai* attack after Pearl Harbor for his pro-Jewish – and general pro-Western – feelings. For his own safety, he moved from Kamakura to Harbin where he was befriended and supported by the Harbin Jewish community until the end of the war. Then, penniless, with his family on the brink of starvation, Kotsuji returned to Tokyo where he was hired by the Jewish owner of a trading company who knew the story of this Japanese who had been so helpful to the Jews in Kobe and Manchuria before the war. In 1959, at the age of sixty, Kotsuji traveled to Israel and formally converted to Judaism, changing his first name to Abraham. Fourteen years later, at his home in Kamakura, he died. Just after the Yom Kippur war in 1973, Kotsuji was buried in Jerusalem with great honor. Zorach Warhaftig, then religious affairs minister of the State of Israel, presided at his funeral which was also attended by many members of the faculty and students of the Mir Yeshiva.

YOSUKE MATSUOKA was imprisoned and indicted as a war criminal. He died in prison in 1946 before his trial was completed.

COLONEL JOSEF MEISINGER was arrested in Japan at the close of the war. After a brief stay in the United States where he attempted unsuccessfully to commit suicide, he was taken to Europe to be tried by the War Crimes Tribunal. In 1946, the "Butcher of Warsaw" was hanged.

THE MIR YESHIVA was the only European yeshiv a
intact. In 1946, its students and teachers came to New York and reestablished the school in Brooklyn. Prior to the war, Europe had been the principal source of rabbis, teachers and scholars for the American Jewish community. Though the Holocaust destroyed an entire generation of teachers, when the hundreds of graduates of the Mir Yeshiva came to America, they filled that vacuum until a new generation of scholars could mature. The Mir Yeshiva, with a branch in Jerusalem, is now one of the major yeshivas in the world, with a student population of over 2,500.

ANATOLE PONVE was in the United States when the war with Japan broke out. (His wife was trapped in the Philippines where she was interned as an enemy national until the war ended.) Ponve returned to Japan after the war. He was instrumental in organizing the Jewish Community Center in Tokyo and in helping the refugees emigrate from Shanghai in the late 1940s. Ponve later returned to California where he became president of the Hollywood Temple Beth El. He died in Los Angeles in 1969.

MOSES SHATZKES arrived in the United States in 1941 and joined the staff of the rabbinical school of Yeshiva University in New York. He died in 1958 at the age of seventy-seven.

MITSUGI SHIBATA, having been expelled from Shanghai, returned to Japan. Believing that he had done the Shanghai Jews a great disservice by mentioning the impending pogrom and causing their imprisonment, Shibata was too ashamed to contact any of the Jews in the Orient after the war. It was not until the research was being done for this book that Shibata was found and informed that, in fact, he had saved the lives of thousands of Jews. Shibata was honored at a Passover *seder* at the Jewish Community Center in Tokyo in 1976. He died in 1977.

NOBUTAKA SHIODEN was elected to the Diet in 1942 on a platform of anti-Semitism. After the war, he was arrested but was not considered important enough to stand trial. Subsequently, until his death in 1962, Shioden lived alone in a small town in eastern Japan, believing to the end that an "international conspiracy of Jews" had caused the war and even that the airplane which brought the first atomic bomb to Japan had Hebrew letters on its tail.

SHANGHAI, as it is today, would be, with on eexcepi on , co mpl a d y unrecognizable to the refugees. Even in the 1940s, it was a huge metropolis, spreading mile after square mile back from the Whangpoo River. But now, the city is also going up and up. Neighborhood by neighborhood, Shanghai is being rebuilt with high-rises and architecturally stunning skyscrapers going up in clusters of five or six at a time. A brand new subway system has been tunneled under the city; elevated highways unroll like ribbons above the crowded streets. And neon lights – even on the staid, pre-war buildings that line the Bund – celebrate the 24/7 energy of the place.

The one exception to the re-building is the one-time home of all the refugees – Hongkew. Former refugees come with their children and grand-children to revisit the places where they lived out the war – and find them still standing. The unpretentious low-rise cement buildings that crowded the streets and lanes are still there. The Ohel Moishe Synagogue is still there, though now it is The Jewish Museum, displaying photos of the refugee period. Hongkew Park is as it was, though the government has erected a monument in the park, inscribed in English, Hebrew and Chinese with an explanation that China was a refuge for Jews during the war and that thousands lived in Hongkew and survived. The Shanghai Jewish School still stands, though now, appropriately, it houses the offices of the Ministry of Education.

Beyond Hongkew, individual buildings can also still be found. The former Jewish Hospital is now a public hospital specializing in ear, nose and throat. The Shanghai Jewish Club is now the Conservatory of Music. The Ohel Rachel Synagogue built by Sir Victor Sassoon, is now, after many years of neglect, again open, and the Hebrew words above the Ark are again visible. There is also one more building that none of the refugees would recognize but certainly all would approve – an Academy of Jewish Studies in Shanghai, with a library and archives devoted to every aspect of Jewish history in China from the 18th century to the present.

SENPO or CHUINE SUGIHARA was the *sina qua non*, the person without whom thousands of Jewish refugees would never have been able to escape from Europe. As to his name, the Japanese characters can be read either *Senpo* or *Chiune*. Originally, he used the reading *Chiune*. After the war, however, he worked for many years in Moscow for a company that specialized in trade between Japan and the Soviet Union. Sugihara knew of Russia's history of anti-Semitism and feared that if someone learned that he had saved thousands of Jews during the war, it might be the end of his career. Therefore, he changed the reading of his first name to *Senpo* until he left Moscow. Sugihara died in Japan in 1986.

The story of Sugihara's life, before and after he issued the life-saving visas, is told briefly in the two Introductions to this edition of *The Fugu Plan*. Sugihara's wife, who was with him in Lithuania in 1940, has written a short book about her husband entitled *Visas for Six Thousand*. And Professor Hillel Levine has written a longer biography titled *In Search of Sugihara*. But the most comprehensive presentation of Sugihara's life is the award-winning documentary *Conspiracy of Kindness*. This 90-minute documentary will be aired on PBS nationwide in the spring of 2004.

MITSUZO TAMURA spent the war years in Japan, under the constant surveillance of the *kempeitai* as one whose ties with America were suspiciously close. After the war, he continued in the metal container business. Tamura died in 1976.

ALEX TRIGUBOFF, exiled with many other foreigners to the small town of Karuizawa for the duration of the war, went to Tokyo after the surrender. He was one of the original founders of the Jewish Community Center there. Triguboff, an exporter, lived in Tokyo for many years. He died in Hawaii.

ZORACH WARHAFTIG left Japan for the United States in mid-1941. In 1947, he emigrated with his family to Palestine. Warhaftig was one of the 37 signatories to Israel's Declaration of Independence. A member of the Knesset from 1949 to 1981, he was appointed Minister of Religious Affairs in 1961 – a post he held until 1974. He was also a founder of the National Religious Party of Israel. Warhaftig died in 2002.

STEPHEN WISE continued after the war to be active in Jewish affairs in the United States. He was president of both the American and World Jewish Congresses and was a champion, particularly before the United Nations, of the Zionist cause. Rabbi Wise died in 1949.

NORIHIRO YASUE spent the war years in Dairen as an advisor to the government of Manchukuo. With the surrender, he did not attempt to flee. Rather, he arranged a family farewell at which he declared that he considered his generation to have been completely responsible for the war. To flee, he felt, would be a dishonorable attempt to evade the consequences. As his wife played on the *koto*, Yasue told his children they should return home to rebuild their country. He himself would remain in Dairen. Within days, he was arrested by the Russians and sent to Siberia. He died in 1950, in the labor camp at Khabarovsk.

LEW ZIKMAN boarded the ship *Tatsuma Maru* on December 1, 1941, bound for the United States. On Pearl Harbor Day, the ship turned around and returned to Yokohama. After the war, Zikman emigrated to the United States where he lived until his death in 1973.

# GLOSSARY

| | |
|---|---|
| Ashkenazim | Jews of Central and Eastern Europe |
| Avodah Zorah | Idolatry |
| Bar Mitzvah | Religious confirmation for a boy at age 13 |
| Cheder | Hebrew school |
| Diet | Japanese parliament |
| Frum | Religiously observant |
| Futon | A heavy quilt used for bedding |
| Gaijin | Non-Japanese |
| Gaimusho | Japanese Foreign Ministry |
| Gaon | Hebrew term for genius – occasionally used as title |
| Goy | Non-Jew |
| Hasid | A disciple of a great rabbi, a pious man |
| Hatikva | Jewish anthem which became the national anthem of Israel |
| Heder | Hebrew school |
| Heim | Refugee living quarters; plural is "heime" |
| Im yirzeh ha-Shem | God willing |
| Kaddish | Commonly, prayer recited by mourners for dead |
| Kaki | Persimmon |
| Kempeitai | Japanese military police |
| Kimono | Traditional clothing of Japan – a full length garment worn by men and women |
| Kum gezunt | Return safely, literally: return in good health |
| L'chaim | To life! A toast offered with wine or liquor |
| Manchukuo | Puppet state created by Japan in Manchuria |

| | |
|---|---|
| Mensch | Honorable and decent person |
| Mikveh | Ritual bath |
| Mitzvah | Commandment, good deed, religious duty |
| Niggun | Spiritual melody without words |
| Ostjuden | Eastern European Jews |
| Pogrom | Violent attack on a Jewish community |
| Sephardim | Jews of Spain or the Middle East |
| Schnorrer | A beggar |
| Shabbos | Sabbath |
| Shiva | Seven days of mourning for the dead |
| Shoji | Sliding door or screen made of wood and paper |
| Shtetl | A village or small town |
| Shul | Traditional synagogue |
| Tallis | Prayer shawl |
| Tallis Katan | Small prayer shawl, generally worn by a male under his shirt |
| Tatami | Thick straw mat that covers the floor |
| Tefillin | Prayer boxes, phylacteries, worn by adult males at weekday morning services |
| Yahrzeit | Anniversary of death of a near relative |
| Yarmulka | Skull cap, head covering worn by religious Jews |
| Yeshiva | Academy of higher Jewish studies. |
| Yiddish | The language spoken by Jews of Eastern Europe |
| Yudayajin | Japanese term for Jew |
| Zhid | Russian word (perjorative) for Jew |

# INDEX

Names in *italic* refer to fictional characters

Abraham, Reuben, 225
Africa, 183, 218
*Agudath Israel*, 221
Akiyama, 228
Alamogordo, 260
Alexandrov, 21–3
American Jewish Congress, 68, 77, 185, 258, 275–6
Amshenover rebbe (Shimon Kalisch): in Vilna, 90–2, 93, 96, 97–8, 101; in Vladivostok, 110–11; goes to Japan, 112–13, 114, 118–20, 132; discovers loophole in visa regulations, 135–7; interrogation of Jewcom, 169–81; in Shanghai, 194–5, 202, 239–42; after the war, 271
anti-Semitism, 9; *The Protocols of the Elders of Zion* and, 47–8; in pre-war Germany, 52; in Japan, 78–9, 141; Nazis, 78–9, 172–4, 177–9
Aoki, Kazuo, 234
Arbitration Board, 256
Arita, Hachiro, 56, 58, 66, 74
Asahina, 141
Ashkenazi, Rabbi, 249
Ashkenazic Jews, 63–4, 65, 71, 220
Association of Central European Physicians, 207

Auschwitz, 269
Australia, 40, 158, 184
Austria, 64, 65, 191, 243
Austro–Hungary, 48
Ayukawa, Gisuke, 51–2, 55, 57, 59, 79, 260, 271

Baikal, Lake, 107
Bailey, 40
Baltic states, 42, 82, 102
Bank of Japan, 45
Baruch, Bernard, 9
Belgium, 29, 135
Belokamen, Zelig, 258–60, 271
Ben Gurion, David, 49
Bermuda, 42
Betar, 272
Beth Aharon Synagogue, Hongkew, 202, 209–11, 249
Bialystok, 36–8, 88
Birobidzhan, 58, 108–9
Bitker, Joseph, 225–7, 232, 252, 254, 255
Black Dragon Society, 257
Bolshevik Revolution, 47, 159
Bombay, 217
Brahn, Fritz, 226–7, 231–2
Bridge House Prison, Shanghai, 232
Bureau of Military Affairs (Japan), 218
Bureau for Refugee Affairs, 224, 247

California, 34–5, 39–40
Canada, 184
Casablanca, 218
Cassel, 68
Catholic church, 44
Central Palestine Committee, 157
Centrojewcom, 256
Chelyabinsk, 107
Chesno, Avram: forced to leave
  Warsaw, 32–41; in Vilna, 87–90,
  92–3, 96; arrival in Japan, 115,
  116, 117–18, 120; in Kobe,
  131–9; in Shanghai, 203–9,
  214–15, 260–7, 269–70; after
  the war, 271
Chesno, Ruth, 33, 34–6, 37–8, 87,
  88, 132, 214
Chiang Kai-Shek, 256–7, 268
Chin, Mr., 214
China, 42, 48; Japanese colonies
  in, 9, 59, 75, 258; war with
  Japan, 44, 62, 71, 76, 122,
  216–17, 218; and Japan's
  interest in Manchuria, 51;
  Japanese control of part of, 218;
  Japan withdraws from, 256–7;
  end of the war, 260, 268;
  recaptures Shanghai, 272
Club, the (Vilna), 32–3
Cohen, Gershon, 146, 147–54, 210,
  211–13
Cohen, Two-Gun, 49
Cohn, Dr. Abraham, 227–31, 234,
  244–5, 249, 272
Committee for Assistance of
  European Refugees in Shanghai
  (CFA), 191, 192, 195–6, 197–9
Communism, 141
'Concrete Measures to be
  Employed . . .', 68
Conference of Jewish Communities
  in the Far East: 1937, 55–6, 123;
  1938, 56, 123; 1939, 66, 77–8, 123
Crok, 82
Cuba, 40
Curaçao, 27–8, 29–30, 79, 117
Czechoslovakia, 243

Daido City, 58
Dairen, 53, 56
Dekker, L.P.J. de, 29–30
Dunkirk, 29
Dutch East Indies, 218

Eastjewcom (Committee for
  Assistance of Jewish Refugees),
  192–3, 195, 202, 221, 242, 256
Einstein, Albert, 60
Ershowsky, Mrs., 241
Estonia, 243
European Refugee Union, 256
Evans, Sam, 133–7, 272
Exclusion Act, 1924(USA), 50

Far Eastern Jewish Council (FEJ),
  55–6, 66, 252
Finkel, Rabbi, 82, 87
Finland, 183
Five Ministers' Conference (1938),
  56–61, 217, 218–19
Fleisher, Benjamin, 48
France, 42, 54, 82, 183, 218
Freud, Sigmund, 60
Friedricks, Dr. Theodore, 253
Fujisawa, 176–7, 179
Fukamachi, Captain, 175, 177, 179

Germany, 82, 218; invasion of
  Europe, 29; invades Poland,
  33–6, 37; alliance with Japan,
  44, 57, 79, 94, 95, 96, 115, 126,
  142; anti-Semitism, 52, 172–4,
  177–9; Kristallnacht, 57; Jewish
  emigrants, 64, 65, 191; annoyed
  by Jewish refugees in Japan,
  126, 141, 142; opposes Japan's
  aid to Jews, 166–7; interrogation
  of Jewcom, 173–5; declares war
  on Russia, 188–9; Nazis 'final
  solution', 222; refugees, 243;
  retreats from Stalingrad, 246;
  end of war, 260
Gerson, Otto, 67, 72, 74, 78
Gestapo, 222
Ghoya, 250–1, 261, 272

*Gilbewitz, Yankel*, 82, 83–7, 144–54, 210–13, 247–9, 261–2
Goa, 254
Great Britain, 40, 218; retreat from Dunkirk, 29; deteriorating relations with Japan, 44; and Shanghai, 62; funds for Jewish refugees, 220
Greater East Asia Co-Prosperity Sphere, 9, 216
*Gripsholm*, 254
Grunebaum, Ernst, 67, 72, 74, 78
Gutwirth, Nathan, 27, 29–30, 130, 272

Hailar, 53
Hayim, Ellis, 77
Halsey, 256
Hanin, Leo, 136–7, 170, 172–81, 200, 272
Hanin, Mrs., 162
Harada, 261
Harbin, 11, 53–6, 123, 192, 236
*Harbin Maru*, 111, 112–15
Hardoon, Silas, 63, 209–10
Hartwich, Lucie, 204
Hasidim, 90, 113
Hayim, Elias, 225–7, 232
Hebrew Immigrant Aid Society (HIAS), 26, 40, 98, 101, 125, 184, 219
Herzl, Theodor, 218
HICEM, 99, 202, 219
Hidaka, Colonel Tomioka, 259–60
Higuchi, General Kiichiro, 51, 56, 123
Higuchi, Tsunaosuke, 141
Himmler, Heinrich, 173, 222
Hirohito, Emperor of Japan, 31, 50, 267
Hiroshima, 267
Hirschland, Franz, 62, 72, 73, 74, 76, 78
Hitler, Adolf, 139, 257, 269; anti-Semitism, 28, 52, 71, 173, 183; invades Poland, 32–4, 36; cultural agreement with Japan,

44; military alliance with Japan, 95, 115; invades Russia, 218
Hokoshi, 141–2
Holiness Church, 134
Holland, 29–30
Hollywood, 69
Hong Kong, 216, 218, 257
Hongkew, Jewish refugees, 64, 196–7, 202, 205; ghetto established in, 234, 235–54, 255–6; ghetto bombed, 262–7; after the war, 269
Hoto, 58
Hull, Cordell, 220–1, 254
Hungary, 243

Ikeda, Seishin, 56, 59
Imperial Japanese Navy, 58, 167, 169, 177–81, 244
Indochina, 42, 216, 218
International Red Cross, 217, 243, 254
Intourist, 92, 93, 96, 97–9, 101, 102–3, 109–10, 137, 183
Inuzuka, Koreshige, 12, 55, 137, 225; belief in Jewish conspiracy, 47–9; evolution of *fugu* plan, 51, 52–3, 60; in favor of Jewish settlement in Shanghai, 58; development of *fugu* plan, 64–72; attempts to establish relations with American Jews, 74, 77; broadcasts on Jewish policy, 94; writes anonymously on Jewish problem, 141; disquiet at number of refugees in Kobe, 165–7, 169; proposal to move refugees from Kobe to Shanghai, 184–8; Japan enters, 215–17; leaves Shanghai, 218; after the war, 272–3
Ionis, Michael, 149–56, 157
Irkutsk, 107, 108
Ishiguro, Shiro, 64–5, 68, 69, 74, 77
Ishihara, Lieutenant Colonel Kanji, 50, 51

Israel, 272, 275;
  see also Palestine
Itagaki, General Seishiro, 50, 51,
  56, 57–8, 59
Italy, 79, 94, 95, 218
Iwo Jima, 260
*Izumo*, 65, 78, 187

Japan; *fugu* plan, 9–12; entry
  requirements, 40–1, 42–3; war
  with China, 44, 62, 71, 76, 122,
  216–17, 218; alliance with
  Germany, 44, 57; recognition
  of Jews, 44–9; westernization,
  45; war with Russia, 45–6, 50;
  Siberian Expedition, 46–8;
  relations with America, 50, 52,
  57, 60; evolution of *fugu* plan,
  51–3, 55–61; captures Shanghai,
  62, 64; development of *fugu*
  plan, 64–79; tries to establish
  links with American Jews, 67,
  68–9, 72–8; military alliance
  with Germany and Italy, 79, 94,
  95, 96, 115, 126, 142; Jewish
  refugees arrive in, 112–20;
  Jewish refugees in, 122–43,
  144–56, 161–7, 182, 183–4;
  stops issuing transit visas, 154–6,
  157–61; neutrality pact with
  Russia, 166, 244–5; interrogation of Jewcom, 168–81;
  refugees moved from Kobe to
  Shanghai, 186–8, 191–3;
  Japanese in Shanghai, 211–13;
  enters war, 214–21; failure of
  *fugu* plan, 217; proposed
  Shanghai pogrom, 223–34;
  creates ghetto in Shanghai, 234,
  235–54; forced to withdraw,
  256–7; reappearance of *fugu*
  plan, 258; tries to end war,
  259–60; surrenders, 267–8
*The Japan Advertiser*, 48, 74
Japanese army, 244
Jewcom, looks after refugees in
  Kobe, 124–31, 133–9, 152–6,

161, 165–6, 201; Navy
  interrogates, 167, 168–81;
  struggle to find destinations for
  refugees, 183–4; closed down,
  192, 200
Jewish Affairs Bureau (Shanghai),
  223
Jewish Agency, 157
Jewish Refugee Committee, 72
Jews, Russian treatment of
  refugees, 80–1, 86–7, 90–3,
  96–111, 183; Japan's recognition
  of, 44–9; evolution of *fugu* plan,
  51–3, 55–61; colony in Shanghai,
  62, 63–4; development of *fugu*
  plan, 64–79; refugees arrive in
  Japan, 112–20, 122–43;
  refugees in Japan, 123–4,
  144–56, 161–7, 182, 183–4;
  Jewcom interrogated, 168–81;
  refugees in Lithuania, 182–3;
  refugees moved from Kobe to
  Shanghai, 186–8, 191–9;
  refugees in Shanghai, 200–13;
  failure of *fugu* plan, 217; Japan
  enters war, 217–21; proposed
  Shanghai pogrom, 221, 222–34;
  Hongkew ghetto, 234, 235–54,
  255–6; reappearance of *fugu*
  plan, 258; Shanghai ghetto
  bombed, 262–7
Joint Administrative Committee,
  256
Joint Distribution Committee
  (JDC), 26, 157, 160, 187; relief
  kitchens, 32; and *fugu* plan, 78;
  finds money to get Jews out of
  Vilna, 99, 100, 101; Kobe
  Jewcom appeals to, 124, 129;
  aid to refugees in Shanghai,
  202, 255, 269; stops sending
  funds to refugees in enemy-
  occupied territories, 219–20
Judaism, 69, 180; Stalinist view of,
  37; role of yeshivas in, 81–2;
  similarities to *Shinto*, 230
*Juedische Gemeinde*, 256

Kadoorie, 206
Kadoorie School, 204, 205–6, 238, 251, 260–1, 269
Kaidan, 82
Kaifeng, 59
Kalisch, Shimon, *see* Amshenover rebbe
Kalmanowitz, Rabbi Abraham, 83, 86, 99, 220–1, 254
Kamakura, 125–6
Kano, 245, 252
Kardegg, Dr., 225–7, 232
Karuizawa, 257
Kase, Hideaki, 11
Kaspé, Joseph, 53–4
Kaspé, Simon, 53–5, 233
*Katznelson, Moishe*, 96; escape from Poland, 24–7; leaves Vilna, 97–8; arrival in Japan, 113–14, 116–17; in Shanghai, 193–9, 206–9, 237–42, 266–7; after the war, 271
*Katznelson, Sophie*, 96, 162, 240, 242; escape from Poland, 24–7; leaves Vilna, 97–8; arrival in Japan, 113, 116; in Shanghai, 193–5, 197–9, 206, 208–9; death, 266
Kaufmann, Fritz, 225–7, 232
Kaufman, Dr. Abraham, 53, 55–6, 66–7, 185, 226, 231, 233, 252, 273
*kempeitai*, 226, 231–2, 257
Kindermann, Dr. Karl, 78, 257–8, 273
Kiseleff, Rabbi Aaron, 53
Kishi, Nobusuku, 271
Kishinev, 46
Kitchen Fund, 256
Kobe, 55, 116; Jewish community, 75, 122–5; Jewish refugees in, 122–43, 144–56, 161–5, 182, 184, 200; refugees moved to Shanghai, 186–8, 191–3
Kogan, Michael, 11, 273
Kogan Papers, 11–12
*Kokusai Hinmitsu Ryoku No*

*Kenkyu* (KHR), 141
Konoye, Fumimaro, 56
Korea, 76, 218
Kotsuji, Setsuzo, 66, 123, 125–8, 139–43, 154, 175–6, 183–4, 273–4
Kovno, 20–1, 27, 79, 80
Krakinava, 82, 83, 86–7
Krasnoyarsk, 107, 108
*Kristallnacht*, 57
Kubota, Tsutomu, 141, 223–4, 228–31, 233–4, 244–6, 249–50, 252, 264
Kucholze, 24
Kuczbork, 40
Kwantung Army, 50, 58

Latvia, 243
Lemberg, 81, 86, 93
Levy, Zev, 82–3, 86, 87
*Lewin*, 240–1
Library of Congress, 11
Lithuania, 243; Jewish refugees, 20–1, 23, 29–31, 32–3, 79, 80–93, 96–102, 124, 182–3; Soviet Union annexes, 29
Lochow, 36
Lodz, 82
Lomz, 170
London, 130, 243
Long, Breckinridge, 184
Lublin, 82

MacArthur, Douglas, 256
Malaya, 218
Manchouli, 53
Manchuria, (Manchukuo), 218; development of *fugu* plan, 9, 11, 64–79; Japan's plans for expansion in, 45, 50–61; creation of Manchukuo, 50; Jewish population, 53–5, 123; reappearance of *fugu* plan, 258; Japan tries to end war, 260
Manchurian Faction, 50–2, 53
Manila, 236, 260
Mao Tse-tung, 256, 268, 271–2

Margolies, Laura, 202, 217, 220, 252, 254, 255
Marx, Karl, *Communist Manifesto*, 48
Matsui, General, 226, 231
Matsuoka, Yosuke, 11, 31; and evolution of *fugu* plan, 51, 66, 94–6; becomes foreign minister, 78–9; allows extension of transit visas, 126–7; disquiet at numbers of refugees coming to Japan, 139–43; stops issue of transit visas, 156; signs neutrality pact with Russia, 166; prevents Shanghai pogrom, 233; after the war, 274
Medical Board, 256
Meiji, Emperor, 46
Meisinger, Colonel Josef, 12, 222–4, 226, 233–4, 274
Middle China Expeditionary Army, 69–70
Minami, 58
Ministry of Greater East Asia, 244
Mir Yeshiva, 96, 146; forced to leave Lithuania, 81–7; goes to Japan, 99; in Shanghai, 202, 209–11, 221, 247–9, 250, 252–3, 269; after the war, 274
Morgenthau, Henry Jr., 254
Moscow, 102–6, 154–6, 218
Moses, 180
Mukden, 53

Nagasaki, 227, 267
Nakada, Bishop, 134
Nakamura, Admiral, 257–8
Nanking, 75, 218
Naval Bureau, Shanghai, 64
Nazis: encourage anti-Semitism in Japan, 78–9; annoyed by Jewish refugees in Japan, 126, 141; anti-Semitism, 172–3, 177–9; pogrom planned in Shanghai, 221, 222–34; *see also* Germany
Neumann, Hans, 223–4
New Mexico, 260

New York, 34, 130
*New York Times*, 71
Newman, Frank, 185–6, 273, 274
Nicholas II, Tsar, 45–6, 53
Nimitz, Admiral, 256
Nippon-Israel Friendship League, 273
Nippon Yusen Kaisha Steamship Company (NYK), 157–61
Nissan Industries, 51
NKVD, 86, 87, 89, 92–3, 96, 100, 104–5, 155, 183

Okuda, 150–2, 154, 212
Okura, 251
Omsk, 107, 108
Organization for Rehabilitation and Training School, 238
*Orliansky family,* 96
*Orliansky, Ephraim,* 39–41, 87–8, 137–9
*Orliansky, Mischa,* 88, 138
Otwock, 90–1

Pacific Trading Company, 66
Palestine, 40, 49, 82–3, 135, 158–9, 184
Palestine Committee, 157, 159, 184
*Pao Chia,* 251, 261–2, 268
Pearl Harbor, 51, 200, 214–15, 217, 219
Pehle, John, 254
Peking, 236
Peritz, Robert, 225–7, 232
Perry, Matthew, 45
*Petrel,* 214
Philippines, 218
'A Plan to Invite Fifty Thousand German Jews to Manchukuo', 52
Poland, 82; Jewish refugees from, 20–5, 32, 36, 243; German invasion, 33–6, 37, 173; Soviet Union annexes part of, 81; Germany controls, 183; government-in-exile, 184, 221, 237, 243

Ponve, Anatole, 123, 124, 125,
152–5, 168–70, 274
Pootung, 224
Portugal, 218, 221
*The Protocols of the Elders of Zion*,
10, 47–8, 58, 142
Puttkamer, Adolph, 223

Radin, 82
Ramailes Yeshiva, 146
Ramigola, 82
Reform Judaism, 72
Ribbentrop, Joachim von, 44
Romer, Count Theodore de, 184
Roosevelt, Franklin D., 49, 59,
60, 72, 217, 258, 259, 260
Rothschild family, 9
Royal Navy, 214
Rumania, 82
Russia: war with Japan, 45–6, 50;
*see also* Soviet Union

St. Louis, 40, 135
Sakai, Shogun, 141
Salvation Army, 247, 249
Sassoon, David, 63
Sassoon (David) and Sons, Ltd.,
63, 216–17
Sassoon, Sir Victor, 63, 66, 71,
216–17
Schat, 82
Schiff, Jacob, 9, 46, 48, 68
Schoyer, Raphael, 74
Sekiguchi, Colonel Tsugio, 257
Semonov, General Gregorii, 47
227–8, 231
Sephardic Jews, 63, 64, 65, 68,
70–1, 191, 218, 219, 243, 268
Shanghai, 158; visa requirements,
27; Jewish community, 54–5,
63–4; and *fugu* plan, 58, 68–9;
Japan gains control of, 62, 64–5;
attempts to stop Jewish
immigration, 70–2; refugees
moved to, 186–8, 191–9, 200–13;
Japan enters war, 218, 219–21;
proposed pogrom in, 222–34;

Hongkew ghetto, 234, 235–54,
255–6; reappearance of *fugu*
plan, 258; ghetto bombed,
262–7; Communists take over,
10, 271–2
Shanghai Ashkenazi Collaborating
Relief Association (SACRA),
245–9, 250, 251–2, 253, 256,
261, 263–4
Shanghai Club, 209
Shanghai Jewish Youth Association
School, *see* Kadoorie School
Shanghai Joint Distribution
Committee, 256
Shanghai Russian Jewish Club,
245, 246
Shanghai Volunteer Corps, 268
Shapiro, Rabbi Shlomo, 172–81
Shatzkes, Rabbi Moses, 170–81,
274
Shibata, Mitsugi, 12, 223, 224–7,
232, 274–5
Shigemitsu, Mamoru, 54–5
*Shinto*, 69, 180, 230
Shioden, General Nobutake, 58,
141, 230, 275
Siberia, 81, 98, 107–9, 155
Siberian Expedition, 46–8
Singapore, 218, 257
Sino–Japanese war, 44, 62, 71,
76, 122, 216–17, 218
Slobodka, 82
South Manchurian Railway, 51–2,
66, 126
Soviet Union, 23; Manchukuo
buffer state against, 9; annexes
Lithuania, 29; annexes part of
Poland, 36–7; treatment of
Jews, 42; relations with Japan,
44; anti-Semitism, 46–7, 48;
Jewish homeland in, 58; Jewish
emigrants, 63–4; treatment of
Jewish refugees, 80–1, 86–7,
90–3, 96–111, 183; Japan stops
issuing transit visas in, 154–6;
pact of neutrality with Japan,
166, 244–5; Germany declares

war on, 188–9; German invasion, 218; Germans retreat from Stalingrad, 246
Spain, 218
Spechman, 195, 199
Speelman, Michael, 225–7, 232
SS, 222
Stalin, Josef, 37, 81, 90, 139
Stalingrad, 246
*Studies in the International Conspiracy*, 141
'The Study and Analysis of Introducing Jewish Capital', 68–70
Sugihara, Senpo, 20–1, 27–9, 30–1, 41–3, 80, 82, 129, 140, 146, 275
Sun Yat-Sen, 49
Sweden, 218
Switzerland, 218, 221, 243
*Syrkin, Cheya*, 96; forced to leave Poland, 21–3; leaves Vilna, 90–1; crosses Russia, 100–2, 108–9, 110; in Kobe, 161–5; in Shanghai, 193, 195–9, 237, 239–42, 266–7; after the war, 271
*Syrkin, Dovid*, 96; forced to leave Poland, 22–3; crosses Russia, 100–1, 108–9, 110–11; in Kobe, 161–5; in Shanghai, 193–6, 199, 206–9, 236, 239–42, 267; after the war, 271
*Syrkin, Getzel*, 96; forced to leave Poland, 21–3; leaves Vilna, 90–3; crosses Russia, 100–2, 103–6, 108; in Kobe, 161–2; in Shanghai, 195, 197, 199; death, 235–42

Taiwan, 218
Takahashi, Baron Korekiyo, 45–6, 51–2, 59
Takarazuka Music School, 57
Talmud, 221
Tamura, Mitsuzo, 12, 67, 72–8, 185, 275
Tanaka, K., 43

TASS, 246, 256
*Tatsuta Maru*, 276
Tels, 82
'ten lost tribes', 134, 180, 230
Tientsin, 258–60
Togo, Shigenor, 217, 233
Tojo, General Hideki, 142, 250, 257
Tokyo, 10, 122, 130, 236, 260
Tokyo Jewish Community Center, 273
*Tookansky, Mrs.*, 204–5
Topas, Boris, 71, 185, 225–8, 231, 232–3, 245, 275
Torah, 81–2
Trading with the Enemy Act, 219, 254
Trans-Siberian Railway, 102, 107, 123
Treaty of Portsmouth, 50
Treblinka, 269
Triguboff, Alex, 115–20, 148, 169, 170–1, 275
Tripartite Pact, 79, 94, 95, 96, 115, 126, 142
Tsitsihar, 53
Tsungming, 224
Tsuruga, 112, 113–20, 129–30, 183, 189

Union of Orthodox Rabbis, 157, 185–6
United Nations, 276
United Nations Relief and Rehabilitation Agency, 271
United States of America, 218; Jews in, 9, 10; Jewish refugees, 26–7, 34–5; entry requirements 39–40; relations with Japan, 44, 50, 52, 57, 60; Japan tries to establish links with Jews in, 67, 68–9, 72–8; refuses to take Jewish immigrants, 82–3, 184, 254; Jewish immigrants, 158–60; immigration regulations tighten, 188; relief funds to Shanghai curtailed, 219–20; relaxes

control on funds for refugees, 254, 255, 256; and reappearance of *fugu* plan, 258; Japan tries to end war, 259–60; bombs Hongkew ghetto, 262–7; end of war, 268
Ural Mountains, 107
US Treasury Department, 220
Utsonomiya, 141

*Va'ad Hatzalah*, 83, 86, 99, 157, 202, 220–1
Vera, 228
Vilna, 25–6, 32–3, 38, 82, 86, 87–93, 97–101, 136, 155, 183
Vladivostok, 47, 107, 108, 109–11, 130, 155, 158, 159, 183, 189
Vogelfut, J. Gustav, 57
Voogd, N.A.G. de, 130, 131

Warhaftig, Zorach, 157–61, 174, 184–8, 192, 202, 274, 275
Warburg, 68
Ward Road Jail, Shanghai, 251, 264–5
Warsaw, 23, 33–6, 37, 131–2, 222, 237
Warsaw Military Command, 33
Washington, 130
Weizman, Chaim, 49
Whangpoo River, 62, 193, 224
White Russians, 45–6, 53, 227
Wilson, Woodrow, 72

Wise, Rabbi Stephen, 10, 72–8, 185, 257, 258, 275–6
World Jewish Congress, 56, 142, 157, 160–1, 174, 185, 254, 276
Wright, Frank Lloyd, 94

Yangtze River, 62, 224
Yano, Seiki, 234
Yasue, Colonel Norihiro, 12, 123; belief in Jewish conspiracy, 47–9; development of *fugu* plan, 51, 55–6, 60, 65, 66, 68, 69; attempts to establish links with American Jews, 74, 77; loses post in Manchuria, 94, 141–2; planned pogrom in Shanghai, 226; prevents Shanghai pogrom, 233; and end of war, 260; after the war, 276
Yenisei River, 107
Yiddish, 203
Yokohama, 75, 122, 124–5, 130, 159, 227
Yokohama Relief Committee, 160
Yonai, Admiral Mitsumasa, 56
Yugoslavia, 166

Zalman, Rabbi Elijah ben Solomon, 89
Zikman, Lew, 68, 72–3, 74, 94–6, 142, 252, 276
Zionism, 72, 135, 276
Zupnik, Moishe, 82, 83–4, 86
Zwartendijk, 30